NEW CENTURY BIBLE COMMENTARY

General Editors

RONALD E. CLEMENTS
(Old Testament)

MATTHEW BLACK
(New Testament)

1 and 2 Thessalonians

D1352925

THE NEW CENTURY BIBLE COMMENTARIES

Other titles are in preparation.

NEW CENTURY BIBLE COMMENTARY

Based on the Revised Standard Version

1 and 2
THESSALONIANS

I. HOWARD MARSHALL

WM. B. EERDMANS PUBL. CO., GRAND RAPIDS

MARSHALL MORGAN & SCOTT PUBL. LTD., LONDON

Copyright © Marshall Morgan & Scott (Publications) 1983
All rights reserved
Printed in the United States of America
for
Wm. B. Eerdmans Publishing Company
255 Jefferson Ave. S.E., Grand Rapids, MI 49503
and
Marshall Morgan & Scott
1 Bath Street, London ECIV 9LB
ISBN 0 551 01006 1

Library of Congress Cataloging in Publication Data

Marshall, I. Howard.
1 and 2 Thessalonians.

(New century Bible commentary)
Bibliography: p. xiv
Includes indexes.
1. Bible.   N.T. Thessalonians — Commentaries.
I. Bible.   N.T. Thessalonians.   II. Title
III. Title: One and two Thessalonians.   IV. Series.
BS2725.3.M36   1983   227'.81077   82-16452
ISBN 0-8028-1946-X

Reprinted, November 1990

*The Bible references in this publication are taken from the Revised Standard
Version of the Bible, copyright 1946 and 1952 by the Division of Christian
Education, National Council of the Churches of Christ in the USA, and used
by permission.*

To
Morag, Aileen, Alison and Neil

CONTENTS

PREFACE

I began work on this commentary more because I had been invited to share in the task of revising *The New Century Bible* than because I felt that a new commentary on Thessalonians was a matter of urgent need or that I was specially qualified to produce a new work on these epistles. The earlier commentary in this series by A. L. Moore remains a helpful and serviceable guide to understanding the epistles, although unfortunately the commentator did not have sufficient space to spread himself and discuss tricky problems at length. The volume by E. Best in *Black's New Testament Commentaries* is recent, detailed and marked by a sobriety and wisdom of judgment from which I have generally been unwilling to differ. The letters to the Thessalonians have also been treated in many excellent earlier commentaries, among which may be particularly mentioned the works of G. Milligan and J. E. Frame in English (together with J. B. Lightfoot's stimulating Notes and J. Denney's fine exposition), of E. von Dobschütz and M. Dibelius in German, and of B. Rigaux and C. Masson in French. Surely nothing more is required?

However, five things have given me some justification for the present work. First, I have become increasingly aware of the continuing problems of exegesis raised by the letters, and it has been tempting to make a fresh attempt to solve some of them (or at least to write 'No entry' opposite some earlier solutions). Second, I have attempted to produce a work in somewhat shorter compass than Best's commentary for students who may find he offers them too much. Third, I have felt able to dispense with detailed discussion of earlier investigations of the epistles up to the time of Best's commentary and to concentrate my attention on the not inconsiderable amount of research published since then. Fourth, the case that 2 Thessalonians is a pseudonymous work has been strongly presented in the last decade by W. Trilling in a monograph and in the first detailed commentary to interpret the epistle on this basis. I have been interested to see whether the position maintained by Best and the vast majority of English writers still stands in the light of these recent publications. Fifth, the thought of the epistles may seem strange and even bizarre to modern readers, and I have tried to indicate what I regard as the abiding message and significance of these writings; I make no apology for asking how they are to be understood as Christian Scriptures. At the end of the exercise I must confess that I have come to appreciate more fully the spiritual value of this section of the New Testament.

I am conscious of my debt to many writers apart from those already named. It was my privilege to be associated with Dr W. H. Burkeen, a post-graduate student in the University of Aberdeen, in the writing of his thesis on the eschatology of the epistles, and I greatly profited from our discussions. I am grateful also to Prof. A. J. Malherbe for his kindness in letting me see a draft of his forth-coming article on 'Hellenistic Moralists and the New Testament' in which the value of a study of Hellenistic writers for understanding Paul is powerfully illustrated. Finally, my thanks go to Prof. M. Black for inviting me to undertake this task and for his help in the accomplishment of it.

I. HOWARD MARSHALL
November, 1981

ABBREVIATIONS

BIBLICAL

OLD TESTAMENT (*OT*)

Gen.	Jg.	1 Chr.	Ps.	Lam.	Ob.	Hag.
Exod.	Ru.	2 Chr.	Prov.	Ezek.	Jon.	Zech.
Lev.	1 Sam.	Ezr.	Ec.	Dan.	Mic.	Mal.
Num.	2 Sam.	Neh.	Ca.	Hos.	Nah.	
Dt.	1 Kg.	Est.	Isa.	Jl	Hab.	
Jos.	2 Kg.	Job	Jer.	Am.	Zeph.	

APOCRYPHA (*Apoc.*)

1 Esd.	Tob.	Ad. Est.	Sir.	S 3 Ch.	Bel	1 Mac.
2 Esd.	Jdt.	Wis.	Bar.	Sus.	Man.	2 Mac.
			Ep. Jer.			

NEW TESTAMENT (*NT*)

Mt.	Ac.	Gal.	1 Th.	Tit.	1 Pet.	3 Jn
Mk	Rom.	Eph.	2 Th.	Phm.	2 Pet.	Jude
Lk.	1 C.	Phil.	1 Tim.	Heb.	1 Jn	Rev.
Jn	2 C.	Col.	2 Tim.	Jas	2 Jn	

DEAD SEA SCROLLS (*DSS*)

1QH	Hymns of Thanksgiving
1QM	War of the Sons of Light against the Sons of Darkness
1QS	Rule of the Community (Manual of Discipline)
1Q27	Book of Mysteries

GENERAL

AG	*A Greek-English Lexicon of the New Testament and Other Early Christian Literature*, by W. Bauer, translated by W. F. Arndt and F. W. Gingrich (Cambridge, 1957)
ANRW	*Aufstieg und Niedergang der Römischen Welt*, edited by H. Temporini and W. Haase (Berlin/New York, 1972–)
Asc. Isa.	Ascension of Isaiah
b. Hag.	Haggigah (Babylonian Talmud)
CBQ	*Catholic Biblical Quarterly*
Const. Apost.	Apostolic Constitutions
Did.	Didache
Diog.	Epistle to Diognetus
1 En.	1 Enoch
Epist. Apost.	Epistola Apostolorum
ETL	*Ephemerides Theologicae Lovanienses*
Exp	*Expositor*
ExpT	*Expository Times*
Gen. R.	Genesis Rabbah
GNB	*Good News Bible*
HTR	*Harvard Theological Review*
IBS	*Irish Biblical Studies*
Idiom-Book	*An Idiom-Book of New Testament Greek*, by C. F. D. Moule (Cambridge, 1953)
JBL	*Journal of Biblical Literature*
Jos. Ant.	Josephus, *Antiquitates Judaicae*
Jos. Bel.	Josephus, *Bellum Judaicum*
JTS	*Journal of Theological Studies*
Jub.	Jubilees
LSJ	*Greek-English Lexicon*, edited by H. G. Liddell and R. Scott, rev. ed. by H. S. Jones (Oxford, 1940)
LXX	Septuagint
MM	*The Vocabulary of the Greek New Testament*, by J. H. Moulton and G. Milligan (London, 1914–29)
MS(S)	manuscript(s)
NEB	*New English Bible*
NIDNTT	*The New International Dictionary of New Testament Theology*, edited by C. Brown (Exeter, 1975–8)
NIV	*New International Version*
NovT	*Novum Testamentum*
NTS	*New Testament Studies*
Poly. Phil.	Polycarp, *Epistle to the Philippians*

Ps. Sol.	Psalms of Solomon
RSV	*Revised Standard Version*
SB	*Kommentar zum Neuen Testament aus Talmud und Midrasch*, by H. Strack and P. Billerbeck (München, 1926–61)
Sib. Orac.	Sibylline Oracles
ST	*Studia Theologica*
Sym.	Symmachus' Greek translation of the *OT*
TDNT	*Theological Dictionary of the New Testament*, edited by G. Kittel and G. Friedrich (Grand Rapids, 1964–76)
ThBl	*Theologische Blätter*
ThZ	*Theologische Zeitschrift*
T. Levi	Testament of Levi
TU	*Texte und Untersuchungen zur Geschichte der altchristlichen Literatur*
TynB	*Tyndale Bulletin*
UBS	*The Greek New Testament*, edited by K. Aland, *et al.* (Stuttgart, 1975³)
ZNW	*Zeitschrift für die neutestamentliche Wissenschaft*
ZPEB	*The Zondervan Pictorial Encyclopaedia of the Bible*, edited by M. C. Tenney (Grand Rapids, 1975)
ZTK	*Zeitschrift für Theologie und Kirche*

SELECT BIBLIOGRAPHY

(Works listed below are cited simply by the author's name in the commentary)

Best, E., *A Commentary on the First and Second Epistles to the Thessalonians* (Black's New Testament Commentaries), London, 1972

Bjerkelund, C. J., *Parakalô*, Oslo, 1967

Burkeen, W. H., *The Parousia of Christ in the Thessalonian Correspondence*, Ph.D. Thesis, Aberdeen, 1979

Calvin, J., *Commentaries on the Epistles of Paul the Apostle to the Philippians, Colossians and Thessalonians*, Edinburgh, 1851 (There is a later translation of *The Epistles of Paul the Apostle to the Romans and to the Thessalonians*, Edinburgh, 1961)

Denney, J., *The Epistles to the Thessalonians* (Expositor's Bible), London, 1892

Dibelius, M., *An die Thessalonicher I II, an die Philipper* (Handbuch zum Neuen Testament), Tübingen, 1937[3]

Dobschütz, E. von, *Die Thessalonicherbriefe* (Kritisch-Exegetischer Kommentar), Göttingen, 1909, reprinted 1974

Ellingworth, P. and Nida, E. A., *A Translator's Handbook on Paul's Letters to the Thessalonians* (Helps for Translators), Stuttgart, 1975

Evans, R. M., *Eschatology and Ethics: A Study of Thessalonica and Paul's Letters to the Thessalonians*, Th.D. Dissertation, Basel, 1967

Frame, J. E., *The Epistles of St Paul to the Thessalonians* (International Critical Commentary), Edinburgh, 1912

Friedrich, G., *Die Briefe an die Thessalonicher* (Das Neue Testament Deutsch), Göttingen, 1976

Giblin, C. H., *The Threat to Faith; An Exegetical and Theological Re-examination of 2 Thessalonians 2*, Rome, 1967

Graafen, J. *Die Echtheit des zweiten Briefes an die Thessalonicher*, Münster, 1930

Grayston, K., *The Letters of Paul to the Philippians and to the Thessalonians* (Cambridge Bible Commentary), Cambridge, 1967

Harnisch, W., *Eschatologische Existenz. Ein exegetischer Beitrag zum Sachanliegen von 1. Thessalonicher 4,13–5,11*, Göttingen, 1973

Hendriksen, W., *Exposition of 1 and 2 Thessalonians*, Grand Rapids, 1955

Henneken, B., *Verkündigung und Prophetie im 1. Thessalonicherbrief*, Stuttgart, 1969

Jewett, R. *Paul's Anthropological Terms. A Study of their Use in Conflict Settings*, Leiden, 1971

Kemmler, D. W., *Faith and Human Reason: A Study of Paul's Method of Preaching as illustrated by 1 – 2 Thessalonians and Acts 17 : 2–4*, Leiden, 1975

Laub, F., *Eschatologische Verkündigung und Lebensgestaltung nach Paulus. Eine Untersuchung zum Wirken des Apostles beim Aufbau der Gemeinde in Thessalonike*, Regensburg, 1973

Lightfoot, J. B., *Notes on Epistles of St Paul*, London, 1904

Marxsen, W., *Der erste Brief an die Thessalonicher* (Zürcher Bibel-kommentare), Zürich, 1979

Masson, C., *Les deux Épîtres de Saint Paul aux Thessaloniciens* (Commentaire du Nouveau Testament), Neuchâtel/Paris, 1957

Metzger, B. M., *A Textual Commentary on the Greek New Testament*, London/New York, 1971

Milligan, G., *St Paul's Epistles to the Thessalonians* (Macmillan), London, 1908

Moore, A. L., *1 and 2 Thessalonians* (The Century Bible: New Series), London, 1969

Morris, L., *The First and Second Epistles to the Thessalonians* (New International Commentary), Grand Rapids, 1959 (references are to this work and not to *id.*, *The Epistles of Paul to the Thessa-lonians* [Tyndale New Testament Commentaries], London, 1956)

Neil, W., *The Epistles of Paul to the Thessalonians* (Moffatt New Testament Commentary), London, 1950

O'Brien, P. T., *Introductory Thanksgivings in the Letters of Paul*, Leiden, 1977

Peterson, R. J., *The Structure and Purpose of Second Thessalonians*, D. Theol. Thesis, Harvard, 1967

Rigaux, B., *Saint Paul: Les Épîtres aux Thessaloniciens* (Études Bibliques), Paris/Gembloux, 1956

Schmithals, W., *Paul and the Gnostics*, Nashville, 1972

Stephens, D. J., *Eschatological Themes in II Thessalonians 2 : 1–12*, Ph.D. Thesis, St Andrews, 1976

Thomas, R. L., *1, 2 Thessalonians* (The Expositor's Bible Commen-tary, Vol. XI), Grand Rapids, 1978

Trilling, W., *Der zweite Brief an die Thessalonicher* (Evangelisch-Katholischer Kommentar zum Neuen Testament), Zürich/Neukirchen, 1980

Trilling, W., *Untersuchungen zum 2. Thessalonicherbrief*, Leipzig, 1972 (cited as Trilling, *Untersuchungen*)

Ward, R. A., *Commentary on 1 and 2 Thessalonians*, Waco, 1973
Whiteley, D. E. H., *Thessalonians* (New Clarendon Bible), Oxford, 1969
Wrede, W., *Die Echtheit des zweiten Thessalonicherbriefs*, Leipzig, 1903
Wrzol, J., *Die Echtheit des zweiten Thessalonicherbriefes*, Freiburg, 1916

INTRODUCTION

to

1 and 2 Thessalonians

INTRODUCTION

The New Testament contains two documents which purport to be letters from one group of people (Paul, Silvanus and Timothy) to another group of people described as the church of the Thessalonians. In order to understand these documents as fully as possible, we need to know something about the partners in this literary conversation, about the circumstances surrounding the composition of the documents, and about the literary character of the documents. One particular problem which arises is whether the documents are what they appear to be at first sight, namely, actual communications from Paul and his colleagues to the church at Thessalonica.

1. THESSALONICA AND ITS CHURCH

The church of the Thessalonians was situated in the town that is now known as Salonica in the north-east of Greece. The original site was called Therme, presumably because of hot springs in the neighbourhood. It became a place of some importance when it was rebuilt as a 'new town' by Cassander, who had served as a general under Alexander the Great, and named 'Thessalonica' after his wife. Founded in this way about 300 BC, Thessalonica rapidly became one of the leading cities in the country of Macedonia. In 167 BC the Romans took over the country, and the city became the capital of one of the four areas into which it was divided. When the whole country was organised as a single province (the Roman administrative unit) in 146 BC, Thessalonica became the capital city. This meant that it was the headquarters of the Roman administration. It received further privileges in 42 BC when it became a free city, i.e. one where the local inhabitants had their own government and rights of citizenship. The local magistrates were called 'politarchs', a title used in Ac. 17:6, 8 and attested in inscriptions from the site. The city was not only an administrative centre; it was also an important centre of communications and trade, being situated on the Roman trunk route, the Via Egnatia, which conveyed traffic to and from the West coast of the Balkan peninsula where it connected with the sea crossing to Italy and hence to Rome. We have no archaeological evidence from the first century of a Jewish element in the population (see Best, p. 59, for later evidence), but the analogy of other commercial centres and seaports strongly supports the *NT* evidence for their presence.

According to the account in Ac. 17 the evangelisation of Thessalonica took place during the second of the major missionary campaigns of Paul. In company with Silas and Timothy he made his way through Asia Minor to Troas and then crossed over into Macedonia. The first place they visited was Philippi, and from there they came via Amphipolis and Apollonia to Thessalonica. They conducted an evangelistic campaign in the Jewish synagogue for three weeks and were successful in converting a number of Jews together with a larger number of Gentiles, both men and women, who worshipped at the synagogue. Paul's success aroused the envy and enmity of the Jews. They instigated a rabble who attacked the house of Jason, where Paul was staying, and hauled both Jason and other converts before the city authorities on a charge of seditious behaviour. The magistrates bound Jason over. He had to give security for the behaviour of his guests, and so to avoid further trouble he got them secretly out of the town. They went on to Beroea, where they had a friendly welcome from the synagogue, until some of the Thessalonian Jews came and stirred up trouble. (For the legal procedure see A. N. Sherwin-White, *Roman Society and Roman Law in the New Testament*, Oxford, 1963, pp. 95–97.)

The narrative in Acts describes how Paul himself then went on to Athens, leaving his companions Silas and Timothy behind in Beroea to follow after him as soon as possible. Paul waited for them in Athens. However, Acts says nothing about their meeting him there, and it was only when he reached Corinth that they rejoined him from Macedonia (Ac. 18:5).

We hear nothing more of Thessalonica directly from Acts. After Paul's lengthy stays in Corinth and Ephesus, however, he departed for Macedonia, and after encouraging the disciples there, he went on south to Greece (Ac. 20:1f.). After three months there, presumably in Corinth, he returned north to Macedonia and sailed from Philippi to Troas, and so made his way to Jerusalem for his last visit (Ac. 20:3–6). It can be taken for granted that on both of these journeys through Macedonia he would have visited Thessalonica. This is confirmed by the fact that a number of Christians accompanied Paul from various churches to Jerusalem, and two names of Thessalonians, Aristarchus and Secundus, are listed, along with a representative from Beroea; no representative from Philippi is named, but a name may be concealed in the 'we/us' used at this point in the narrative. Acts says nothing about Paul writing letters at any point to Thessalonica, but there is nothing unusual about this, since no mention is made of any letters written by Paul.

It must be admitted that all this information is very formal and tells us little about the actual character of the church and the way in which it was founded. It is rather like the problem of trying to form a picture of a modern church simply on the basis of the official minutes of its business meetings; we should know very little about what actually happened at its services and other activities or about the kind of people who made up the congregation. Acts does not give us much help in understanding the correspondence of Paul with the church. What we can learn is as follows: (1). The church was composed of both Jews and Gentiles, and included a number of people with some standing in the community. (2). Paul's message was about the Messiah. He explained from the *OT* what would be the career of Messiah, namely, that he would suffer (i.e. die) and rise from the dead, and he claimed that the career of Jesus fitted this pattern. (3). Paul's message could be understood to mean that he was proclaiming another ruler in opposition to the Roman emperor; more precisely, he may have been thought to be predicting a change of ruler (E. A. Judge, 'The Decrees of Caesar at Thessalonica', *Reformed Theological Review* 30, 1971, pp. 1–7). (4). As a result the Christian community was under attack. All this is very general, and similar things could be said about other towns where Paul worked, but this does not make the account any less credible as far as it goes; it is indeed likely that Paul's message would be essentially the same in different towns, and that reactions to it would be similar.

2. THE BACKGROUND TO 1 THESSALONIANS

Let us now compare the picture in Acts with what can be gleaned from 1 Thessalonians. According to ch. 1 the letter was written by Paul, Silvanus and Timothy. Since 'Silvanus' is an alternative form for 'Silas' we have the same three missionaries mentioned as in Acts. In chs. 1 and 2 there are references to the visit of the missionaries to Thessalonica and to the conversion of the members of the church. This visit appears to have taken place in the recent past, since it is described in a fresh manner. There is no indication that the missionaries, or rather Paul himself in particular, had paid more than one visit to the town. Other people in Macedonia and Achaia had spoken about the conversion of the Thessalonians to Paul in a way which suggests that it was still comparatively fresh news (1 Th. 1:8). The description of the way in which the readers had responded to the gospel suggests that they were Gentiles who 'turned to God from idols' (1 Th. 1:9), and stood in some danger of living 'like heathen who do not know God' (1 Th. 4:5). This suggests that the church consisted of former pagans rather than of Jews or Gentiles who worshipped the one God at the synagogue. Is there a difference between Acts and Paul's report at this point? This suspicion would be strengthened if those writers are correct who think that 1 Th. 2:14f. means that the readers suffered at the hands of their own *Gentile* fellow-countrymen, just as the churches in Judea suffered from their fellow-countrymen, the Jews. However, this is a dubious understanding of the text, since it fails to explain why Paul mentions the Jews at all in this context and it does not take v.16 into account where Paul relates how the Jews hindered him personally from speaking to the Gentiles (see commentary, *ad loc.*). What does emerge is that the Gentile element in the church was larger than Acts indicates and that it included Gentiles who had not been attached to the synagogue as worshippers of the one God. At the same time, however, the picture of persecution surrounding the formation of the church is confirmed. In 1 Th. 2 we can read between the lines that there was a 'smear' campaign against the missionaries, and this fits in with the picture in Acts of opposition directed against the missionaries and (doubtless) also affecting the converts.

From 1 Th. 2:1f. we have confirmation that Paul came to Thessalonica via Philippi. This is further attested by Phil. 4:15f. where Paul describes how the Christians at Philippi sent him financial help while he was at Thessalonica, which would be very natural if this was the next point on his itinerary. Two points arise here. First, if Paul received financial help from Philippi, which was approximately 100 miles away, it would seem that he must have stayed in Thessalonica for a somewhat longer period than the three weeks of his mission in the synagogue mentioned in Ac. 17:2. Further, 1 Th. 2:9 states that the missionaries had to work with their own hands to keep themselves in Thessalonica. However, Morris, pp. 17f., has insisted that even for a short period the missionaries would have needed to work for their keep (especially if they were determined on principle not to be dependent on the hospitality of their converts, 1 C. 9:14f.), and that Phil. 4:15f. need not imply that more than one gift was sent to Paul at Thessalonica. The three weeks mentioned in Acts may well refer just to the period of Paul's initial mission in the synagogue, but it is unlikely that he remained much longer in the town. Second, the way in which Paul states that news of the conversion of the Thessalonians had spread in Macedonia and Achaia (1 Th. 1:7f.) and that the Thessalonian Christians loved all their Christian brothers throughout Macedonia (1 Th. 4:10) indicates that we must allow for a period of at least some months between their conversion and the writing of the letter.

This period, though short (1 Th. 2:17), was long enough for Paul to wish to revisit the town. But he was unable to do so because, as he puts it, 'Satan hindered us'. This was probably because of adverse circumstances affecting Paul himself (see 1 Th. 2:18 and commentary). Therefore, Timothy was sent instead in order to encourage the church in the midst of its afflictions. When he returned to Paul, he brought good news of the church which filled Paul with thanksgiving and joy—and with increased longing to revisit the church himself. The letter in which these words occur is best understood as Paul's joyful reaction to the news brought by Timothy.

Here again there is tension with the account in Acts. In 1 Th. 3:1f. Paul says that he was willing to be left behind at Athens alone and sent Timothy to the church, but according to Acts neither Timothy nor Silas was with Paul in Athens (although Paul was expecting them to join him there) and they rejoined him later in Corinth. Two solutions to this discrepancy have been suggested. The first is that Silas and Timothy, who had been left behind at Beroea, did in fact rejoin Paul in Athens and that he immediately sent Timothy back to Thessalonica (and Silas to some other destination), and that they rejoined him after this journey at Corinth; Acts simply omits part of the story. The second view is that when he reached Athens Paul sent a message back to Timothy at Beroea (Ac. 17:5) telling him to revisit Thessalonica before rejoining him (von Dobschütz, pp. 15f., 131). Best, p. 131, argues that this view does not give sufficient force to 'we were willing to be left behind' (1 Th. 3:1) and to the plural 'we' which implies that Silas was with Paul in Athens. These objections seem to be decisive, and it is better to accept the former view.

This is all the information that we can gather from 1 Thessalonians with regard to the narrative in Acts. Neither source gives us a full picture of Paul's relations with the church – as is only to be expected.

3. THE STRUCTURE OF 1 THESSALONIANS

There are a number of inter-connected problems in determining the historical setting and the character of the letter. First, we shall assume that it is a genuine writing by Paul, on the grounds that there is no need to defend what nobody disputes. This is not to say, however, that there are no doubts about the integrity of the letter.

It is disputed whether it is a unified writing or a combination of fragments and also whether some passages are non-Pauline.

The analysis of the letter as it stands is fairly clear, although there are some difficulties in detail. Marxsen, pp. 26–9, has correctly perceived that basically the letter falls into two parts. In chs. 1–3 the author is concerned with the past life of the church, the difficulties which it has faced and its success in overcoming them. In chs. 4–5 the author is concerned with the future of the church and aims to help it in continuing on its Christian way. Put otherwise, the first part of the letter explains why Paul has not been able to revisit the church and help it in its difficulties, and the second part is in effect a substitute for Paul's presence in which he sets down in writing what he would have said to the church if he had been able to revisit them. This way of analysing the letter recognises the equal importance of both parts.

Somewhat similar is the analysis of Bjerkelund, pp. 124–35, that the letter consists of thanksgiving and request, the former forming the basis for the latter. This two-part structure can be traced in other Pauline letters (especially Philemon) and corresponds to an ancient epistolary pattern. On this view the point of the letter lies in 4:1f., 10b–12.

More precisely H. Boers has analysed the letter in terms of ancient epistolary patterns ('The Form Critical Study of Paul's Letters. 1 Thessalonians as a Case Study', *NTS* 22, 1975–6, pp. 140–58):

Prescript	1:1
Thanksgiving	1:2–10
Apostolic Apology	2:1–12
Apostolic *Parousia*	2:17–3:13
Exhortation	4:1–5:22
Conclusion	5:23–28

The opening greeting is a regular part of Paul's letters and is a Christian adaptation of the normal greeting in a secular letter. Similarly, the closing personal greetings (5:23–28) are part of the conventional framework of a letter. We would doubt, however, whether Boers is right to regard the expression of prayer in 5:23f. as part of the conclusion; in our opinion it is more probable that it should be regarded as closing the previous section (cf. Phil. 4:19f.).

All of Paul's letters, with the notable exception of Galatians, begin with an expression of thanksgiving for the spiritual state of the readers, and 1 Thessalonians is no exception. Problems arise, however, in determining where the thanksgiving ends, and these are accentuated by the fact that again in 2:13 and 3:9 Paul expresses his thanksgiving for the readers to God.

The difficulty in analysis is partly due to the fact, brought out particularly by P. Schubert in his basic study (*Form and Function of the Pauline Thanksgiving*, Berlin, 1939), that the content of the thanksgiving is never formal but is intimately related to the main concerns of the letter. Schubert himself argued that the thanksgiving section ran as far as 3:13 and contained two 'digressions' (1:6–2:12; 2:17–3:8) which were organically related to it (cf. O'Brien, pp. 142–4). The solution adopted by Boers, following suggestions by other scholars (especially J. T. Sanders, 'The Transition from Opening Epistolary Thanksgiving to Body in the Letters of the Pauline Corpus', *JBL* 81, 1962, pp. 348–62; cf. W. G. Doty, *Letters in Primitive Christianity*, Philadelphia, 1973), is that the thanksgiving is followed by the 'body' or central section of the letter, which contains its main teaching. Two sections are distinguished. The first is 2:1–12 which is in content an 'apostolic apology', a section in which Paul is concerned with himself and his ministry (cf. 2 C. 1:12–17; 7:5–16; 10:7–12:13; Gal. 1:10–2:21; Phil. 1:12–26; 3:2–14; see also Rom. 1:14–16a). The second is 2:17–3:11 which deals with the coming of Paul, as an apostle to the church. A number of motifs can be found in similar passages in other Pauline letters (Rom. 1:8–13; 15:14–33; 1 C. 4:14–21; 16:1–11; 16:12; 2 C. 8:16–23; 9:1–5; 12:14–13:13; Gal. 4:12–20; Phil. 2:19–24; 2:25–30; Phm. 21f.): they include Paul's purpose in writing, his desire to visit the readers, possible hindrances in the way, the dispatch of a colleague, his own travel plans, an invocation of God's help, and the benefits to be expected from his visit. (See R. W. Funk, 'The Apostolic *Parousia*: Form and Significance', in W. R. Farmer (*et. al.*, ed.), *Christian History and Interpretation: Studies Presented to John Knox*, Cambridge, 1967, pp. 249–68.) This characterisation of both sections of the letter is justified in terms of their content and the parallels detected with similar material in other letters. However, a closer analysis of the parallels suggests that it is over-precise and perhaps misleading to think of these as two specific 'formal' parts of Pauline epistles which constitute structural elements in them. It would appear rather to be the case that here we have two themes which recur—for good contextual reasons—in various of Paul's letters and in which he naturally expresses himself in similar ways.

If we understand this section of the letter in this way, namely, as a combination of the themes of thanksgiving, apology and future visit, then we are on the way to a solution to the alleged problem of the repetition of the thanksgiving by Paul. Boers (art. cit., p. 152) finds no great difficulty with 3:9f.: 'although iii.9f. has all the *formal* characteristics of a thanksgiving formula, it does not function as such, i.e. to introduce a thanksgiving period'. With this judgment we may well concur, underlining the fact that Paul should not be regarded as being tied to a formal structure in his letters from which deviations are not permitted: the evidence of his other letters demonstrates this point abundantly (cf. 1 C. 1:14; 14:18). However, Boers has considerable difficulty with the thanksgiving and the comments on the Jews in 2:13–16, and adopts the solution that these verses constitute an interpolation into the letter. According to this theory Paul passes straight from his 'apology' (2:12) to his forthcoming visit (2:17). However, this deletion appears to be completely unnecessary so far as the attempt to recognise a clear structure in the letter is concerned. In fact these verses round off the 'apology' by claiming that the Thessalonians themselves accepted Paul's message as God's Word and thereby rejected any insinuations that might be made against him, and they also give the motivation for the following section by indicating something of the problems which made Paul long to revisit the church (see Marxsen, pp. 47f.). Boers' problems arise from attempting to find too formal a structure in this part of the letter. As in 3:9f., again we do not have a formal thanksgiving, but rather a means of introducing a statement about the readers and what they had endured from their fellow countrymen.

The clear break at the end of ch. 3 is universally recognised. What follows is exhortation. We should not, however, draw a line between teaching and exhortation. The answer to some of the practical problems in the church lay in fuller teaching. Thus we have a series of sections in which Paul deals with Christian morality, love for one another, worries concerning the fate of those who had died, uncertainties aroused by teaching about the parousia, and more general admonitions about life together in the church. The opening sections are introduced by comments that the readers need little further instruction on how to live, but rather encouragement to carry on the way they are already doing. It need not be doubted that the instruction was related to the particular needs of the church, although some of it is paralleled in other letters in a way which suggests that, like any preacher, Paul had his favourite themes which he thought it right to put before any of his congregations rather than because there was a specific need to do so.

Understood in this way, the letter makes good sense as a unified whole. It shows the broad formal characteristics of a first-century letter, but is not tied down in detail to a precise pattern. Rather, Paul remains broadly within the general pattern in order to compose a letter whose content is determined by the particular needs of this congregation. The situation is that of a congregation which he had not been able to instruct as fully as he wished before his hasty departure; while he was basically confident that, having made a good start on the Christian way, they would continue to stand firm and make progress despite opposition, he had a natural concern to help them and to this end he had sent Timothy to give him news of the situation. Timothy's return with good news led him to write this letter which is a combination of thanksgiving and encouragement.

The whole letter is a masterly piece of pastoral encouragement based on the existing progress made by the readers (see Marxsen for an excellent development of this point). So the letter begins with a reminder of the foundation of the church in the joyful response of the converts to the Christian message despite opposition. It moves on to a defence of the missionaries against possible charges of impure motives—a section which is intended to reassure the converts if they had any doubts about the character of the missionaries and their message. Then Paul comes to the actual situation, his own inability to visit the church, which might have been construed as a lack of concern for his friends. He affirms his longing to see them again, his anxiety for their welfare which led him to send Timothy when he himself could not make the journey, his joy at the good news with Timothy brought back, and his own hope that he would yet be able to visit them.

From this point it was natural to move on to exhortation, to write the things that he would have said if he had been able to be with them, and here he no doubt takes up themes that were suggested to him by the news brought by Timothy. These covered three main areas. First, there were questions of general morality; we can presume that some of the readers needed a reminder about sexual morality and about working for their living instead of bringing the church into disrepute by idleness. Second, there were problems arising from teaching about the parousia which needed to be clarified. Third, there was need to say something about their life together in the church. Finally, Paul could conclude his letter with warm greetings.

On the basis of this discussion we can divide up the letter for the purposes of this commentary as follows:

4. THEORIES OF INTERPOLATION AND REARRANGEMENT

We have given a reasonably simple and straightforward account of the circumstances which led to the writing of the letter and of the composition of the letter itself. In our discussion, however, we have assumed that the letter, as we have it, is a unified composition by Paul. This view has been challenged in various ways (see the survey by R. F. Collins, 'A Propos the Integrity of 1 Thes', *ETL* 55, 1979, pp. 67–106):

1. There is the possibility that the letter has been subjected to small interpolations.

(*a*) We have already mentioned the view that 2:13–16 is a later interpolation into the letter. This view was defended by B. A. Pearson, '1 Thessalonians 2:13–16: A Deutero-Pauline Interpolation', *HTR* 64, 1971, pp. 79–94). Earlier scholars had proposed that some or all of these verses were post-Pauline. The arguments offered by Pearson are: (i). Verse 17 refers to a final verdict upon the Jews, which is inconsistent with Paul's hopeful outlook in Rom. 11:25f. (ii). Verse 17 refers to a past judgment upon the Jews, which is most plausibly identified as the destruction of Jerusalem in AD 70. (iii). Verses 15f. contain traditional, formulaic language which reflects anti-Semitic feeling such as was current after AD 70 and which could not have been penned by Paul. Verse 14 speaks of persecution by Jews which is unattested at the time of the letter. And would Paul have used Jewish congregations as an example for other Christians to imitate? Elsewhere he uses only the apostles as an example. (iv). Verse 13 formally introduces a 'thanksgiving' which is out of place in the letter. If we remove vv. 13–17 we get rid of this unexpected element and produce a smoother transition from 2:17 to 3:13. In any case, the link between 2:12 and 13 is harsh. (v). We can account for the interpolation as the work of a writer encouraging his readers in the post-70 period when Jewish-Christian relationships had collapsed—a period reflected in the anti-Jewish polemic in Matthew.

This case falls down under examination. (i). Verse 17 is wrongly interpreted if it is seen as an attack on the Jews *in toto*. The use of the term to refer to unbelieving Jews and the use of strong language to condemn them are both found in Paul alongside his hopes for Jews to be converted (2 C. 11:24; Phil. 3:2; J. Coppens, 'Miscellanées bibliques. LXXX. Une diatribe antijuive dans 1 Thess., II, 13–16', *ETL* 80, 1976, pp. 90–5). (ii). The language of v. 17, which is probably inspired by the teaching of Jesus, most likely refers to an imminent judgment rather than a past one. (iii). The language is indeed traditional, but the tradition has early roots both in Judaism and in the teaching of Jesus. Persecution of Christians by Jews went back to the earliest days of the church. While the degree has often been exaggerated, the fact of it cannot be denied. (iv). The formal considerations regarding the place of 2:13–16 have already been discussed above. (v). No good reason has been adduced why a reference to Jewish persecution should have been interpolated at this particular place in this particular letter. On the contrary, Marxsen, pp. 47f., has demonstrated that the theme of persecution unites the whole of 2:1–16. For further details, see the commentary, *ad loc*. See further, W. D. Davies, 'Paul and the People of Israel', *NTS* 24, 1977–8, pp. 4–39, especially pp. 6–9, who suggests that Paul's words may be somewhat emotional and that he may not fully have made up his mind about the place of the Jews in God's plan.

(b). G. Friedrich ('1. Thessalonicher 5, 1–11, der apologetische Einschub eines Späteren', *ZTK* 70, 1973, pp. 288–315) has proposed that 5:1–11 is an interpolation by a later writer who wished to correct Paul's belief that the parousia was very near and to deal with the problem caused by the delay of the parousia. (i). He argues that the passage deals with a false security in view of the parousia which is different from the fear expressed in 4:13–18. (ii). The section is characterised by unoriginal, traditional phraseology. (iii). The language and thought show unpauline signs (such as Christ died for [*peri*] us, and the lack of differentiation between the dead and the living at the parousia). (iv). The structure of the section is modelled on that of the previous chapter. (v). The readers envisaged in 4:13–18 expected an imminent parousia, but 5:1–10 shows that this hope had evaporated. The stress is no longer on imminence but on suddenness and unexpectedness. The term 'parousia' is replaced by the day of the Lord, and while ch. 4 is comforting, ch. 5 is full of warning. (vi). There are parallels with Rom. 13:11–14, but while these verses still regard the parousia as imminent, the present passage no longer does so. (vii). There are also parallels with Luke. (viii). The interpolator wished to counterbalance the effect of the plain meaning of 4:15 which is that Paul expected to be alive at the parousia. He therefore, like Luke, replaced imminence with suddenness. If the interpolation is removed, the remaining text of the letter runs smoothly.

Friedrich's thesis has been characterised by B. Rigaux as more ingenious than convincing ('Tradition et rédaction dans 1 Th. V.1–10', *NTS* 21, 1974–5, pp. 318–40) and rejected as unconvincing by Marxsen, p. 27; their verdicts are justified. There is nothing uncompatible at all in Paul dealing with the worries of his readers, not about the imminence of the parousia but rather about the place of their dead relatives and friends, and his stress on its unexpectedness; as the commentary will show, the point of 5:1–11 is that the parousia will take the world unawares and unprepared *but not believers*. The alleged antithesis between two points of view is simply not there. The thought of the section is very much Pauline, as Best, pp. 220–2, has demonstrated. The parallels with Romans do not show that this passage is later, and the links with Luke's attitude to the parousia indicate that both authors are dependent on traditional Christian material. It is mistaken to draw a distinction between the imminence and the suddenness of the parousia, as if the latter were a later development. Finally, the content of v. 10, 'whether we wake or sleep', is sufficiently motivated by the desire to include both the dead believers of 4:13–18 and the readers who might be alive at the parousia; it is unlikely that it is meant to correct false impressions that could be drawn from 4:15.

Both the suggestions of interpolations thus lack cogency.

2. A second type of theory is that the letter has been subjected to a whole series of interpolations. C. Demke ('Theologie und Literarkritik im 1. Thessalonicherbrief', in G. Ebeling (*et al.*, ed.) *Festschrift für E. Fuchs*, Tübingen, 1973, pp. 103–24) argues that post-Pauline material has been added in 1:2–2:16; 3:12–4:8; 5:23–27 (and apparently 5:14f.) to material drawn from a genuine Pauline epistle to produce a two-part writing in which Paul is made to appear as an example to the church, and the church is called to sanctification and maintenance of apostolic tradition. (i). Demke begins by observing that Paul uses 'parousia' in 3:13 and 5:23 where the analogy of Phil. 1:6, 10; 1 C. 1:8 leads us to expect 'day', and that in 2:19; 3:13 he uses *emprosthen* where we would expect *enōpion*. What is the cause of this variation? (ii). In 1:9f.; 3:12f.; 5:23 salvation is entirely future, and the Pauline 'already' is unknown. (By contrast the latter *is* present in 5:1–11.) Further, the readers are not described as already 'holy', and the Spirit is simply the power that assists in sanctification rather than an eschatological gift to believers. The verb 'call' does not refer to God's effectual summons at conversion, but is simply his call to faithful service. In other words, Paul's concept of present, eschatological existence is missing. (iii). This difference from Paul's other letters is confirmed by an examination of the relation of Word and faith which shows

that the Word is concerned more with how the apostles and their converts behave than with the saving action and gift of God. The writer presents Paul not as someone really known to the readers but rather as an example to people who never knew him. The writer is concerned with imitation of the apostle and with the effects of faith rather than its content.

Demke expressly describes his essay as a *'Diskussionsbeitrag'*, and therefore it is perhaps unfair to criticise a case which is put forward in a provisional and incomplete form. Nevertheless, it raises serious questions about the credibility of a writer who could go to work in the manner described, producing a composition with so small a Pauline content. Second, there is a major methodological problem running through the essay. Demke does not consider how long a composition must be in which a writer does not express his characteristic theological motifs. Thus the Pauline 'already' is present in 5:1–11 (a passage which Friedrich was, however, prepared to regard as non-Pauline!): what grounds has Demke for asserting that since another section of the same letter does not contain this motif it cannot be from the same author? This sort of chopping up inspires no confidence. A third point is that Demke's starting point assumes that Paul must always express himself in the same way and use the same vocabulary. Demke is apparently prepared to allow such variation only if 1 Thessalonians was written at some considerable time before Paul's other letters. But there is no reason whatever why Paul should not have used the term 'parousia' in some cases and 'day' in others; he shows a growing tendency to use the latter, and that is all that we are entitled to say. As for *emprosthen*, Paul uses it in an eschatological context in 2 C. 5:10 (why does Demke not regard this verse as non-Pauline?), and it is found in eschatological contexts in Lk. 12:8; 21:36; Mt. 25:32; Fourth, Demke's understanding of the theology of 1 Thessalonians—salvation as purely future—is quite mistaken. This is shown by the occurrence of the 'in Christ' formula (and its variants) throughout the epistle (1:1; 2:14; 3:8; 4:1, 16; 5:12, 18). Demke gives the impression of trying to be more Pauline than Paul. The real test of his and all similar theories is whether the epistle in its present form makes sense as a Pauline composition.

3. A third type of theory is that which sees our letter as a combination of two or more existing documents.

(*a*). K.-G. Eckart ('Der zweite echte Brief des Apostels Paulus an die Thessalonicher', *ZTK* 58, 1961, pp. 30–44) argued that 1 Thessalonians is a combination of two letters by Paul to the church which have been joined together by a redactor who added his own interpolations in the process of editing. Letter A was taken by Timothy

to the church during the visit mentioned in 3:1–5 and consisted of
1:1–2:12; 2:17; 3:4; 3:11–13. Letter B was sent after his return to
take up various points which he reported to Paul and consisted of
3:6–10; 4:13–5:11; 4:9–10a; 5:23–26, 28. The material added by the
redactor was 2:13–16; 4:1–8, 10b–12; 5:12–22 (with 3:5 and 5:27 as
linking passages). This theory has not found any support among
scholars, although aspects of it have been developed by Demke (the
theory of post-Pauline interpolation—see above) and Schmithals
(the theory of combination of Pauline letters—see below). It is
generally agreed that the methods used by Eckart to defend the
theory were defective. There is no need to go over the ground again
here (see Best, pp. 29f., and the full study by W. G. Kümmel,
'Das literarische und geschichtliche Problem des ersten Thessalonicherbriefes', in W. C. van Unnik, *Neotestamentica et Patristica:
Freudesgabe O. Cullmann*, Leiden, 1962, pp. 213–27; reprinted in
W. G. Kümmel, *Heilsgeschichte und Geschehen*, Marburg, 1965,
pp. 406–16).

(*b*). W. Schmithals (like Demke) has insisted that the refutation
of Eckart's theory does not rule out in principle the possibility that
the letter is a secondary composition. His own theory takes in
2 Thessalonians as well as 1 Thessalonians and claims that four
genuine letters of Paul have been combined to produce the two
which we now have (Schmithals, pp. 123–218; cf. 'Die Thessalonicherbriefe als Briefkomposition', in E. Dinkler (ed.), *Zeit und Geschichte: Festschrift für R. Bultmann*, Tübingen, 1964, pp. 295–
316):

A. 2 Th. 1:1–12; 3:6–16
   (sent on first hearing news of disturbing happenings in the
   church)
B. 1 Th. 1:1–2:12; 4:2–5:28
   (further attempt to help the church to withstand influence of
   visiting preachers with a 'Gnostic' message)
C. 2 Th. 2:13–14; 2:1–12; 2:15–3:3, (5), 17f.
   (Paul's reply to news that a letter, falsely ascribed to him, has
   been circulated and has encouraged apocalyptic enthusiasm)
D. 1 Th. 2:13–4:1
   (Paul's reactions after he has sent Timothy to clear up the
   problems in the church)

So far as 1 Thessalonians is concerned, this theory has the merit of
proposing a simple partition of the letter into two parts, one included
within the other, which is a much more plausible proceeding than
the elaborate interweaving of material proposed by Eckart and

Demke. The real basis for the theory is the argument that 3:11–4:1 contains the elements of the concluding section of a letter and that 2:13 contains an introductory thanksgiving. 2:13–4:1 can thus be regarded as an independent letter. However, both of these points are unfounded. We have already seen that 2:13 need not be regarded as the formula introducing an opening thanksgiving and that the section 2:13–16 belongs closely with what precedes it. The case for seeing an epistolary conclusion in 3:11–4:1 has been fully criticised by C. Demke (art. cit., pp. 104–7) and Best, pp. 32f., who have shown that there is no fixed pattern represented in all Paul's letters, and that in particular the prayer in 3:11–13 is not necessarily the sign of a conclusion and the inclusion of paraenesis (4:1) after a prayer or doxology at the end of a letter is never found in a Pauline letter. Best further argues (pp. 31–5) that there are no discrepancies in though between the postulated two letters but rather a unity of theme. He concludes rightly that Schmithals has not established this part of his hypothesis (see further A. Suhl, *Paulus und seine Briefe*, Gütersloh, 1975, pp. 92–110; Bjerkelund, pp. 125–39).

It emerges that none of the theories proposed for dividing up 1 Thessalonians carries conviction. Although the possibility that the letter contains disparate material is not to be dismissed out of hand, it is sound exegetical sense to see whether the letter can be understood as a unity.

5. THE PROBLEMS ARISING IN THE CHURCH

In our earlier discussion we have described the situation in the church which led to the composition of the letter in terms of the external difficulties faced by the members and the problems which they had in living according to the gospel. A number of attempts have been made to give a more precise account of the situation, particularly in terms of possible opposition with which Paul had to deal. Four main types of opposition have been suggested:

1. The view that the church was subject to pressure from Judaisers was adopted by F. C. Baur and members of the Tübingen school in the nineteenth century. Judaisers is a term to describe Christians, usually of Jewish race, who insisted that Gentile converts must be circumcised and keep the Mosaic law; the early church in Jerusalem, Antioch and Galatia was certainly affected by such people, as Acts and Galatians clearly show. But there is not the slightest evidence in the Thessalonian correspondence that such influence had infiltrated the church at Thessalonica. There is simply no mention of the characteristic points of argument, and the Pauline vocabulary

that recurs in such debates is simply absent (such words as sin, law, justification and works).

2. However, the church could well have been subject to pressure from non-Christian Jews, and this is in fact attested by the account in Ac. 17. It has been argued that 1 Th. 2:14 implies that the opposition to the church came exclusively from the Gentile fellow-countrymen of the converts, but this view is not substantiated. Such opposition came from outside the church, and Paul's letter is not directed to outsiders. Nevertheless, it is quite plausible that people outside the church attacked it by denigrating the character of Paul and the other missionaries, and we should probably see an attempt to ward off such accusations in 2:1–12. Here Paul defends himself against the suggestion that he uses the same methods as the less honest and honourable types of travelling philosophers and preachers in the ancient world.

3. The hortatory parts of the letter have given rise to the view that Paul is dealing with teaching that was being spread in the church by people who held a different understanding of the Christian faith from his own. W. Schmithals in particular has claimed that each of Paul's churches was invaded by Gnostic teachers who advocated a different kind of Christianity from his. Specifically the Gnostics did not believe in a future resurrection of the body but held that a spiritual resurrection had already taken place, as a result of which believers were now transformed and living in a new age. In this situation the true messengers of the gospel had special spiritual powers, and the true believers were set free from ethical constraints in respect of sexual relationships.

Schmithals goes through the letter and argues that we can read between the lines and see evidence of Paul attacking such notions. In 1:2–2:12 Paul defends himself against the charges of being weak and lacking the power of the Spirit in his preaching and also of preaching from deceitful and avaricious motives. The sexual sins which Paul attacks in 4:3–8 are said to arise from Gnostic libertinarianism. The laziness and rejection of manual labour criticised in 4:9–12 arose from Gnostic 'enthusiasm'. Paul's eschatological teaching was necessary because his opponents had caused the church to doubt that the dead would be raised, and also because his opponents lacked any sense of future expectation at all. In 5:12–14 Paul had to defend the leaders of the church from being usurped by Gnostic rivals. All of these references are taken from Letter B in Schmithals' reorganisation of the epistle.

The remainder of the epistle, which constitutes Letter D, is a joyful letter which indicates that the problems in the church had been resolved; Schmithals suggests that the afflictions mentioned in

3:3f. which the church had experienced were both outward persecution and the internal problems caused by the presence of the
Gnostic teachers.

This thesis has been accepted and made the basis for further
study of 4:13–5:11 by W. Harnisch, but it has been generally rejected by other scholars (Best, pp. 17–19; A. Suhl, op. cit.;
G. Lüdemann, *Paulus, der Heidenapostel*, Band 1, Göttingen,
1980, pp. 221–6), and with good reason:

(*a*). The existence of a developed first-century Gnosticism remains
completely unproven despite constant protestations and assumptions
to the contrary (E. M. Yamauchi, *Pre-Christian Gnosticism: A Survey
of the Proposed Evidences*, London, 1973). Admittedly, this is partly
a question of definition. Some of the phenomena identified by
Schmithals and others in the Pauline churches and elsewhere in
first-century Christianity may well belong to what has been variously
called 'Gnosis' (as a broader and less developed stream of thought
than fully-fledged second-century Gnosticism) or 'pre-Gnosticism'.
However, the question is more than one of mere definition, for it
is concerned with the interpretation which we put upon the phenomena and with the question whether we are entitled to draw inferences
from attested second-century phenomena as regards the first-century
situation.

(*b*). Nothing in the evidence found in 1 Thessalonians offers
independent proof of the existence of Gnosticism in the first century.
It was quite possible for people to believe that some kind of resurrection had already happened, or to be libertinarians, or to lay stress
on the power of the Spirit, without being Gnostics, and the combination of these features would not be peculiar to Gnosticism. If
there really were Gnosticism in Thessalonica, we should expect to
find evidence of salvation by knowledge and of the existence of
Gnostic mythology, none of which is present.

(*c*). If the church were threatened by Gnostic teachers, we would
expect that Paul would be much more concerned about their presence and would attack them more strongly. In fact, there is nothing
of the sort. The letter indicates that Paul was basically happy with
the situation in the church. Schmithals is able to establish his case
only by dividing up the two letters to the Thessalonians, by pos-
tulating that at the outset (letter A) Paul was not fully informed
about the situation and responded in a fairly mild manner and also
by claiming that Paul's expressions of satisfaction with the state of
the church belong to a later letter (D) after the trouble had died
down. But we have seen that this dissection of 1 Thessalonians, on
which the case for Gnostic influence depends, is not justified.

(*d*). Schmithals' case requires that Thessalonica should have been visited by the same kind of Gnostic teachers who visited the churches in Corinth, Philippi and elsewhere. But it is extremely improbable that any such teachers existed at the time of Paul's second missionary campaign when he evangelised Thessalonica; the existence of a rival brand of Christianity so soon in the Macedonian area is most unlikely. To avoid this fatal difficulty Schmithals has to date the letters at the time of Paul's third campaign when he was involved with similar problems in Corinth. This dating, however, is to be rejected (see below).

(e). Several of the passages in which Schmithals finds evidence of Gnosticism at Thessalonica have been misinterpreted by him. Nothing in the letters suggests that some of the readers thought that the resurrection had already taken place and that there were no significant future events to be expected. Nor is it at all clear that Paul had to defend the church leaders against Gnostic rivals. Nor again is it probable that the afflictions in 3:3f. are internal tensions in the church.

These considerations show that the theory of Gnosticism at Thessalonica has no real basis.

4. R. Jewett ('Enthusiastic Radicalism and the Thessalonian Correspondence', *Society of Biblical Literature 1972 Proceedings*, Vol. I, pp. 181–232) has revived the view of W. Lütgert that some of the members of the church had developed a radical enthusiastic self-consciousness resulting in libertinism and idleness. Jewett utilises the evidence which was also gathered by Schmithals, and argues that the readers had identified their experience of the Spirit with the parousia. Consequently they believed that the resurrection was already past and they had no future expectation. They regarded Paul as lacking in spiritual power. They felt free from the order imposed by God and by society, and so were living in sexual licence and idleness. They were consequently shocked by the persecution which was disturbing the church and also by the deaths of some of the members which contradicted their understanding of the new age in which they thought they were living. All in all, they were a group showing similarities to the 'divine men' whose activities have been suspected in Corinth.

The exegetical basis of this hypothesis has been carefully examined by Best, pp. 19–22, and nothing needs to be added to his critical comments. There is nothing to show that the readers believed that the resurrection and parousia had already happened; Jewett misinterprets 2 Th. 2:2 as teaching the latter. Paul assumes that the parousia is still in the future, and makes no effort to prove the point. Paul's emphasis that his message was accompanied by the power of the Spirit appears to be not so much a form of self-defence as rather a means of assurance to the readers concerning the reality of their conversion. The sexual licence displayed by some of the readers was simply a carry-over from a pagan way of life (4:5), and the idleness probably arose from a heightened sense that the parousia was imminent. The problems felt over the deaths of some members of the church arose from a failure to appreciate the connection between the parousia and the resurrection of the dead. Finally, there is no evidence in the letter to suggest that there was a group opposed to Paul and teaching a view of the Christian faith that differed substantially from his.

5. We come, therefore, to the view of Best, p. 22, who rightly sees a combination of factors causing unease in an infant Christian congregation. There was persecution from outsiders, including attacks on Paul's character and the uprightness of his motives as a preacher; he was being compared with the less respectable type of wandering philosopher and preachers. There was the novel experience of the power of the Spirit which was causing different reactions. Some were responding over-enthusiastically, while others wished to damp down this excess of enthusiasm. There was a carry-over of pagan standards in sexual ethics, though it does not appear to have been on a worrying scale, and Paul's remarks are more in the nature of a warning against possible failure than a condemnation of existing practices. And there were the problems caused by an over-emphasis on the imminence of the parousia and by a lack of detailed teaching, probably due to the short time that the missionaries had been able to spend with the church. This may not be as exciting a hypothesis as those which find an organised and hitherto unsuspected group of opponents of Paul in Thessalonica, but it has the distinct advantage of doing better justice to the evidence.

6. THE DATE OF 1 THESSALONIANS

1. The information that can be gleaned from the letter itself shows that Paul had sent Timothy from Athens to Thessalonica to encourage the church and to bring back news; Timothy duly returned with good news about the state of the church (3:1–10). Paul hoped that the way would open up for a visit by himself, but it is clear that in the meantime he had to content himself with sending a letter instead, and the general tone of the letter suggests that it was sent shortly after Timothy's return from Thessalonica. The question now arises as to whether this situation can be fitted into a broader pattern of Paul's activities. According to Ac. 17–18, when Paul left Thessalonica he went to Beroea, where he left Silas and Timothy, and

then went on to Athens, where he waited for his companions to join him. Before they could do so, he moved on to Corinth, and it was there that they rejoined him from Macedonia. It is tempting to link the two accounts together despite the fact that they do not contain exactly the same itineraries and to conclude that 1 Thessalonians was written after Timothy had rejoined Paul at Corinth and during the extended period that Paul spent there. This dating of the letter can be supported by the following points:

(a). The letter is characterised by numerous references to the initial visit of the missionaries to the church, and there is nothing to suggest that more than one visit had been paid by Paul to Thessalonica. The vivid character of the language strongly suggests that the letter was written not long after the foundation of the church and indeed that this was Paul's first letter to it.

(b). The general character of the teaching suggests an early date in relation to Paul's other letters. This is particularly so with regard to Paul's teaching about the parousia; here only does he reckon earnestly with the possibility that he will be alive to experience it (4:15), whereas in his other letters he appears to think much more in terms of his own death before the parousia. The teaching about church order also appears to be very primitive. A good deal of Paul's characteristic doctrine is also absent from this letter, although this may well be because it was not relevant to the situation which he was addressing rather than because it was not yet developed in his mind.

(c). Paul writes in the context of a mission in Achaia and Macedonia and says nothing about Ephesus and other places in Asia which he evangelised during his third campaign. He names Silas as a co-author of the letter, but we have no certain evidence that Silas worked with Paul after the second campaign.

These points have appeared decisive to most scholars, but there are some difficulties with this view and some evidence that may favour a later date.

2. The view that Paul wrote the letter during his third missionary campaign has gained some supporters, notably Schmithals, pp. 181–91, who makes the following points:

(a). The differences between the accounts in 1 Th. 3 and Ac. 17–18 are irreconcilable.

(b). According to 2:18 Paul wanted to revisit the church several times, but there would not have been time for this during his brief visit to Athens. In any case was there really any obstacle to his revisiting the church at this juncture?

(c). Sufficient time must be allowed for the report of the mission at Thessalonica to become known 'everywhere' (1:8).

(*d*). It is unlikely that sufficient people had died in the brief period before Paul's first visit to Corinth to cause the problems reflected in ch. 4.

These considerations lead Schmithals to argue that Paul wrote the letter during a subsequent visit to Corinth, but he recognises some problems attached to this view:

(*e*). The 'fresh recollections' of Paul's initial visit to the church do not fit a later date. But Schmithals argues that this is a subjective impression, and the impressions are no more 'fresh' than in Phil. 4:15.

(*f*). The naming of Silas as co-sender is awkward, but Schmithals argues that he could well have been with Paul briefly during his third campaign.

(*g*). A second visit by Paul to Athens is unlikely. But if Paul travelled by sea from Ephesus to Corinth, he must surely have called at Athens en route.

(*h*). Schmithals argues that Paul had heard several times about the state of the church before he sent Timothy to bring it encouragement; this was not possible in the short time before his first visit to Corinth.

These arguments have not convinced other scholars. With regard to (*a*), we have already seen that Ac. and 1 Th. give us two incomplete accounts of the situation and are not incompatible with each other. As for (*b*), Paul could have wanted to revisit Thessalonica two or three times within a short period of weeks. With regard to (*c*), Best, p. 10, notes that it was news of the *conversion* of the Thessalonians which was causing excitement rather than news of the continuing development of the church. (*d*) is a subjective point; two or more people could easily die in as many months. In (*e*), the point about the recollections is not just that they are fresh but that they dominate the first part of the letter. (*f*) carries no weight one way or the other, and the same is true of (*g*). As for (*h*) there is no real problem here either, especially if Timothy rejoined Paul in Athens before he was sent to Thessalonica and brought news from Macedonia. Contact with Christians from Philippi (who would travel via Thessalonica) is also probable.

Thus none of the reasons for dating the letter later in Paul's career is decisive. Schmithals' case is also disputed by G. Lüdemann (op. cit., pp. 224–6). He argues that the evidence of Acts must not be used since it is a secondary (and, in Lüdemann's view, unreliable) source, that it is false to claim that difficulties with his churches prevented Paul from revisiting Thessalonica, that 1:8 is rhetorical in character just like 2 C. 9:1ff., and that the period between the letter and the founding of the church was sufficient for some of the

members to have died. Lüdemann seriously underestimates the
historical value of Acts and appears to deprive 1 Th. 3:1ff. of its
full force, but nevertheless he is right to conclude that no considerations demand a late date for the letter. Lüdemann's own chronology of Paul's career is very different from traditional outlines in that
he dates Paul's visit to Corinth to found the church as early as AD
41 and the Macedonian ministry correspondingly earlier, but he still
maintains the composition of 1 Thessalonians at the same relative
point, namely, when Paul moved south from Macedonia to Corinth.
Likewise, R. Jewett (*Dating Paul's Life*, London, 1979) adopts the
same relative dating, but is more traditional in his absolute dating.
A detailed discussion of Lüdemann's absolute chronology is not
possible in the present context; for criticism of the early date which
he offers for the Macedonian ministry, see R. Jewett, op. cit.,
pp. 81–5.

7. THE CONTENTS AND PURPOSE OF
2 THESSALONIANS

The second letter to the Thessalonians begins in very much the
same way as 1 Thessalonians, i.e. as a communication from the
same group of authors to the same group of readers. It is evident
that three main topics dominate the letter. First, in the opening
chapter the author (assuming that one person is responsible for the
composition) comments on the steadfastness of the readers under
persecution and proceeds to draw a contrast between the fate of
persecutors and the fate of the readers at the revelation or parousia
of the Lord. We have to envisage a situation of fairly fierce opposition to the church to call forth the strong language of the author.
Second, there was teaching current in the church that the day of
the Lord had already arrived and that consequently the parousia of
the Lord and the gathering of his people to meet him was very
imminent. This was a mistaken view in the opinion of the author,
and he argued that the day of the Lord could not yet have arrived
because certain other events must precede it, namely, the revelation
of a rebellious person who is at present restrained from appearing;
once he has been revealed, the Lord will also appear and destroy
him. Those who follow the rebel will come under condemnation,
but the readers are God's people and will be saved, provided that
they hold fast to the gospel as they have been taught it. Third, some
of the members of the church were living in idleness and sponging
on the better-off and generous members. Such people were to be
placed under discipline if they did not mend their ways.

These three parts of the letter indicate three elements in the situation to which the letter was addressed. Otherwise the letter contains no concrete information about the situation of the readers or the author which would enable us to place it more easily.

One important indirect clue is that both in structure and in style the letter is a close relative of 1 Thessalonians. Like 1 Thessalonians it has a fairly simple epistolary structure:

Greeting	1:1–2
Opening Thanksgiving	1:2–12
Instruction	2:1–17
Exhortation	3:1–16
Conclusion	3:17–18

As for the style, this will be considered in more detail below; suffice it to say that there are considerable parallels in subject-matter and in language.

If we take the letter at its face value, this similarity suggests that it was probably written close in time to 1 Thessalonians. It is not difficult to envisage a situation developing in which the letter would be necessary:

1. Already in 1 Thessalonians there are hints of the afflictions which the church was undergoing, sufficiently serious for Paul to be worried about the church and to send Timothy to give encouragement. The intensity of Paul's language in 1 Th. 2:14–16 reflects the seriousness of the situation. There would be nothing surprising about further outbursts of persecution directed against the church. Nothing suggests that organised, state persecution is necessarily in mind.

2. The belief that the day of the Lord had already come would not be a surprising development in a church where an intense expectation of the parousia existed. Paul's first letter had laid much stress on the parousia as an event that could be expected within the lifetime of the readers. It would not require much encouragement to make people believe that they could already see the signs of the end of the world. The author of 2 Thessalonians recognised that a prophetic message or a piece of teaching to this effect could easily have been given in the church. Not only so, but what had been said in 1 Thessalonians could have given a basis for this belief. In short, the apocalyptic enthusiasm reflected and perhaps unwittingly encouraged in 1 Thessalonians could well have led to the unbalanced views that are countered in 2 Th. 2.

3. 1 Thessalonians also testified to the fact that some members of

the church were living in idleness, and it would be altogether natural for intense apocalyptic excitement to foster this mood.

There is thus no difficulty in seeing how the situation reflected in 2 Thessalonians could have developed in the church at Thessalonica, and it may be worth remarking that we do not have independent evidence of a precisely similar state of affairs anywhere else. (The nearest parallel would probably be that of the Montanists in the second century, but Montanism was characterised by a dependence on spiritual revelations which would have aroused much more comment than the casual reference in 2 Th. 2:2. In any case Montanism was considerably later.) Moreover, such a situation could have developed fairly soon after the writing of 1 Thessalonians. But time must be allowed.

If this is the case, then the letter will have been written shortly after 1 Thessalonians, and it may well date from later in Paul's first visit to Corinth. But there is no concrete evidence in the letter to enable us to be more specific.

8. ALTERNATIVE VIEWS OF THE ORIGIN OF 2 THESSALONIANS

However, this apparently straight-forward account of the matter has not found anything like general acceptance, especially in recent years, and various theories have been advanced to meet the difficulties, real or imagined, which surround the traditional theory. We shall consider first of all those theories which maintain that Paul was the author of the letter. These are broadly speaking attempts to deal with difficulties in the situation presupposed by the letter.

1. A number of scholars have found it difficult to see why Paul should send a letter so similar to 1 Thessalonians to the same church soon after the first letter: why should he need to go over the same ground once again? Coupled with this problem is the claim that the general tone of 2 Thessalonians is cooler and more formal than that of 1 Thessalonians; there is a distinct lack of the personal comments and reminiscences that characterise the first letter. One solution to this problem is to argue that the two letters were written in the reverse order, with 2 Thessalonians being the earlier communication. Since Paul's letters were grouped in descending order of size for the most part, it is understandable that the longer letter was placed first in the corpus. It can be argued that a better presentation of the situation results. Thus: (*a*). The persecution of the church is at its height in 2 Th. 1:4-7, but is diminished or past in 1 Th. 2:14. (*b*). The problem of idleness in the church is said to sound like a

new topic in 2 Th. 3:11, whereas it sounds old in 1 Th. 4:11; moreover, it is strange that Paul refers back to his own example in 2 Thessalonians rather than to his previous letter. (c). The exhortation not to worry about the time of the parousia in 1 Th. 5:1 would gain more force if it had been preceded by the teaching in 2 Th. 2. (d). The emphasis on Paul's autograph in 2 Th. 3:17 would be pointless except in his first letter to the church. (e). 1 Thessalonians can be understood as a reply to questions raised by the church (possibly in a letter) in response to what Paul had said in 2 Thessalonians (cf. 1 Th. 4:9, 13; 5:1, where Paul introduces topics raised by his readers in the same way as in 1 C. 7:1; et al.). (See T. W. Manson, *Studies in the Gospels and Epistles*, Manchester, 1962, pp. 259–78.)

This interesting theory has failed to win support. It can equally well be argued that the problems of persecution, idleness and expectation of the parousia had intensified since the writing of 1 Thessalonians, that the emphasis on Paul's signature was due to the special problems in the church, and that, while 1 Thessalonians does answer questions in the minds of the church, the case that these questions arose out of what Paul said in 2 Thessalonians has not been made out. In addition, the more personal tone in 1 Thessalonians is much more natural in the earlier letter. Moreover, 2 Thessalonians contains references to an earlier letter from Paul (2 Th. 2:2, 15), and these must surely be to 1 Thessalonians and not to some other, lost letter.

2. A second type of hypothesis is that the two letters were written to different groups of readers. We can set aside the theory of E. Schweizer that 2 Thessalonians was really sent to Philippi (see Best, pp. 40f.), and earlier suggestions that Beroea was the destination; nothing in the letter supports such a view, and no good explanation of the mix-up in the address has been given.

More weight can be given to theories that the two letters were sent to two different sections in the church. One view is that the first letter was sent to the Gentile members of the church, while the second letter was sent to the Jewish members (A. Harnack, 'Das Problem des zweiten Thessalonicherbriefs', *Sitzungsberichte der Kgl. Preuss. Akademie der Wissenschaften*, Phil. Hist. Klasse 31, Berlin, 1910, pp. 560–78). This view is supported by the more Jewish colouring of the second letter and by the suggestions in 1 Th. 5:26f. and 2 Th. 3:18 that the church was divided. But most subsequent scholars have rejected this view because there is Jewish colouring in other Pauline letters written to Gentile (or partly Gentile) audiences (e.g. Romans) and also because one can hardly imagine Paul toler-

ating a divided church without saying something about the situation
(see Best, pp. 38–40).

A second suggestion is that one letter was written to the church
as a whole and the other to a group within it. M. Dibelius thought
that 1 Thessalonians was written in an intimate manner to the
leaders of the church while 2 Thessalonians was written to the whole
community (Dibelius, pp. 57f.). This theory has been stood on its
head by E. E. Ellis (*Prophecy and Hermeneutic*, Tübingen/Grand
Rapids, 1978, pp. 19–21). He accepts Harnack's claim that 2 Thessalonians was written to a minority group in the church, but argues
that this group was composed not of Jewish Christians but of the
church leaders. Three arguments are utilised: (*a*). The term 'brothers' is taken to be a reference to Paul's colleagues who acted as the
leaders of the church. (*b*). The term 'first-fruits' (2 Th. 2:13) refers
to the first converts who are consecrated to the work of God (cf.
1 C. 16:15). (*c*). The instructions to the 'brothers' in 2 Th. 3:6–15
are concerned with Christian workers who were supposed to imitate
Paul in forgoing their claim to support from the church but were in
fact living in idleness and depending too much on the church to
keep them.

This view has been examined and criticised by W.-H. Ollrog
(*Paulus und seine Mitarbeiter*, Neukirchen, 1979, p. 78 n. 93); he
argues that, while Paul can *refer* to his fellow-workers as 'the brothers', this term does not come to *mean* a basically limited group of
workers. He rejects Ellis's view of 2 Thessalonians without, however, advancing his reasons in detail. In fact, the letter is addressed
to the church in the same way as the first letter. Further, the word
'first-fruits' is a variant reading in the text of 2 Th. 2:13 and the
reading 'from the beginning' is probably to be preferred. At most,
2 Th. 3 could refer to a group of 'brothers' who were dependent on
the church for support, but it seems more probable that the allusion
is to members of the church in general who were dependent on the
richer members, especially since the earlier references to the same
fault in 1 Th. 4:11f.; 5:14 give no hint that the church leaders were
in mind. On the whole, the theory is not very persuasive.

3. A third type of hypothesis is that the letter should be regarded
as composite. Schmithals, pp. 191–218, holds that Paul's first letter
to Thessalonica, consisting of 2 Th. 1:1–12; 3:6–16, has been expanded by the inclusion of his third letter, slightly rearranged in
order, 2 Th. 2:13f., 1–12, 15–3:3 (5), 17f. The first letter, written
some time after the foundation of the church, is a warning in general
terms to avoid the Gnostic teachers who were infiltrating the church
and to give no place to their fanaticism. At this point Paul was not
well-informed about their teaching and wrote in general terms. After

the second letter, discussed earlier, in which Paul refuted Gnostic attacks on himself, came the third letter in which he tackled the actual Gnostic teaching that the day of the Lord had already come, teaching which was held to be supported by his own letter (1 Th. 5:5ff.).

The arguments in favour of this view are that it gives a plausible reconstruction of Paul's dealings with the church and that it does justice to the peculiar structure of the letter, as it stands at present, with its second thanksgiving in 2:13f. and its apparent conclusion in 2:16–3:5. However, it cannot be said to be persuasive. The setting of the letters during Paul's third missionary campaign is implausible, as we have already noted. Further, the reversal in the order of the letters which results is open to some of the same objections as have been made against the simpler theory that 2 Thessalonians in its present form is earlier than 1 Thessalonians. Finally, there is no real problem in Paul reverting to thanksgiving in 2:13 and following this with exhortation. Schmithals, in other words, is too rigid in his insistence that a Pauline letter must follow a particular pattern in detail. (See Best, pp. 45–50, for a detailed examination.)

Schmithals' theory is of particular interest because he uses it to argue for the Pauline authorship of the letter. He insists that the only real argument against authenticity is the literary structure of the letter, a point that may be significant as we come to look at other views of the origin of the letter.

9. THE AUTHENTICITY OF 2 THESSALONIANS

When E. Best published his commentary on the epistles in 1972, probably a majority of scholars regarded 2 Th. as a genuine letter of Paul, or at least held that the arguments advanced by some scholars against its authenticity were not convincing. The question of authenticity seems to have been raised originally by J. E. C. Schmidt in 1798. He argued that 2:1–12 was un-Pauline and was a later interpolation into an otherwise genuine letter (the essential part of his argument is reprinted in Trilling, *Untersuchungen*, pp. 159–61).

It was the work of W. Wrede, published in 1903, which launched a full-scale attack on the letter, principally on the basis of its literary relationship to 1 Th. For Wrede, 2 Th. was based on the earlier letter and showed numerous points of literary dependence which have a cumulative force; he paid less attention to the eschatological teaching, which he regarded as a less forceful argument. Replies to Wrede came from J. Wrzol and J. Graafen as well as from commentators. Subsequent critics of authenticity included C. Masson (one of the few commentators to deny authenticity), H. Braun, 'Zur nachpaulinischen Herkunft des zweiten Thessalonicherbriefes', *ZNW* 44, 1952-3, pp. 152-6 (= *Gesammelte Studien zum Neuen Testament*, Tübingen, 1962, pp. 205-9) and W. Marxsen, *Introduction to the New Testament*, Oxford, 1968, 37-44. The views of these scholars are discussed by Best, pp. 50-8, who himself concludes in favour of authenticity. Other defenders of the same point of view include Rigaux, pp. 124-52, Whiteley, pp. 9-18, and W. G. Kümmel, *Introduction to the New Testament*, London, 1966, pp. 187-90.

Since 1970, however, the tide of critical opinion has shifted decisively in favour of inauthenticity as the solution to the problems raised by the letter. A useful article by J. A. Bailey, 'Who wrote II Thessalonians?' *NTS* 25, 1978-9, pp. 131-45, summarises the reasons commonly given. Surprisingly it was written in ignorance of the major work by W. Trilling (*Untersuchungen*) which attempts to bring new factors into the discussion. Simultaneously there has been a general trend in favour of the inauthenticity of the letter among Continental scholars. We shall summarise briefly the case against the authenticity of the letter before considering the various points in more detail.

1. The basic reason for suspecting the genuineness of the letter is its relationship to 1 Th. Historically, the starting point was the eschatological teaching in the letters. 1 Th. emphasises the imminence and unexpectedness of the parousia, whereas in 2 Th. the author attacks the view that the Day of the Lord has come and insists that various other events must precede the parousia. This contrast between the emphasis on imminence and the dampening down of eschatological hope raises two questions. First, how can we explain the different situation in the church at Thessalonica which led to the different teaching given in 2 Th.? If the letters were written close in time (as the literary evidence would seem to imply, if they are both genuine), is such a swift change in the situation at Thessalonica credible? Second, how can this aberration in Paul's teaching be explained, especially since elsewhere in his letters there is no comparable teaching about the delay of the parousia?

2. The structure and wording of 2 Th. show impressive similarities with those of 1 Th. One can draw up, as Wrede has done, a synoptic table of the parallels. How can one explain why Paul should so slavishly have followed his earlier letter, particularly when one bears in mind that there is no other example in Paul's writings of such parallelism?

3. This close parallelism is accompanied by various theological

differences between the letters, not only in eschatology but also in other areas. How can this difference in teaching be explained in the case of writings which, on the assumption of genuineness, were written close in time to one another?

4. There is said to be a difference in tone between the warmth, freshness and specific relationship to the readers found in 1 Th. and the solemn official tone and the lack of personal allusions in 2 Th. At the same time one can also detect differences in style and theology between the letters.

5. These points all cast doubt on the genuineness of 2 Th. as compared with 1 Th. It then becomes natural to extend the investigation and assess the relationship of 2 Th. to other Pauline letters. It can be argued that its literary style differs from that of Paul and that its theology is post-Pauline.

6. Hence, it can be argued, the letter is best understood as a pseudepigraph. An unknown author wrote this letter to deal with a group of apocalyptic enthusiasts who were claiming Paul's authority for their belief in the imminence of the parousia; he sought to quench their views by himself assuming the mask of Paul and insisting on the delay of the parousia. His very insistence on the authenticity of his letter (2 Th. 3:17) betrays its inauthenticity; letters falsely ascribed to Paul are unlikely to have circulated during his lifetime.

Such is the essence of the case: 2 Th. is best understood as an imitation of 1 Th. designed to teach a different lesson (cf. the acute presentation of the case by P. Vielhauer, *Geschichte der urchristlichen Literatur*, Berlin/New York, 1975, pp. 95–103). We shall now analyse the arguments.

1. *Literary arguments.*

(*a*). *Structure*. It is argued that the general structure of the letter as a letter is very similar to that of 1 Th. In particular, both letters have the peculiarities of a thanksgiving in the middle of the 'body' (1 Th. 2:13; 2 Th. 2:13) and of a benediction at the end of it (1 Th. 3:11–13; 2 Th. 2:16). According to Peterson, p. 46, 2 Th. can be said to have more form than content, in that it has the complicated skeleton imitated from 1 Th. but has little flesh on the bones.

It is doubtful whether much weight can be placed on this point. If the traditional ascription and dating of the letters is correct, 2 Th. would have been written not long after 1 Th. and at a time when Paul was not writing many other letters. It would not be at all surprising if in these circumstances the letters should follow the same general plan. The similarities in any case are largely due to the fact that both letters follow the typical first-century epistolary pattern, and they are thus of no significance in determining author-

ship. The renewed thanksgiving and the benediction are not surprising in letters written about the same time.

A further point is that it is hard to estimate the significance of
the similarities when we have no generally agreed basis for comparison in other Pauline letters. The integrity of 1 and 2 Corinthians,
Philippians and even to some extent of Romans is a matter of doubt
to some scholars, and in any case only Philippians is comparable in
length with the Thessalonian epistles. All the other Pauline letters
stand under suspicion of being inauthentic, particularly in the eyes
of scholars who dispute 2 Thessalonians. We have, therefore, no
accepted 'control' against which to gauge the significance of the
similarities in structure between 1 and 2 Th. It would certainly
seem that we have no evidence which would enable us to say that
because the general structure of 2 Th. is so close to that of 1 Th.
it must be an imitation by a pseudonymous author.

For Wrede the decisive point lay not so much in the common
epistolary structure as rather in the common wording and structure
of numerous passages in the letters. He argued that the order of the
material and the nature of the verbal parallels suggest that 2 Th. is
a literary echo of 1 Th. (cf. further Peterson, pp. 48–71). Best,
pp. 50–4, admits that Wrede's case is very strong, but goes on to
argue that the similarity in structure is not as significant as he
claimed and that the cumulative effect of the linguistic parallels is
much less than appears at first sight. Our problem again is that we
have no 'control' which would enable us to determine whether the
phenomena are consistent with composition by Paul shortly after
1 Th. The defence that Paul composed 2 Th. within a few days of
2 Th. (Graafen, pp. 35–52), even before he heard of the reception
of the earlier letter at Thessalonica, seems most improbable, and
there is more to be said for the view of T. Zahn (taken up by Wrzol,
p. 90; Neil, p. xxiii; Morris, p. 30) that Paul retained a draft copy
of 1 Th. and was able to read it before composing 2 Th. Dismissal
of this view on the grounds that it is purely hypothetical is open to
the objection that the construction of a pseudonymous situation is
even more hypothetical. It must be remembered that we simply do
not know how Paul's mind would have worked in composing a
second letter soon after an earlier one on the same topic; we have
no other example of two letters written by Paul to the same church
within a matter of months of each other. What we do know is that
Paul did write a letter which contained teaching which was partly
misunderstood and then had to write and go over the same ground
again (1 C. 5:9–13). Given that Paul was writing to the same church
about the same topics in two letters not far distant in time, it would
not be surprising if his wording in the second letter should be

similar to that in the first. Wrede's case is at the very least not
proven.

(b). *Vocabulary*. It is admitted by Trilling, *Untersuchungen*, p. 47,
that no weight can be placed on the vocabulary of 2 Th. taken on
its own. Von Dobschütz, pp. 39f., proved that there is nothing
un-Pauline about the vocabulary, and his figures are basically unaffected by any subsequent text-critical discussions (*pace* Trilling,
ibid., who quibbles over the point).

A new point is raised by K. Grayston and G. Herdan, 'The
authorship of the Pastorals in the light of statistical linguistics',
NTS, 6, 1960–1, pp. 1–15. They argue that there is an unusually
low number of words (58) peculiar to 1 and 2 Thessalonians when
compared with the other Pauline epistles; on the basis of the length
of the letters one would expect 80–90. They conclude that the most
probable explanation is that the author of 2 Thessalonians has copied
from 1 Thessalonians. Unfortunately, this argument proves too
much: the number of words peculiar to 1 Thessalonians (38) is also
'unusually low' and would suggest that this letter too is not genuine.
The figures indicate rather that each letter has a somewhat small
vocabulary.

This last point is taken up by Trilling, pp. 62f., who quotes
evidence originally assembled by W. Bornemann to show that a
large number of words and expressions are each used twice or more
often, and uses this as a sign of poverty of expression. However,
when the list is examined, it seems much more likely that we should
accept Bornemann's explanation in terms of the eschatological purpose of the letter rather than Trilling's explanation in terms of a
writer with a limited vocabulary.

Trilling asserts that no weight can be placed on arguments from
vocabulary. However, this is not an altogether fair judgment. When
we find a document which claims to be by Paul and which demonstrates a Pauline vocabulary, it is fair to claim that the argument
from vocabulary must be held to give some support to the document's claim to Pauline authorship.

There are in fact various small features which it would have been
difficult for an imitator to produce (the use of the Pauline particle
eiper in 1:6; the use of *anesis* in 1:7; the creation of the Pauline-type
compound *hyperauxanein* in 1:3).

(c). *Style*. No generally accepted precise methods have been formulated to cope with style, and much depends on subjective judgment as to what a given author may or may not do.

A. Q. Morton and J. McLeman, *Paul, The Man and The Myth*,
London, 1966, have attempted to make a statistical survey of such
matters as sentence-length and the proportionate occurrence of var-

ious common words in Paul's epistles, and they conclude that
Romans, 1 and 2 Corinthians and Galatians form one stylistic group;
the other letters traditionally assigned to him all show different
styles, but 1 and 2 Th. show the same style as one another (see also
S. Michaelson and A. Q. Morton, 'Last Words: A Test of Authorship for Greek Writers', *NTS* 18, 1971–2, pp. 192–208). Few, if
any, scholars have taken these findings seriously. An approach
which denies that the Paul of the *Hauptbriefe* wrote Philippians
stands condemned since every other kind of argument favours its
Pauline origin. If 2 Th. is inauthentic by this criterion, so also is
1 Th. One wonders whether one can place any weight on the conclusion that 2 Th. shows the same style as 1 Th. in terms of these
tests.

Trilling, *Untersuchungen*, pp. 48–61, takes over Frame's lists
(pp. 32f.) of unusual phrases in 2 Th., but fails to ask whether
many of these may not be accounted for by the subject-matter, and
also whether similar lists of unusual phrases may be made for other
Pauline epistles. Frame, in fact, has drawn up comparable lists for
1 Thessalonians, but Trilling ignores these and their significance.
He proceeds to work through the material in Rigaux, pp. 85–94,
and draws attention to the presence of parallel expressions and
groups of threes; 2 Thessalonians is poorer in such phenomena than
1 Thessalonians. He notes that 2 Thessalonians contains very little
metaphor by comparison with 1 Thessalonians. (This may be the
place to note the remarkably high frequency of *kathōs* in 1 Thessalonians by comparison with Paul's other epistles: this may suggest
that this letter has its own peculiarities and 2 Thessalonians should
not be expected to correspond in every detail with it.)

Trilling next notes what he regards as unusual phenomena. (i).
Fullness of expression. This is seen in the use of compound verbs
(1:3, 4, 5, 10) – but ignores the fact that Paul likes such verbs and
the unique form *hyperauxanein* is the kind of word that he likes to
coin. Again, there is the frequency of phrases with *pas* which Trilling sees as a mark of generalisation. But the same phenomenon can
be seen in Philippians. Third come various phrases in which nouns
are linked together in a manner reminiscent of Ephesians. But, as
von Dobschütz, p. 43, remarks, any of Paul's letters can produce
unusual forms of expression.

(ii). *Unusual expressions.* Trilling lists about nine of these, recog-
nising that individually they carry little weight, but claiming that
collectively in a short document they are significant.

(iii). *Preferred words and phrases.* These include the use of the
stems *dox-*, *axio-*, *dik-* and *tass-* and the use of *kyrios*. No doubt
some of these can be explained by the fact that authors tend to

repeat words which they have already used. Others are due to the subject matter (e.g. the use of *tass-*) in the discussion of the idlers, and the use of *dik-* in reference to the vindication of the persecuted. The frequency of *kyrios* is the continuation of a tendency already visible in I Thessalonians.

Trilling makes two further observations. The one concerns the formal, 'official' tone of the letter which he regards as very impersonal and stiff. He rejects von Dobschütz's explanation of this in terms of the situation of the readers who needed to be addressed in a fairly strong and impressive manner. But surely something like this was the actual situation if the letter is authentic. Paul was faced, not by personal opponents, but by a church which despite all its good points was being led astray into unrealistic attitudes and ways of life. The Paul who could come in a spirit of gentleness or with a rod (I C. 4:21) could vary his tone to the occasion. But in any case it is surely time that the myth of the cold tone of the letter was exploded. Granted that it is not as full of personal references as I Thessalonians nor written on such a crest of emotion, it is nevertheless by no means cold in tone. The claim that 'we ought to give thanks as is fitting' (1:3) is a cold and formal expression is quite unfounded (cf. Phil. 1:7). The personal concern of the author for the readers shines through the letter.

The other observation concerns the lack of Pauline features that might be expected in the letter, particularly the use of brief sentences, rhetorical questions, sharp imperatives and the like. This letter has more the character of solemn teaching and lacks Paul's originality. One may grant that there is something in this comment, but it is hard to see that it justifies a verdict of inauthenticity.

Trilling would no doubt emphasise that it is the total impression of all the arguments that counts rather than the individual weight of each, but it is very doubtful whether a set of weak arguments adds up to one powerful one. So far at least as questions of vocabulary and style are concerned, there is nothing of sufficient weight to make Pauline authorship really dubious. We must see whether any of the other arguments are stronger.

(*d*). *Form criticism*. Trilling, *Untersuchungen*, pp. 67–108, has attempted to introduce a new method of tackling the problem by undertaking what he calls a form-critical analysis of the epistle, on the basis of which he concludes that it is from one author who is not Paul, that the various individual forms have similar characteristics which link them together, and that the epistle is not a letter to a particular community but a didactic and paraenetic tract which claims apostolic authority. It is extraordinarily difficult to see how the analysis justifies these conclusions.

The prescript is close in wording to that of 1 Thessalonians but is slightly fuller. Trilling argues that Paul does not repeat himself word for word, that the additional words are awkward, and that there is nothing personal in the details. But is there any reason why Paul should not give substantially the same greeting in a second letter to the same community? The differences between 1 C. 1:1–3 and 2 C. 1:1f., written some considerable time afterwards, are not all that great. There is an equal lack of personal details in 1 Th. 1:1, and the overladen style can be paralleled elsewhere in Paul (see commentary for details).

The opening thanksgiving in 1 Thessalonians is lively in style and filled with personal allusions. By contrast, 2 Th. 1:3–12 is one long and complicated sentence, and it clothes teaching in the form of a thanksgiving. To Trilling it does not sound like a living address to an actual community. It shows the biblical knowledge, particularly of apocalyptic material, and the didactic tendency of a later period. Trilling further contrasts the genuine thanks in 1 Th. 2:13 with the dogmatic and didactic section in 2 Th. 2:13f. These differences in style can certainly be readily admitted, but it is not clear that they suggest difference of authorship. A didactic and paraenetic tendency can be detected in other Pauline thanksgivings, and the contents are usually linked to the theme of the letter. As for the second thanksgiving in 2:13f., this is, as Trilling rightly notes, closely tied to the preceding context and has the function of reassuring the readers that they will not suffer the fate of those who are to perish; it is hard to see why Paul could not have expressed himself in this way.

Trilling's analysis of 2:1–12 is mainly concerned to separate off vv. 3b, 4, 8–10a, and to argue that the writer has adapted this apocalyptic material to the situation of the church in his own day. Since defenders of Pauline authorship would agree that traditional material is being used – indeed material that comes from the tradition of Jesus' apocalyptic teaching and that also lies behind 1 Th. 4:13–18 – again there is no real basis here for challenging Pauline authorship.

Trilling argues that the material about prayer in 3:1–5 is formal compared with that in 1 Thessalonians; it shows literary dependence but has lost the personal tone. But one may question whether the tone is really any less personal than in, say, Phil. 4:4–7 which is even more general in content.

As regards the paraenesis in 3:6–13, Trilling notes that it deals with only one topic and heavily stresses the apostolic authority of the writer; he argues that the topic is broader than laziness and belongs to a period when Christian profession and life-style were not in agreement with each other. Here Trilling is disputing the fact that in reality the paraenesis does deal with a concrete situation in the church and is trying to show that there is a false impression of concreteness. As the commentary will attempt to indicate, his exegesis of the passage is dubious in detail, and in particular the impression that a later writer is claiming apostolic authority is read into the material.

Trilling is uncertain how to regard the closing greeting. He draws attention again to the lack of personal details and warmth. In his earlier study he takes v. 17*b* to be a means of stressing the authority of the apostolic contents of the letter, but in his commentary he reverts to the more usual explanation that it is meant to be a sign of authenticity, but—as Wrede observed—one that over-reaches itself and in fact betrays inauthenticity. J. A. Bailey, art cit., p. 138, seems to imply that Paul did not always write his own signature at the end of a letter, and he argues that the verse is an attempt to allay suspicion by a pseudonymous writer. But it is questionable whether the purpose of v. 17*b* is to authenticate the letter against forgeries; it is more plausibly regarded as a means of underlining the authority and importance of the contents of the letter and it has clear analogies in other Pauline epistles (cf. 1 Th. 5:27). As for the tone of the greeting, one may question whether that in 1 Th. is so very much warmer.

It is difficult to find all these considerations compelling. The most that has been established by critics of authenticity is that the letter is less personal than 1 Th.; it concentrates on teaching and paraenesis rather than on personal news and interests. But then the same might be said of the main body of Romans which is conspicuously lacking in personal material. The force of this parallel may seem to be weakened by the personal matter in the introduction and conclusion of Romans, but the point is that Romans does illustrate Paul's didactic style. The lack of personal greetings can also be paralleled in Galatians, a letter from which we learn remarkably little about the congregations addressed.

(2). *Theological arguments*

(*a*). *Eschatology*. Opinions differ considerably as to whether the eschatology of 2 Th. is contradictory to that of 1 Th. (so Whiteley, pp. 13–15, but he does not regard this as fatal to authenticity) or complementary to it. J. A. Bailey, art cit., pp. 136f., poses the problem: 'Either the end will come suddenly and without warning like a thief in the night (1 Thessalonians) or it will be preceded by a series of apocalyptic events which warn of its coming (II Thessalonians). Paul might have said both things – in differing situations to one church, or to different churches – but he can hardly have said both things to the same church at the same time, i.e. to the

Thessalonian church when he founded it. Moreover, corresponding to Paul's different messages to them, the situations in the two churches are quite different.' Bailey also argues that 2 Th. 2:2 implies correction of statements in 1 Th. which had been misunderstood as teaching that the End had come. He claims that such misunderstanding was unlikely at the time of receiving the letter, and that it is more likely that later misunderstandings are being corrected by a writer other than Paul.

Against the second part of this argument we may observe that 1 Th. implies that teaching about the imminence of the parousia was part of Paul's original preaching at Thessalonica, and that probably the arrival of 1 Th. encouraged existing hopes of the near parousia rather than caused them. This explains the language of 2 Th. 2:2, which suggests that a variety of causes lay behind the misunderstanding of the Thessalonians. It is impossible to see why Paul himself should not have corrected such misunderstanding, since he was careful to do so with a similar case at Corinth (1 C. 5:9–13). Furthermore, the somewhat obscure teaching of 2 Th. 2 is hardly likely to be the work of a later writer who was trying to correct Paul's teaching in a convincing way; it presumes some knowledge on the part of the readers. (It is true that one might argue that the Thessalonians could not have forgotten what Paul had taught them about coming events, but this is hardly a realistic objection; people can easily ignore unwelcome facts under emotional stress.)

Further, it is well known that in Jewish eschatology the coming of the End is preceded by signs, and that the gospel tradition contains the same juxtaposition of the suddenness and unpredictability of the End and of the prophecy of premonitory signs as we find in the two epistles. There is no real problem in Paul having taught that the End was coming soon and unpredictably and that certain events would precede it, and equally there is no problem in the Thessalonians overstressing the imminence and ignoring what Paul had said about events that must first take place. It is also worth noting that nothing in 1 Th. shows that Paul expected the parousia immediately; at most he reckoned with the possibility of it in his lifetime (1 Th. 5:10), but his teaching about its unpredictability and imminence could have led his readers to assume that it could happen immediately. In any case, Paul's teaching in 1 Th. 5 is that the parousia will take non-believers by surprise, whereas believers will be ready for it and will not be taken by surprise.

There is, then, no real disharmony between the two letters, and there is no problem about envisaging how the situation in Thessalonica may have led to the presentation of the two aspects of teaching in the two letters. It does not seem necessary to posit a development in Paul's teaching, such as is envisaged by C. L. Mearns, 'Early Eschatological Development in Paul: the Evidence of I and II Thessalonians', *NTS* 27, 1980–1, pp. 137–57. He argues that originally Paul regarded the resurrection of Jesus as his parousia. However, the deaths of believers meant that this view lost some of its attractiveness, and so Paul reconceptualised the parousia in the form of a 'second coming' of Jesus accompanied by the resurrection of dead believers. Then at a later stage he had to damp down over-enthusiastic acceptance of his new emphasis on a futurist eschatology and did so by intercalating a signs-sequence as a prelude to the Day of the Lord. But this scheme of development is very hypothetical. A speedy change from Paul's thinking in 1 Th. to another stage in 2 Th. is not likely, and Mearns is forced to hold that Paul's oral teaching at Thessalonica about the Antichrist (2 Th. 2:5) was not tied in to his teaching about the parousia.

(*b*). *Other aspects*. Trilling attaches considerable importance to his claim that the theological structure of 2 Thessalonians shows signs of a period later than Paul and is better understood in a post-Pauline context. What is important is not whether Pauline theological terms are used but whether they are used with different nuances. He investigates three samples of the thinking in the letter. First, there is the appeal to Pauline tradition. The concepts of gospel, witness and truth have been more or less identified with the authoritative teaching of the apostle and thus narrowed down and intellectualised. (This explains the theological poverty of the epistle.) It is, therefore, the Pauline tradition containing this teaching which the readers must accept and hence arises the stress on Paul's epistles (2 Th. 2:2, 15; 3:17). Further, the actual way of life of the apostle is made into a pattern to follow, in a way that impresses Trilling as un-Pauline.

Second, the picture which we gain of the Christian life is not one of freshness and joy, as in the early days of the Pauline mission, but of difficulty and weariness, a situation in which courage and exhortation are needed. The delay of the parousia has introduced uncertainty and given time for the development of doubt. There is no sense of mission to the outside world. The delay of the parousia has led to attempts to claim that it is already at hand. The parousia is increasingly seen as judgment, and the joy of expectation for it has disappeared.

Third, the picture of God and of Christ has taken on *OT*-cultic and apocalyptic-dramatic traits. His judging activity is emphasised. The coupling of Jesus with the Father is seen in a purely formal way. The frequent designation of Jesus as Lord indicates a late phase when he was increasingly given the *OT* title of Yahweh. The 'in Christ' formula is only weakly present, and Christ is depicted in a hieratic manner. The Spirit is scarcely mentioned. Trilling takes up a point made by W. Bornemann to the effect that if one simply removes the references to Jesus we are left with a document that could be purely Jewish in character.

Thus, although the epistle preserves some traces of Pauline theology, it is on the whole pretty weak theologically. Its main contribution is to give fresh life to traditional eschatology, and in this respect its use of the Antichrist figure in a new way can be compared with that in 1 John.

In attempting to assess this picture of the theology of 2 Thessalonians we would draw attention first of all to the comparable character of 1 Thessalonians. An investigation of the theology of 1 Thessalonians reveals that many of the fundamental theological ideas of Paul, as they are known to us from the *Hauptbriefe* (Rom., 1, 2 C., Gal.), are more or less completely missing. There is a ready explanation for this in the fact that Paul was not facing the same situation in 1 Thessalonians as in these others (I. H. Marshall, 'Pauline Theology in the Thessalonian Correspondence', in M. D. Hooker and S. G. Wilson (ed.), *Paul and Paulinism*, London, 1982, pp. 173–83). He did not need to discuss the law and justification, for example, because these were not issues at Thessalonica. Much of the silence over characteristic Pauline doctrines in 2 Thessalonians can be traced to the same clause. Second, the scope of theological interest of 2 Thessalonians is even narrower than that of 1 Thessalonians. If 2 Thessalonians is understood as a follow-up to 1 Thessalonians, dealing with one or two particular topics that needed further attention, the comparative lack of Pauline theology is adequately explained. Third, despite these gaps something of the fundamental structure of Pauline theology can be traced in 1 Thessalonians and also (though admittedly not quite so fully) in 2 Thessalonians. In particular, the idea of being 'in Christ' is well represented in both epistles.

It is, then, in the light of the similar problem in 1 Thessalonians and of the special character of the letter itself that the theology of 2 Thessalonians must be assessed. The problem boils down to the question of whether the theology is post-Pauline and reflects a post-Pauline situation. First, it must be insisted that the appeal to tradition which Trilling finds in the letter is exaggerated by him and corresponds in fact to appeals to tradition found in other Pauline epistles. In our opinion the view that the letter emphasises the apostolic authority of Paul is mistaken, a small pointer in this direction being the total absence of the word 'apostle'. Nor is it true that the concept of the gospel is intellectualised. Trilling ignores the moral element in the use of the word 'truth' in 2:12.

Second, Trilling reads the delay of the parousia into the epistle by trying to claim that assertions that the day of the Lord had come represent a lack of patient waiting during the period of delay. It is more probable that such assertions arose out of the enthusiasm in the church generated by Paul's preaching and fostered by 1 Thessalonians itself (and also reflected in Paul's own sense of imminence in 1 C. 7:26, 29). The element of judgment associated with the parousia is related to the persecution and the apostasy of which the writer speaks. The sense of joyful expectancy is present in 1:7, 10; 2:14, and the general tone of the letter as regards the readers is entirely hopeful.

Third, the christology is close to that of 1 Thessalonians. In both letters Jesus is placed alongside the Father, and the frequent use of 'Lord' in 2 Thessalonians is matched in 1 Thessalonians. If the christology of 2 Thessalonians is highly developed, the same must be said of 1 Th. Some difficulty arises at 2 Th. 1:12 where it is possible that Christ is called 'God', but the Greek phraseology is so ambiguous that nothing can be built on this reference. It is the stress on the parousia and the attendant events which leads to the rather lofty position ascribed to Jesus; 'cultic' and 'hieratic' are hardly appropriate terms to apply to the depiction, since no priestly traits are ascribed to him.

As for the claim that the theology of the letter is essentially Jewish rather than Christian, something similar has been said of James. In both cases, however, the sub-structure of the appeal to the gospel tradition (in this case, the apocalyptic teaching ascribed to Jesus) and to Christian paraenesis is sufficient to refute the suggestion. (We may note in passing that the similar use of apocalyptic tradition in 1 and 2 Th. favours identity of authorship.)

These brief comments, along with the discussion of individual points in greater detail in the commentary, will, we hope, show that the reasons alleged for the view that the theology of 2 Th. is post-Pauline will not bear the weight assigned to them. The greatest weight should probably be given to turns of phrase not attested elsewhere in Paul or varying from his usual practice (e.g. 2 Th. 1:10; 2:10, 12), but such phenomena can be observed in any Pauline epistle.

(3). *The situation of the letter.*

If the letter is not by Paul, it is necessary to offer a more plausible account of the situation which led to its composition, i.e. to provide it with a more credible setting in the life of the early church. It has indeed been argued in the past that the failure of scholars to offer a credible alternative setting for the epistle is an argument in favour of its authenticity.

Wrede, pp. 67–9, envisaged a situation late in the first century when a group of enthusiasts, basing their belief on dreams and visions and also using 1 Th. 5 as Pauline teaching, argued that the Day of the Lord had at last come. A more sober-minded opponent sought to refute their teaching by composing a fictitious letter in the name of Paul. We do not know precisely when or where this happened. The form of a letter to 'Thessalonica' was chosen simply because the original letter of Paul to Thessalonica was being used by the enthusiasts. The letter is to be dated before AD 110. It cannot be dated before Paul's death and must come from a time when 1 Thessalonians was regarded as a letter that was not meant only for Thessalonica.

An obvious difficulty for this view is that in 2 Th. 2 the temple at Jerusalem is apparently still there and there is no hint of its destruction. Wrede, pp. 96–114, devotes some space to this problem and admits that he has no completely convincing solution to offer; one must assume that the saying about the temple was included in the tradition which the author incorporated in 2 Th. 2, and that he simply took it over because it was included in an authoritative, possibly written, tradition without thinking at all about the destruction of the temple. Wrede argues that this is credible, and that the difficulties in accepting this view are far less than in assuming that the letter is Pauline or that it is a pseudonymous writing from the period before AD 70.

J. A. Bailey adopts a somewhat similar position. For him the author's opponents were Gnostics who had abandoned belief in a cosmic parousia in favour of the view that salvation had fully come; probably they claimed that the resurrection was already past and that they now lived 'in the light'. The author opposed them and sought to prepare the church for a long period of waiting for the parousia by insisting on the need for hard work. His recourse to apocalyptic is to be seen against the background of the resurgence of apocalyptic interest in Judaism and Christianity after AD 70 (cf. 2 Esd.; Rev.; Mt. 24–25; Mk 13; J. M. Robinson and H. Koester, *Trajectories through Early Christianity*, Philadelphia, 1970, pp. 153f.). The writer had no intention of disputing Paul's authority – indeed, he makes use of it for his own purposes. The letter is to be dated *c.* AD 90–100.

A rather different interpretation is offered by A. Lindemann ('Zum Abfassungszweck des Zweiten Thessalonicherbriefes', *ZNW* 68, 1977, pp. 35–47). He adopts the view of A. Hilgenfeld and H. J. Holtzmann that 2 Th. was written to discredit and replace 1 Th.

He argues that the fact that 2 Th. closely resembles 1 Th. and yet makes no positive reference to it is a sign that it was meant to be understood as Paul's *only* letter to Thessalonica. 2 Th. 2:2 is to be understood as a reference to 1 Th. as a letter purporting to be from Paul, and this critical allusion to 1 Th. is then followed in 2 Th. 2:15 by a reference to 2 Th. itself as the true source for Pauline traditions. 2 Th. 3:17 is intended to exclude 1 Th. from the corpus of Pauline letters in that 1 Th. did not contain Paul's own greeting. The author's aim was to rid early Christianity of belief in the imminence of the parousia. His opponents were not Gnostics but apocalyptically-minded Christians who believed that the Day of the Lord was immediately at hand. It was written in a time of persecution towards the end of the first century. The reference to the temple is part of the pseudepigraphic machinery: the writer puts himself into the situation of Paul and sees the approaching destruction of the temple as part of the divinely-willed programme of events which was still slowly pursuing its way in his own time. He writes purely in order to deal with the problems of his own day and in particular with the eschatological problem, and this explains the lack of theological discussion of other issues.

In his commentary W. Trilling rejects the view of Lindemann. He disputes his exegesis of the critical texts, and he finds it incredible that a writer should want to discredit the whole of 1 Th., particularly when he does not in fact attempt to deal with all of its eschatological statements. The detailed presentation in 2 Th. 2:3–12 is a strange way of dealing with the eschatological teaching of 1 Th. Trilling himself is dubious of the view that 2 Th. was meant to correct or revise 1 Th. and sees it rather as a supplement to it. The author was not concerned with Thessalonica as such, but saw in 1 Th. a good model on which to base his own teaching about the parousia and apostolic authority. The situation of the letter is to be seen in the need to dampen down belief that the parousia was directly at hand, to help the church in time of persecution, and possibly to deal with some disorder in the church (although Trilling argues that it is very doubtful whether the 'disorder' reflected in 3:6–12 was on a large scale or was related to expectation of the parousia). The author is unknown. He was probably not a member of a Pauline school and was no theologian, but simply tried to deal with the actual situation by sensible advice. He knew 1 Th. and probably 1 C. but there is no proof that he was familiar with a corpus of Pauline letters. It is not certain that 2 Th. was known to Polycarp. The letter, therefore, can be dated anywhere between AD 80 and the early second century. It is unlikely to have been written to Thessalonica, and is best associated with Asia Minor.

From this survey of various recent attempts to 'place' 2 Th. as a pseudepigraph it will be seen that there is considerable difference of opinion regarding the actual circumstances leading to its composition within broad agreement that it is to be dated towards the end of the first century.

The identification of the opponents attacked in the letter as Gnostics has nothing to be said for it. It is unlikely that Gnostics would have spoken of the Day of the Lord (an apocalyptic term) as having come or being at hand (so rightly, A. Lindemann, art cit., p. 41; P. Vielhauer, *Geschichte der urchristlichen Literatur*, pp. 93f.). Nor can the letter be regarded as a response to the delay of the parousia. It is concerned to deal with an enthusiastic apocalyptic belief that the Day of the Lord had already arrived, a belief which could certainly have arisen or gained fresh currency in the late first century. The writer's aim was to insist that the Day of the Lord had not yet come, and not to kill that hope. Lindemann's understanding of his aim seems quite false at this point; on his view that the writer understood the destruction of the temple as part of the end-drama, it would seem that the effect of the letter would be to encourage belief that the end could not be far distant rather than to quench expectation of the imminent parousia altogether. The emphasis on the need for orderly behaviour is no indication that the End was regarded as far distant; such advice would be appropriate at any point in the history of the church, and Rom. 13 starkly juxtaposes the need for orderly, civil behaviour and a fervent belief that the day is at hand. In any case, however, there is no reason to suppose that such a situation could not have arisen in Paul's lifetime, or that such a situation is more plausible historically late in the first century.

The relation of 2 Th. to Paul's other letters raises problems. Some of the writers whom we have discussed imply that the author *chose* 1 Th. as the most suitable model for his own letter—apparently out of a corpus of other Pauline writings. However, there is no clear evidence of use of any of the other Pauline letters (Trilling mentions 1 C. as being probably known), and no proof that the author even knew them. This point argues against setting 2 Th. at a late date and also against any idea that the author 'chose' his model. It would follow that the author knew only 1 Th. and that the recipients of his letter were also familiar with it; here Wrede seems to have been wiser than some of his followers. But such a setting is of course provided by the actual relationships between Paul and the church at Thessalonica; once again, the assumption of a later date has nothing intrinsically in its favour. In fact, the later the date assigned to 2 Th. the more implausible it becomes that the writer can have been familiar only with 1 Th.

A further point is that the setting of 2 Th. does appear to be distinctly local. In particular, the teaching about disorderly behaviour is directly linked with that in 1 Th. and presupposes the same situation. But it is surely most improbable that this same situation should have arisen in a different community from that at Thessalonica (or even in Thessalonica upwards of thirty years from the date of 1 Th.). Put otherwise, the way in which 2 Th. does follow closely the same problem areas as 1 Th. strongly favours that it was written to the same situation rather than to a mirror-image of it almost a generation later.

Wrede saw the Achilles' heel of his reconstruction in the mention of the temple in 2 Th. 2 as though it were still standing. His own attempt to deal with this problem is quite unconvincing. It is inconceivable that the author of the letter should simply have ignored the destruction of the temple. Lindemann does not fare any better. On his view the destruction of the temple was part of the end-drama 'prophesied' by 'Paul'. However, what 2 Th. describes is not the destruction of the temple, but the enthronement of the man of lawlessness in the temple and *his* destruction; it is improbable that a writer could 'prophesy' such an event after the temple no longer existed. Moreover, if the already-past destruction of the temple was recorded in 2 Th. 2, this would indicate that the End was now imminent—the very point that, according to Lindemann, the letter was meant to deny.

If, then, the reference in 2 Th. is to an event envisaged as taking place in the actual temple in Jerusalem, then a date after AD 70 must be regarded as impossible. There remains, however, the possibility discussed in the commentary, *ad loc.* that the writer was using existing imagery metaphorically; he used the motif of sitting in the temple and claiming to be God as a picture for opposition by evil to God (cf. Trilling, p. 86). Such imagery could have been used after the destruction of the temple. We cannot, therefore, say that 2 Th. 2:4 absolutely rules out a date for the letter after AD 70.

There are, however, a number of features in the letter, pointed out by Best, pp. 57f., which suggest that 2 Th. is a primitive rather than a late document. He lists the primitive character of the eschatological expectation, close in spirit to that of 1 Th., the lack of reference to office-bearers in the church (particularly when one might have expected them to be mentioned in connection with the problem of discipline), the informal nature of the disciplinary process which is envisaged, and the lack of interest in how tradition is to be handed on. These points show the contrast between 2 Th. and the Pastoral Epistles, and they indicate that the characteristics of 'early catholicism' are missing from this letter. It does not bear the marks that we should expect in a document coming from the post-Pauline period. To these points we may add the lack of any awareness of the type of theology found in Paul's letters written later than 1 Th.; it is incredible that a post-Pauline writer should reflect such a total ignorance of Paul's later expressions of his theological position.

These comments show that a date in the late first century faces considerable difficulties; it certainly has no advantages over an early date in Paul's career.

When we examine all the arguments, then, it emerges that neither singly nor cumulatively do they suffice to disprove Pauline authorship. That 2 Th. contains some unusual features in style and theology is not to be denied, but that these features point to pseudonymous authorship is quite another matter. Moreover, the early church had no doubts about the Pauline authorship of 2 Th. The later we set the date of the letter, the more difficult it becomes to explain its unopposed acceptance into the Pauline corpus; indeed, it is hard to envisage how an alleged Pauline letter addressed to a particular church could have escaped detection as a forgery.

THE FIRST LETTER OF PAUL

to the

Thessalonians

1:1 When a person writes a letter, he usually follows a set pattern prescribed by social and literary custom at the beginning and the end. He writes his address and the date at the top of the sheet of paper, and then begins the letter with 'Dear Mr Mackenzie'. At the end he puts a conventional greeting and his name: 'Yours sincerely, Ian Bruce'. He can introduce variations into the pattern —he addresses his wife as 'My darling Sheona'—but the pattern is still visible. Ancient letters also had their standard form of opening. In the Greek-speaking world it was: 'Lucius (says) to Sosthenes Greeting.' Christian writers followed the convention, but developed it in a distinctive manner to bring in various elements that expressed their faith. Paul himself may have been responsible for some of these elaborations, and in 1 and 2 Th. we have a comparatively simple development of a Christian greeting. Such a greeting could become formal and meaningless with repeated use and the passage of time, as when we say 'Goodbye', not aware that it used to mean 'God be with you.' In a letter like 1 Th. the greeting is full of meaning and alive with sympathetic feeling.

Paul names himself along with Silvanus and Timothy as the writers of the letter. In all his other letters (except 2 Th.) he adds a self-description such as 'an apostle' or 'a prisoner for Christ Jesus' which expresses his position in the church and his authority to address his readers. But in these early letters, when his status was not in question (as it was later in some churches where doubts were cast on his apostolic authority), he is content simply to name himself and his co-authors. **Silvanus** is the Latin form of the name of the man known in Acts as Silas (the Aramaic form of 'Saul'); he was Paul's associate in the founding of the church at Thessalonica. Third comes **Timothy** whose presence at the founding of the church can be assumed despite the fact that Ac. 17:10 mentions only the two principal missionaries. He had just returned from a visit to Thessalonica and brought back news of the church to Paul (3:1–10).

The recipients are **the church of the Thessalonians**. The genitive phrase describes **the church** in terms of the people who composed it. **church** here is a local group of people, but the word can also refer to the entirety of Christians (1 C. 12:28; Col. 1:18). The word reflects *OT* and Jewish usage where it refers to those who belong to God as his people. Paul expresses this relationship—one that would be especially significant for former pagans—by the unusual phrase

in God the Father (2 Th. 1:1; Col. 3:3). Its meaning is determined by the associated phrase **and** (*sc.* in) **the Lord Jesus Christ**, which is a common Pauline term. It probably refers to the way in which the existence of the Christian is determined by the fact of Christ crucified and risen (F. Neugebauer, 'Das paulinische "In Christo" ', *NTS* 4, 1957–8, pp. 124–38). The Christian stands in such a relationship to Jesus that his life is determined by his death and resurrection, both in that through Christ he is a new being and in that he is summoned to live a new life in the fellowship of the church. The church, then, is constituted by its relationship to God the Father and to Jesus. Its members know God as their **Father**, since he has made them his children (cf. 2 Th. 1:1, where the fact that God is 'our' Father is made explicit), and they know Christ as their Lord. Significantly Paul places **Jesus Christ** alongside God the Father without any sense of doing anything strange. For Paul and his readers God as Father and Jesus the Lord were closely bound up together as the source of spiritual blessings. They are placed on the same level, and the use of **Lord** to describe Jesus strongly suggests that for Paul he stands 'on the divine side of reality'. The explanation for this understanding of Jesus no doubt lies in Paul's belief that Jesus was the Son of God (1:10).

The element corresponding to 'Greeting' in the introduction to a secular Greek letter is **Grace to you and peace**. Usually Paul goes on to name the source of these blessings (as he does in 2 Th. 1:2), but here he may have felt that this was superfluous after the mention of God and Jesus in the previous phrase. The formula may be paraphrased: 'May God be gracious to you and give you peace.' **Grace** (Gk. *charis*) may be a deliberate pun on the secular form 'Greeting' (Gk. *chairein*), and is probably a Christian development of a Jewish formula which refers to 'mercy and peace' (cf. Gal. 5:16; Tob. 7:11; 2 Bar. 78:2) and may reflect the Aaronic blessing, 'The Lord be gracious to you . . . and give you peace' (Num. 6:24–26). 'Grace' is the word that Christians seem to have preferred to 'mercy'; it brings out more powerfully the thought of God's undeserved and unmerited generosity to mankind. To the Jew **peace** was the spiritual well-being that came from a right relationship with God. For the Christian it comprehensively expressed reconciliation to God and the consequent blessings given to his people through his gracious action in Jesus. Thus these few words sum up the Christian gospel; it is good news of what God offers to men and of the new community into which he wants to bring them.

One of the main themes of the letter is Paul's joy at knowing that the members of the Thessalonian church were continuing to live as Christians during his enforced absence from them and despite every outward obstacle. The same people who had succeeded in making Paul leave Thessalonica doubtless continued to harass the friends whom he left there; yet despite it all, Paul's fears for their faith had proved groundless. Right at the beginning of the letter he expresses his thankfulness to God for the way in which they had originally responded to the gospel and in which they were now continuing. This expression of thankfulness fits in neatly with the typical introductory pattern of many an ancient letter which started with an expression of joy. In this case, however, what begins as a description of how Paul thanks God in prayer for the lives of the Thessalonian believers slides over into a recollection of Paul's visit to them and the way in which they responded to the message. The description is no doubt partly a reminder to the readers of the spirit which they showed when they became Christians, and hence an encouragement to them to continue in the same way, but above all it is an expression of Paul's deep satisfaction with the results of his mission in Thessalonica.

2. The thanksgiving is expressed in a form which appears in most of Paul's other letters, but which is none the less fresh and spontaneous. (See P. T. O'Brien, *Introductory Thanksgivings in the Letters of Paul*, Leiden, 1977; G. P. Wiles, *Paul's Intercessory Prayers*, Cambridge, 1974.) Paul's use of **we** in this letter has been much discussed (Best, pp. 26–9). When used in contrast to 'you the recipients' it probably is meant to associate Silvanus and Timothy with Paul in what he is writing. He and his companions **give thanks to God** at all times for **all** the members of the church whom he has brought to faith. Whatever the shortcomings of some of the members, the fact that each of them has been the object of a divine call is reason for thanksgiving to God. It is sometimes said that prayers of thanks are meaningless and pointless, since God would act according to his will quite independently of any human response. Paul's practice, however, gives the lie to any suggestion that God is to be regarded as an arbitrary bestower of favours on those whom he chooses for his own inscrutable reasons. While Paul recognises the right of God to do as he pleases with his creatures (Rom. 9:21), here he envisages God as a person who acts kindly and lovingly and who is therefore to be thanked, just as any human friend should be thanked for showing kindness. In his prayers, therefore, Paul constantly speaks about the Thessalonian church to God. **Constantly** can be taken with 'mentioning' (*RSV*) or with 'remembering' (v. 3), but the sense is unaffected, since the two activities are simultaneous. It means 'unceasingly', and is applied to prayer in 2:13 and 5:17; it must refer to continual rather than continuous prayer and is a forceful indication of how much Paul lived in an atmosphere of communion with God.

3. As Paul prays he is inspired by what he **remembers** about his friends, and so he gives thanks for three specific aspects of their Christian lives. In each case a pair of nouns is coupled together and the latter expresses the source or origin of the former. Paul writes of the **work** which results from **faith**, the **labour** which results from **love** and the **steadfastness** which results from **hope**. (It is less likely that the three activities as a group are based on the three virtues as a group, *pace* Whiteley, p. 34.) The outward and visible signs of work, labour and steadfastness confirm the reality of the spiritual attitudes which inspired them. These attitudes are the three basic characteristics of the Christian; they are linked together elsewhere and were regarded as a group (5:8; Rom. 5:2–5; 1 C. 13:12; Gal. 5:5f.; Eph. 4:2–5; Col. 1:4f.; Heb. 6:10–12; 10:22–24; 1 Pet. 1:3–8, 21f.). **faith** (1:8; 3:2, 5–7, 10; 5:8; cf. 1:7) is acceptance of the gospel message, trust in God and Jesus, and obedient commitment. **love** (3:6, 12; 5:8, 13; cf. 1:4) is the affection which is expressed in unselfish care for someone, the kind of love shown by God himself in sending Jesus to die for us (Rom. 5:8); Christians must show it to one another and to all men (3:12), and their attitude to God is to be of the same quality, expressing itself in complete devotion to him. **hope** (2:19; 4:13; 5:8) is confident expectation that God will continue to care for his people and bring them through trials and suffering to future bliss in his presence.

Such faith will express itself in action (Gal. 5:6; 2 Th. 1:11). Although Paul contrasts the faith that gladly accepts God's free gift of salvation with the works of the law that men do in order to win or maintain his favour, true faith is not a matter merely of the heart but affects the whole person and leads to a new way of life, expressed in serving God (1:9); faith works by love (Gal. 5:6; Masson, p. 18). Similarly, such love is seen in action, and here Paul uses a word indicating laborious toil, the hard work that a person is prepared to do out of devotion and affection for somebody else (cf. 2:9; 3:5). Finally, such a hope will enable a person to stand firm in the midst of inducements to give up the struggle; confidence that one is on the winning side enables one to survive apparent setbacks. The phrase **in our Lord Jesus Christ** is to be attached to 'hope' (*RSV*) rather than to all three phrases (Rigaux, p. 367); it is because the hope is in the One who will come from heaven and is grounded in the fact that God has already raised him from the dead that it is so firm and confident (1:10). The words **before our God and Father** are linked with this last phrase by Masson, p. 19 n. 1, and Morris, p. 53, in view of the word-order, but *RSV* and other versions link them with 'remembering'. Paul can use the phrase both of being in God's presence at the last day (2:19; 3:13; cf. 2 C. 5:10) and of being with him in prayer (3:9; see also Ac. 10:4). Masson's view is difficult in that it requires that the phrase be taken in a somewhat pregnant sense, and so with some hesitation we would uphold the *RSV* rendering.

4. Although *RSV* begins a new sentence at this point, the verb is actually a participle 'knowing', syntactically parallel to 'remembering' in v. 3. The sentence is thus rather loosely constructed, and the logical relation of **For we know** to what precedes is not entirely clear. The phrase could give a further reason for Paul's thanksgiving to God. It might also be linked to v. 3 to give the thought that as a result of the evidence of their Christian behaviour Paul is confirmed in the knowledge that the Thessalonians have been chosen by God. This thought is then further developed as Paul reminisces on the way in which they responded to the gospel. Paul addresses his readers as **brethren** (the archaic plural of 'brother' retained by *RSV*), a word which occurs 21 times in the two epistles and is expressive of the particular affection that he felt for his readers. The word naturally includes women as well as men. Originally it was used for members of the same religious group and was used especially by the Jews for one another. It was natural for Christians to take over the word; Paul speaks of his racial brothers, the Jews (Rom. 9:3), as well as of his Christian brothers. The word fitted well into the concept of Christians as the children of God (Rom. 8:14–16; Gal. 4:5–7) and the brothers of his Son Jesus (Rom. 8:29). Paul uses it in the vocative, as here, when he is moving over to another theme, and in the present case he elaborates on the term in the light of his immediate subject. The brothers are **beloved by God** (Rom. 1:7; 2 Th. 2:13; Jude 1; Dt. 33:12); they are the objects of his affection and care. To say this is the same as to say that they are God's chosen people. **that he has chosen you** is literally 'God's choice of you' (Ac. 9:15; Rom. 9:11; 11:5, 7, 28; 2 Pet. 1:10). Paul attributes the fact that his readers are Christians to God's choice of them, a choice that was put into effect by the preaching of the gospel. This choice rests upon God's love and not on any worth of the recipients of it (cf. Dt. 7:7f.). Although in the *OT* Israel was the chosen people of God, here Paul recognises that both Gentiles

and Jews have been called by God to salvation. It follows that for Paul election leads to present salvation: the readers are already God's people. It is also a corporate idea: the individuals whom God calls are summoned to be part of his people. Further, although the term stresses God's choice of people and his initiative in salvation, it is generally used of people who have responded to God's call; God's 'elect' are the people who show the marks of belonging to him, such as the evidence of faith, love and hope already mentioned. Finally, Paul's use of the language of election here does not imply that God has withheld the possibility of salvation from others, or that anybody can say that he has not been saved because God did not call him. It is true that Paul recognises elsewhere that God can grant or withhold mercy to sinners as he pleases (Rom. 9:18), and that he will judge sinners, but nothing suggests that the offer of the gospel is withheld from other people in Thessalonica simply because God has so decided it.

5. It makes little difference to the sense whether we regard v. 5a as explaining the reason (**for** = 'because') that led Paul to believe that his readers were God's elect or as a description of the consequence of election (**for** = 'how that'). It could well be that Paul made the connection loosely and would have found it as difficult as modern commentators to be specific about the logic of it. The point is that God's choice of the readers was seen in the powerful way in which the gospel came across to them and in the joyful response of the hearers. **our gospel** means the Christian message preached by the missionaries, but there is probably a hint of the idea that there was a specifically Pauline formulation of the gospel. It was not simply a message proclaimed **in word**, although, as D. Kemmler has rightly insisted (*Faith and Human Reason*, Leiden, 1975, pp. 149–68), this expression does not make the 'word' element unimportant; there is a proper place for reasoned appeal to the mind in the presentation of the gospel. Human words would be useless if the message was not given **in power**. The human message must be seen to be the powerful word of God (2:13). The contrast here may be simply between words that are merely human and thus spiritually ineffective and words that carry conviction because the Spirit makes them vehicles of God's powerful word (1 C. 2:4; 4:20); but it is possible that the power which Paul has in mind is the accompaniment of the spoken message by miraculous deeds which were seen as divine confirmation of the word (Gal. 3:5; 1 C. 1:6f.; 2 C. 12:12; Rom. 15:18f.; Heb. 2:3f.; W. Grundmann, *TDNT* II, p. 311). Although this kind of phenomenon may seem strange to modern western readers and is only spasmodically attested, there is no doubt that the early Christians believed that such deeds accom-

panied the preaching of the gospel and the life of the church. Power
is closely linked with **the Holy Spirit** as its source. **full conviction**
must refer to the assurance and confidence with which the missionaries presented the message (1 Clement 42:3), rather than to the
effect on the hearers, which is discussed in v. 6. (The word might
mean 'fullness', *sc.* of divine working [G. Delling, *TDNT* VI,
pp. 310f.; Rigaux, pp. 377f.], but this idea seems less suitable in
the context.) Paul appeals to the memories of his readers that this
was indeed how the missionaries had appeared to be when they were
in Thessalonica (cf. 2:1–12); their demeanour had arisen out of their
intense concern for their hearers in order that they might be saved.
The work of a missionary is at one and the same time service
rendered to God (Rom. 15:16f.) and carried out in the interests of
those who need to hear the gospel. It will be ineffective if he is not
divinely convinced of the truth of his message.

6. The fact that God had chosen Paul's readers was to be seen
not merely in the effective presentation of the gospel by the missionaries but also in the response of those who heard it. They
became **imitators** of the missionaries **and of the Lord** by their
reception of the message in the midst of **affliction**. To imitate is to
follow an example, usually in an active sense. Paul's own acceptance
of Jesus as his Lord had led him into persecution from the Jews,
and he now says that the Thessalonians had followed his example
by accepting the gospel despite the fact that this plunged them into
persecution. But they did not resign themselves to a life of suffering.
In the midst of suffering they displayed a profound joyfulness which
Paul attributed to the Spirit being active in their lives.

The two thoughts here are deeply etched into the fabric of early
Christian experience. Christian joy is experienced in the context of
suffering, and it enables the believer to bear suffering and not to be
overcome by it (3:7; 1 Pet. 1:6; 4:13; 2 C. 8:2; Phil. 2:17; Col.
1:24). The joy which comes from the experience of salvation is of
such intensity that a believer is prepared to put up with what are by
comparison minor trials; he sees his sufferings from a new perspective. Although Paul is making the point with specific reference to
persecution, the general principle applies to all the other pains and
irritations which can fill the attention of the non-believer but which
are of trivial importance to the believer. The other thought is that
joy is due to the presence of the Spirit in the believer (Ac. 13:52;
Rom. 14:17; Gal. 5:22). It is not merely a human emotion, but is
ascribed to a divine influence, and is thus one of the marks of a
person who has been regenerated. It may seem strange that in all
this the Thessalonians are said to have been imitators **of the Lord**,
i.e. Jesus, since he cannot be said to have received the word; the

point of comparison is rather the way in which Jesus displayed joy
in the midst of suffering (see Heb. 12:2); if this characteristic of
Jesus is not described in so many words in the Gospels, it could
certainly be argued that he must have exemplified the principle
which he taught his disciples: 'Blessed are you when men hate
you. . . Rejoice in that day, and leap for joy, for behold, your
reward is great in heaven' (Lk. 6:22f.).

7. Reception of the gospel in this way made the Thessalonian
believers into **an example to all the believers in Macedonia and in
Achaia**. The two names are those of the Roman provinces into
which Greece was divided. The northern area, **Macedonia**, and the
southern area, **Achaia**, had come into the possession of the Romans
in the middle of the second century BC. Both were administered as
one province until 27 BC when Augustus separated off Achaia and
made Corinth its seat of government. From AD 15 to 44 the provinces
were again united for administrative purposes, but from then on-
wards they were once more separated. Their close connections explain why Paul links the two names together (cf. v. 8). Paul had
already evangelised in the Macedonian town of Philippi before coming to Thessalonica, and from Thessalonica he went on to Beroea,
where a Christian group was formed, before moving on to Athens
and Corinth in Achaia. There were, therefore, groups of believers
throughout the two provinces, both in the towns mentioned and
probably in others also (possibly Amphipolis and Apollonia (Act.
17:1) by the time that Paul wrote these words. The account in Acts
indicates that the preaching of the gospel throughout these areas
was accompanied by opposition, especially from the Jews. The way
in which the Thessalonian Christians had joyfully received the message despite the opposition which they faced would thus have been
both an incentive to these other Christians and also a pattern for
them to follow. The word **example** denotes a model or mould or
the impression made by a stamp. In the former sense it may indicate
not just an example which others are to follow but also a pattern
which influences them. The example of the Thessalonians could be
said to exercise a formative influence on the other Christians, just
as they themselves were to imitate the formative example of Paul
(2 Th. 3:9). It was, then, insofar as the Thessalonians imitated Paul
and the Lord that they became an example for others to follow.

8. If the Thessalonian church had become an example for other
Christians in the two provinces to follow, how had this happened?
The word of the Lord had **sounded forth** from Thessalonica
throughout **Macedonia and Achaia. the word of the Lord** is the
gospel message (the phrase is found only here and in 2 Th. 3:1 in
Paul, and also in Ac. 8:25; 12:24; 19:10, 20; Paul usually has 'the

word of God', 1 Th. 2:13). **sounded forth** suggested to Chrysostom
the sound of a trumpet. As used here the word indicates the spreading out of a sound from a central point in all directions, and the
perfect tense indicates the continuing influence of the sound. The
Thessalonian Christians themselves had spread the gospel through
the surrounding areas (*contra* W.-H. Ollrog, *Paulus und seine Mitarbeiter*, Neukirchen, 1979, p. 130 n. 81, who denies that the Thessalonians themselves engaged in mission and thinks that other
people talked about what had happened to them). But not only
there; with a pardonable touch of exaggeration Paul speaks of an
effect **everywhere** (cf. Rom. 1:8; 16:19). Presumably he means
everywhere that he himself had travelled since he left Thessalonica;
but so far he had not gone further than Macedonia and Achaia.
Morris, p. 61, notes that Aquila and Priscilla had just joined Paul
from Rome (Ac. 18:2) and such travellers as they could well have
picked up news in the capital itself, especially since Thessalonica
lay on an important line of communication with Rome. The **faith**
of the Thessalonians **in God** was a news-topic far and wide, so that
Paul and his companions found that they had no need to tell the
story themselves. This suggests, incidentally, that part of the message of the missionaries was a recounting of how the gospel had
affected the lives of the people to whom they had preached (cf. 3:6;
J. Jervell, 'The Problem of Traditions in Acts', in *Luke and the
People of God*, Minneapolis, 1972, pp. 19–39). Since Paul talks
about **faith in God** and then goes on to speak about turning to God
from idols in the next verse, it is likely that the thought of conversion
from idol-worship is already in his mind in this verse.

9. Paul justifies his statement that there is no need for him to
recount the conversion of the Thessalonians to the people whom he
visits by affirming that **they themselves** (the antecedent is the inhabitants of the places named in v. 8) are telling about the visit of
the missionaries to Thessalonica. It is noteworthy that the report is
about the missionaries rather than about the converts; the point was
that the missionaries had had a successful visit, and this report was
making the people whom they visited more willing to receive them
eagerly and listen to them (some MSS have 'concerning *you*' instead
of **concerning us**; see Masson, p. 23 n. 2). The word translated
welcome in *RSV* is translated 'visit' in 2:1, and this meaning should
also be adopted here; the stress at this point in the verse is on the
conduct of the missionaries rather than on the response of the
Thessalonians.

In the second part of the verse, however, the accent shifts to the
Thessalonians and we receive a classic description of what it meant
for a group of Gentiles to become Christians. The language used is

not characteristically Pauline, and this has led to the well-founded
suggestion that Paul is here echoing the vocabulary of missionary
preaching, particularly of preaching to the Gentiles. G. Friedrich
has made the more precise proposal that what we have here are the
words of a baptismal hymn with which the assembled church would
greet the persons who were being baptised and describe their conversion ('Ein Tauflied hellenistischer Judenchristen', *ThZ* 21, 1965,
pp. 402–16). This claim probably goes further than is warranted,
and there is more to be said for the view of T. Holtz that Paul is
using traditional mission phraseology to relate how people described
the conversion of the Thessalonians, and that this phraseology shows
some kinship with the language and ideas of Jewish missionary
propaganda (' "Euer Glaube an Gott". Zu Form und Inhalt von
I Thess I, 9f.', in R. Schnackenburg (*et al.*), *Die Kirche des Anfangs*
(Festschrift für H. Schürmann), Leipzig, 1977, pp. 459–88). The
most obvious links of the passage are with Paul's speeches to pagan
Gentiles in Ac. 14:15–17 and 17:31.

The basic response is that the Thessalonians **turned to God from
idols**, and this led to a new relationship to God and to Jesus. The
verb **turn** is used by Paul of turning to God (2 C. 3:16; contrast
Gal. 4:9, of relapse into idolatry). But it is in Acts that we find it
used in the same way as here of conversion (Ac. 3:19; 9:35; 11:21;
14:15; 15:19; 26:18, 20; 28:27), whether of Jews or of Gentiles. In
the case of Jews conversion is from a false attitude to God to a true
one, but in the case of Gentiles it is from the worship of false gods
to worship of the true God. **idols** is a word which can be used both
of the images worshipped by pagans and also of the false gods
represented by the images. This use of the word developed in the
LXX (it was not used of religious objects in Classical Greek) and
conveys the suggestion that pagan gods are no more real than their
images (F. Büchsel, *TDNT* II, pp. 375–8). Christian preaching
took over the same thought (I C. 8:4; 10:19; 12:4). By contrast
Christians spoke of their God as **living** or active and **true** or real,
again basing their language on the *OT*; for the former thought see
Dt. 5:26; Jos. 3:10; Ps. 42:2, and for the latter see Exod. 34:6
LXX; 2 Chr. 15:3. The closest *OT* parallel is Jer. 10:10: 'But the
Lord is the true God; he is the living God and the everlasting King'
(the verse is omitted by LXX but appears in other Greek versions).
To be converted is to own this God as God, to accept his existence,
to trust in him as the source of life and to give him love and
obedience. Conversion is 'a fundamentally new turning of the human will to God, a return from blindness and error to the Saviour
of all' (F. Laubach, *NIDNTT* I, p. 355).

Thus Paul can say that the conversion of the Thessalonians led them **to serve God**. The devotion which a person renders to his god is described as that of a slave who is required to obey his master; this devotion is expressed not simply in worship but also in the activity of daily life, and for Paul it is particularly concerned with the doing of what is good and right instead of being in bondage to sin (Rom. 6:6, 16–20). Paul can thus say that the person who serves God is truly free, since he has been delivered from bondage to evil and is now free to do what is right. At the same time, he is aware that the term 'slave' is a one-sided and possibly misleading description of the believer's relation to God, and so he can also say that the believer is not a slave but a son of God (Gal. 4:7). The Christian missionary is in a special sense the servant of God (Rom. 1:1; Phil. 2:22), and it is probable that Paul saw the service of the Thessalonians in their work and toil (1:3) and especially in their spreading of the gospel (1:8).

10. The second result of the Thessalonians' conversion was that they began **to wait for** God's **Son from heaven**. The hope (1:3) of the coming of Jesus was an integral part of the Thessalonians' religion; it was something that they anticipated as a real possibility in their own lifetimes (4:15, 17; 5:4). This hoped-for imminence of the parousia made it a vital part of their Christian belief. The verb **to wait for** is a colourless expression and says nothing about the character of the expectation. The point is that the present existence of the Thessalonian Christians was determined by their expectations regarding the future. From what Paul says later in the epistle we can see that at the coming of Jesus his people were to be blameless and holy (3:13; 5:23), sober and filled with faith, love and hope (5:8f.); waiting for the coming of Jesus meant that Christians would seek to manifest these qualities, although their attainment of them could also be attributed to the power of God working in their lives. The coming of Jesus was thus an incentive to moral behaviour, and if any of the Thessalonians were tempted to inaction and laziness in view of the imminence of the parousia, Paul warned them to be diligent (4:10–12; 2 Th. 3:6–13). It can be objected that waiting for the parousia leads to a self-centred kind of morality, in which a person does what is good for the sake of the reward which he hopes to obtain rather than for the sake of the other people whom he should unselfishly love. But Paul would probably have replied that waiting for the parousia is the evidence of love for God and obedience to his command to love one's neighbour; it expresses love for God rather than a selfish desire for reward from him, although it is true that Christians may be tempted to serve God simply for the sake of reward.

The object of hope is the coming of God's **Son**, **Jesus**. Since elsewhere the title of **Son** is not linked with the parousia, it has been suggested that originally the reference was to Jesus as the Son of man, whose coming is prophesied in the Gospels (Mk 8:38; 13:26; 14:62; G. Friedrich, art cit., pp. 512–15). But this suggestion is purely hypothetical, and it can be urged that the title of Son is used here at the climax of Paul's statement to stress the fact that it is the One who stands closest to God whom Christians await, and also that it is the One whom God declared to be his Son by raising him **from the dead**. The mention of the resurrection here is probably motivated by the desire to give a basis for the future hope. If God raised Jesus from the dead, it follows that he is now where God is, namely, in **heaven**, and the God who raised him can and will bring him back to earth for his people. It is this Jesus **who delivers** believers **from the** coming **wrath**. The End will witness the outpouring of God's wrath upon sinners, but Jesus is able to deliver men from that fate. How he does so is not stated here, but in 4:9f. we learn that it is because Jesus died for us; and the thought is elaborated in Rom. 5:9 where future salvation from the wrath of God is based on present justification or acquittal by the blood, i.e. the sacrificial death, of Jesus.

But what about **the wrath**? The word is one that usually means anger, and many people find it inappropriate to use such a word about God. It has been observed that when Paul uses the word it generally means not an emotion felt by God but the unpleasant measures which are taken against sinners. There is no sense in which God feels angry like a human person whose pride has been hurt and who bursts out with a fit of temper and passion. Rather, if God is holy, pure and righteous, then his wrath represents a just reaction to the wickedness of those who spoil and destroy the perfect society which it was his intention to create. God's wrath is always directed against evil and is not arbitrary and unprincipled. Some scholars have still not been satisfied with the concept and have argued that 'wrath' is a way of describing an impersonal process in which sin reaps its own reward. It is doubtful if this avoids the problem, since the existence of such a process is surely ultimately due to the will of God who actively allows or passively permits it. Perhaps the real problem is the coexistence of love and wrath in the same person. Both aspects of God's character are firmly attested in the biblical evidence, but the Bible sees no tension between them. It is perfectly consistent for God to display his holy and righteous character by judging sinners if they persist in their sin and at the same time by loving them to the limit in giving his Son to be their Saviour from sin and its consequences.

Finally, what has Paul achieved in this section of his epistle? He has in effect congratulated his readers on their steadfast Christianity and has reminded them that they truly became God's people when they accepted the gospel despite the opposition which they faced. They have been an example to other groups of believers. All this constitutes an implicit encouragement to the Thessalonians to carry on as they have begun, despite continuing opposition. Right from the start Paul's aim in this letter is to express his joy at their progress in the faith and to encourage them to continue in the same way, surrounded as they are by many witnesses who rejoice in their example. Christian pastoral care builds on the foundation of what God has already done in the life of the individual or congregation.

THE BEHAVIOUR OF THE APOSTLES IN THESSALONICA

2:1–12

If the basic theme of 1:2–10 was the sincere response of the converts to the gospel, which indicated the fact of their election as God's people, the accent now shifts to the way in which the apostles comported themselves during their stay in Thessalonica. Their visit was truly in accordance with the nature of the gospel which they proclaimed. It was characterised by courage in proclaiming the word despite opposition. There was no attempt to deceive the hearers, but they were faithful to what God had committed to them. And so they sought to please God and not to claim anything for themselves, whether material gain or human prestige. They could have claimed respect as God's messengers, but they preferred to be gentle and to care for their hearers rather than make any demands on them. They were therefore prepared to work for their keep while they preached the gospel, rather than burden anybody with the cost of their hospitality. Both the Thessalonians and God could be cited as witnesses to the blameless behaviour of the missionaries and to their fatherly attitude in exhorting their hearers to live a life that would be worthy of God.

The flow of thought is not always easy to follow, and the motivation for the section is complex. Paul's statements sound on first hearing like a defence against accusations made against him and his colleagues: he had run away from Thessalonica like a coward; while there he deceived his hearers and flattered them in order that he might gain some financial return and personal prestige from them; and his motives and character as a preacher would not stand up to examination. It is certainly improbable that such accusations were being entertained, still less initiated, by any members of the church; nothing suggests that there was any Christian opposition to Paul (cf.

3:6). Nor is it likely that Paul is contrasting himself with Gnostic rivals (*pace* Schmithals, pp. 142–51). Frame, p. 90, claimed that Paul was replying to specific accusations made by the Jews outside the church in an attempt to undo his work by casting aspersions on the preachers.

But a number of commentators (von Dobschütz, pp. 106f.; Dibelius, pp. 10f.) have questioned whether specific accusations are in mind. In particular, A. J. Malherbe ('Gentle as a Nurse', *NovT* 12, 1970, pp. 203–17; 'Hellenistic Moralists and the New Testament', in *ANRW*) has developed the view of Dibelius: the accusations which Paul rebuts were also made by Dio Chrysostom against some Cynic philosophers, and the positive statements which he makes about himself can be paralleled from Dio's concept of the true philosopher. The parallels in language and thought are striking. Paul is thus dissociating himself from any suggestion of behaving like a philosophical charlatan. Malherbe queries whether Paul was making a personal apology against specific charges any more than Dio was; the use of antitheses was part of the philosopher's way of depicting himself and does not prove that negative statements were being made about him. He suggests, therefore, that here and throughout chs. 1–3 Paul's purpose is largely exhortation: he is presenting the missionaries as a pattern for the converts to follow in their own lives.

But while Malherbe is right to see this underlying hortatory function in the section, there is no specific reference here to imitating the apostles, and the comments are more concerned with the characteristics of missionaries and pastors than of ordinary members of the congregation. Moreover, it is difficult to see why Paul, a Christian preacher, should have gone to such pains to describe himself in terms of the ideal philosopher if there was nothing in the situation to make him do so. He must have felt that he was being accused or stood in danger of being accused of behaving like a second-rate philosopher, and he defended himself by claiming that his standards as a preacher were in no way inferior to those of the best philosophers. Since we know that the church was facing opposition, it would not be at all surprising if part of the campaign included attacks on the missionaries, and hence Paul felt it right to defend himself against actual or possible criticisms from outside the church. Perhaps too he was still worried at having left the Thessalonian converts in the lurch by his hasty departure from the town and felt the need to defend himself against the possibility of continued misunderstanding (von Dobschütz, pp. 106f.).

1. When a sentence begins with **For** we expect it to give a reason or an explanation for something that has preceded it. One possible

connection in the present case is with 1:9a where Paul mentions briefly the kind of visit (*RSV* 'welcome') which he had to Thessalonica. There would then be a line of thought: 'Everywhere the people themselves report what kind of a visit we had among you . . . for you yourselves know that our visit was not in vain . . .' In other words, 2:1ff. gives an explanation of the kind of visit that it was reported that Paul had made to Thessalonica. This explanation perhaps stresses overmuch the implied contrast between 'the people themselves' and 'you yourselves,' whereas it seems clear that Paul's main point was to describe the *character* of his visit. Again, Paul has already referred briefly to the nature of his preaching in 1:5, and it can be argued that he is now developing at greater length the hints in 1:5 and 9a about the nature of his visit, so far as the preaching and demeanour of the missionaries were concerned. It looks then as though the connection is a more general one. Already in 1:2–10, which is concerned primarily with the Thessalonians' response to the gospel, Paul is thinking of the missionaries' side of the matter. Having reached the climax of his statement in 1:9f. with his description of the kind of visit that he had made and the kind of response which it evoked, he now explains more fully both of these points. In 2:1–12 he appeals to the Thessalonians' own knowledge in detail of his behaviour; or rather he calls on them to testify from their own knowledge to the truth of the description which he offers them, and so implicitly to recognise the falsity of any charges made against himself; and then in 2:13–16 he reverts again to the response of the Thessalonians to the gospel (developing the theme of 1:6).

The opening **you know** (1:5; 2:2, 5, 11; 3:3–4; 4:2; 5:2; 2 Th. 2:6; 3:7) is thus not particularly emphatic, and is not meant to provide a contrast with, or rather an advance on, the 'they themselves' of 1:9. The thought is rather: 'they themselves report what (a successful) visit we had among you . . . For (as you yourselves know) our visit to you was not in vain.' This understanding of the sentence is strengthened by the fact that the words **our visit** occupy an emphatic position in it and clearly echo 1:9a. The verb **was** is actually a perfect tense in the Greek and thus offers a verdict on the visit in the light of subsequent events: the visit *had not proved to be in vain*. This last phrase can be taken to mean 'lacking in content' or 'lacking in effect.' If we adopt the former rendering, the sense will be that Paul's visit was 'hollow, empty, wanting in purpose and earnestness' (Lightfoot, p. 18), and the description is of the *character* of the mission. If we adopt the latter rendering, the point is that the mission was ineffective and produced no *results*. The former view is supported by the parallels adduced by Malherbe and gives a good parallel with 1:5. The latter view is supported by Pauline

usage elsewhere (cf. Paul's use of the phrase 'in vain,' 3:5), and by
the fact that here Paul is looking back on the effects of the mission.
However, Paul could be commenting that the Thessalonians could
see from the effects that the visit had not been lacking in power and
substance; it had brought the gospel to them. The former understanding of the phrase is thus to be preferred, but we should remember that a Greek writer or reader could probably detect both
nuances simultaneously in the word where we tend to find an either/
or (Moore, p. 33). Since v. 2 goes on to speak of the character of
the apostles' visit rather than its results, this confirms our view of
the main nuance in the word.

2. That the apostles' visit was not an 'empty' affair is seen in the
circumstances in which it took place. It followed a visit to **Philippi**
where they had already suffered and been shamefully treated. The
reference is to the story recorded in Ac. 16:19–40 which tells how
Paul and Silas were summarily arrested, beaten and thrown into
prison when their preaching of the gospel affected local vested
interests. **Shamefully treated** refers to insulting and outrageous
treatment and expresses the public degradation which the apostles
experienced. There may be the thought that the treatment meted
out to Paul was particularly degrading for a Roman citizen, who was
theoretically immune from such procedures. (Best's scepticism on
this point and his suggestion that we cannot rely on all the details
in Luke's narrative [p. 90] seem gratuitous). Paul's point is that
such treatment might have dissuaded the missionaries from courting
further trouble; but, as the readers well knew, they had not been
deterred from moving on to Thessalonica and there they displayed
their **courage in . . . God** by declaring the gospel. **we had courage**
translates a word particularly used of speaking out with boldness
and openness, and was an attribute claimed by the Cynics. It is used
often in the *NT* to describe both the Christian's freedom to come
into the presence of God (Heb. 4:16; 10:19; 1 Jn. 3:21) and also his
bold confidence in openly preaching the gospel (Ac. 9:27; 18:26;
Phil. 1:20; Eph. 6:19f.). Such boldness is not a merely human
natural attribute, but springs from trust **in God** that he will uphold
his servants in the task of evangelism. As Best, p. 91, rightly
comments, there is no 'God-mysticism' here in this 'in God' phrase;
it means 'as a result of our confidence in God,' a confidence which
had been shown to be justified by his protection of the apostles in
Philippi. Such confidence was needed, for the preaching of **the
gospel of God** (2:8–9; Rom. 1:1) took place at Thessalonica despite
considerable difficulty. The phrase, which is translated in *RSV* as
in the face of great opposition, is not absolutely certain in meaning.
The Greek word *agōn* originally meant a contest or struggle, and

it can be used of external circumstances which create conflict or of
an inward struggle. Most commentators take the phrase in the sense
adopted by *RSV*, i.e. as a reference to the outward opposition to
the gospel, despite which Paul and his companions fearlessly proclaimed the message (Phil. 1:30; 1 Tim. 6:12). Others take it to
refer to the inward anxiety which the apostles felt as they came to
Philippi, struggling to overcome the fear of further opposition, or
to the zealous effort which they put into prayer for the Thessalonians. There can be little doubt that *RSV*'s interpretation is correct,
especially since it is clear from elsewhere in the letter that efforts
were made to prevent Paul from preaching and the readers from
accepting the gospel (1:6; 2:14–16; 3:3f.). For Paul's use of the term
to describe the Christian life and the task of the missionary in terms
of an athletic contest, see V. C. Pfitzner, *Paul and the Agon Motif*,
Leiden, 1967, especially pp. 112–4. Here, however, the friendly
rivalry of the arena is absent, and the thought is of a life-and-death
struggle with determined opponents.

3. Again the connection with **For** is not easy to see. Probably
Paul is elucidating the statement in vv. 1–2. He is showing further
how it was that his preaching of the gospel was not lacking in
substance and was based on his confidence in God. For his preaching
did not arise from false, self-seeking motives, and was therefore not
a sham, offering people an empty gospel; on the contrary he spoke
out the message with which he had been entrusted by God, and he
did so regardless of whether it secured him any cheap popularity.
appeal refers to the act of preaching, and indicates that what the
apostles said was not simply a recital of facts or some kind of
intellectual entertainment; it was an urgent summons to the hearers
to respond to the good news by believing in Jesus Christ (2:13) and
living worthily of the God who called them into his kingdom (2:12).
The Greek word can also mean 'comfort' (2 Th. 2:16), but this
sense is excluded here, and the thought is akin to that expressed by
the use of the verb to signify urgent exhortation in 2 C. 5:20; 6:1
(see further on 2:11). Although no verb is supplied in the Greek,
which can omit forms of 'to be' quite freely, *RSV* is right to adopt
a present meaning (**does not spring from**) in view of the parallel
with v. 4; Paul is thinking of his normal practice as an evangelist,
although he lapses into the past tense in v. 5 as he thinks particularly
of his behaviour in Thessalonica.

Three nouns are used to express the characteristics which Paul
repudiates as being inconsistent with Christian preaching. First,
Paul's preaching does not spring from **error** (2 Th. 2:11; 1 Jn 4:6).
The word means not 'deceitfulness' (nothing in the context suggest
that the reference is to Paul's defrauding the Thessalonian congre-

gation of money, as Schmithals, pp. 143–6, suggests), but rather
Paul's ignorance or error concerning the truth about God. The use
of 'springs from' confirms that Paul is speaking about the source or
motive of his preaching, not its manner. Second, Paul's motive was
not **uncleanness**. It is generally recognised that the thought here is
not of physical or ritual impurity but of moral impurity; in 4:7 Paul
contrasts it with holiness. A number of commentators think that the
reference here is specifically to sexual impurity, drawing attention
to the context of 4:7 and to such parallels as Rom. 1:24 and Col.
3:5 (where it is associated with sexual immorality). Some of the
Greek religious cults were associated with ritual prostitution. The
implication would then be that Paul sought converts in order to
indulge in sexual excesses with them. Others (especially Best, pp.
93f.) argue that the word has a more general sense and can refer to
impure motives such as ambition, pride and greed; the context does
not require a sexual content for the word, and there is never anywhere else any suggestion that Paul's conduct was open to this
particular misrepresentation. To these points we may add that the
word was also used by the Cynics; they sought 'to purify the mind
by reason, trying to free it from the slavery to lusts and opinions'
(A. J. Malherbe, art. cit., p. 215). This rather general sense should
be given to the word here (as in Rom. 6:19). It will include sensual
elements, but is not confined to them. The third characteristic which
Paul denies is that he acts **with guile**; the change of preposition in
the Greek shows that here he is thinking of the manner of his
mission, rather than his motives. Paul used no dishonest methods
to trick people into believing his message, by contrast with some of
the wandering Hellenistic preachers who would go to any lengths
to gain adherents. The man who even rejected eloquence (1 C. 2:4)
was not likely to resort to cunning and deceit, although he knew
that Christian preachers were open to this temptation (2 C. 11:13).

4. It was impossible that Paul should have conducted himself in
the manner just described since he spoke as a person **approved by
God to be entrusted with the gospel**. Paul claimed that he and his
associates had been tested by God and approved by him for the
work of the Christian mission. The point is emphasised by repetition. At the end of the verse Paul refers to **God who tests our
hearts**. Here the verb (Gk. *dokimazō,* is used primarily in the sense
of examining or testing, and the reference to the heart (for the
phraseology, see Jer. 11:20; 12:3) indicates that God is concerned
not merely with the outward impression made by men but above all
with the inward motives which dictate their conduct. The verb here
is in the continuous aspect (a present participle) which suggests that
God's scrutiny is not, as it were, a once-for-all entrance examination

for his servants but a continually operative process of what might nowadays be called 'quality-control'. In the earlier part of the verse Paul uses the same verb with its other sense of approving somebody who has been tested. He and his companions have been accepted by God as fit people to do his work. There was, so to speak, an initial test of the missionary, as well as the ongoing scrutiny. As Best, p. 96, observes, there is some tension between this statement and Paul's conviction that God chose him for his work even before his birth and moulded him for his purpose. This tension is inevitable because any one type of human language about God and his relationships with mankind is inadequate by itself to do justice to One who is infinite. The language of predestination used by Paul elsewhere rules out any deduction from the language of testing and approving that Paul had human qualities on the basis of which he could boast that God had chosen him (1 C. 1:28–31). It was in virtue of this divine approval that Paul had been **entrusted with the gospel**. The implication is that **the gospel** is not of human origin; it is good news from God, and its content is determined by him. However much he might express the gospel in his own individual way, Paul was quite clear that the gospel was something that had been given to him (1 C. 15:1–5; Gal. 1:11f.), and that he had to act as a steward or trustee of the mysteries of God (1 C. 4:1). A person with such a consciousness would claim that his motives and method were not associated with his own selfish ends.

Having received this commission, Paul makes it his aim to fulfil it. He could have spoken in a way that would **please men**. There is, of course, a right and proper way for the Christian to please other people, by serving their interests instead of his own selfish ends (Rom. 15:1f.; 1 C. 10:33). Paul is here thinking of the kind of action involving flattery (2:5) and similar devices which superficially pleases other people but is really dictated by self-interest and thus stands in sharp contrast with pleasing **God**, in the sense of serving his purpose (4:1; Gal. 1:10). If Paul has been called to be a servant of God, then it is his duty to please his Master (1 C. 4:1–5). It is with this controlling thought in mind that he shapes what he says in his evangelism.

5. Having stated the general principles on which the Christian missionaries work, Paul now elaborates the point by referring specifically to how they had behaved while they were among the readers, and confidently appeals to the latter once again (1:5; 2:2; see further, 2:9, 10, 11) as people who **know** that what he says is true from their personal observation. He again adopts the style of making negative statements followed by positive ones, and he starts with the thought of pleasing men still in his mind. He explains his

previous statement by affirming that the missionaries never used
words of flattery; they did not put on an obsequious air towards
those whom they were trying to influence, giving them empty praise,
and so cajoling them into acceptance of the preachers' message.
These were well-known tricks used by wandering philosophical
lecturers of the baser sort. The Thessalonian Christians could have
observed for themselves that Paul did not act in this way. They
might not, however, have been able to penetrate Paul's motives in
preaching or see what he did when their backs were turned, and so
he calls God as his witness that he did not use **a cloak for greed**.

The word translated 'greed' (Gk. *pleonexia*) indicates covetousness
of all kinds, and hence the desire to rob other people of what belongs
to them. There is not necessarily any sexual connotation in the word
(and hence it provides no contextual support for a sexual understanding of 'uncleanness' in 2:5), although it can take on this meaning (see 4:6 note).

The other half of the phrase is not altogether easy to translate.
RSV adopts the translation **cloak** (Gk. *prophasis*—a word unfortunately not discussed in *TDNT* or *NIDNTT*), understanding the
word to express 'a means of hiding one's real motives'. Rigaux,
p. 414, offers the paraphrase 'we have not used hypocrisy in order
to exploit you,' which suggests that he takes the word to mean the
act of hypocrisy. The word might also signify 'an ulterior motive,'
a motive which is kept hidden (cf. Best: 'with a veiled desire to
exploit you'). The usage elsewhere (Ac. 27:30; Lk. 20:47; Phil.
1:18) suggests that the word refers to the putting forward of a false
reason or a specious form of conduct as a cover-up for a real motive.
Here, therefore, the point is that the apostles did not use the apparently good action of preaching the gospel as a means of covering up
(and so achieving) their real aim, which was to get some material
gain out of those who responded to their message. The *RSV* translation is thus appropriate, laying the stress on the *deception* that was
employed in the service of greed, rather than on the *motive* of greed.

6. Paul now rejects a third charge, in addition to the two discussed
in v. 5. He denies that he and his colleagues were seeking **glory
from men**, whether from the readers who responded to their message or indeed from anybody else. The thought has moved here
from the desire for material gain to the equally potent longing for
honour and a position of prestige which could easily become a
motive in the Christian preacher, just as it was also for the non-
Christian philosophical teacher. There may be an implied contrast
in the wording between seeking honour from **men**, and from *God*,
just as in 2:4 Paul comments that he sought not to please men but
God (Rom. 2:7; 1 C. 4:5). To seek approval and reward from God

is a proper motive (cf. 2:20), provided that it does not degenerate into self-seeking, and this should not happen as long as the true nature of divine reward is recognised. Paul's words probably also convey an implicit contrast between *seeking* honour from men and *receiving* it. Some of the joy and satisfaction which is felt by those who accept the gospel is bound to be expressed in thankfulness and appreciation shown to the messenger who is instrumental in bringing it to them just as by contrast Paul was aware that rejection of the gospel also involved rejection of the messenger (Gal. 4:15f.). Such a relationship becomes sour when the preacher aims to cultivate it rather than to serve God faithfully. Best, p. 99, rightly comments on the subtlety of this and similar temptations inspired by spiritual pride. The fact that they are so subtle and so hard to avoid should put Christians all the more on their guard against them.

In the second half of the verse (numbered as v. *7a* in Greek texts, *TEV* and *NIV*) Paul admits that he and his companions **might have made demands as apostles of Christ**. Their refusal to seek honour took place despite the fact that they had a legitimate right to it. The Greek phrase is literally 'being able to be a weight (*en barei*)'. The construction, which is paralleled in 1 Tim. 2:2, refers metaphorically to the way in which the missionaries could have made use of a position of 'weight' or influence. In virtue of their position they could have stood on their dignity (cf. how Paul's opponents in 2 C. 10:10 accused him of writing weighty letters) and handed out commands in the church. This view fits in neatly with v. *6a* and above all it gives the appropriate contrast with the depiction of the missionaries as behaving gently in v. 7; we may compare the similar contrast in 1 C. 4:21.

Some commentators have argued that the phrase refers to the missionaries being a 'burden' to the church in the sense that they could expect the latter to provide for their material needs (1 C. 9:14; Gal. 6:6). Paul was well aware that he was entitled to this right, but, while he defended it strenuously (1 C. 9:3–12), he insisted even more strongly that he himself would make no use of it, preferring to support himself by his own part-time labour and by gifts from churches other than the one in which he happened to be working (1 C. 9:15–18; 2 C. 11:7–11; 2 Th. 3:8). He goes on to write explicitly about this theme in v. 9, and it is difficult not to detect an echo of the present verse in the verb (*epibareō*) used there. However, this can hardly be the primary thought in the present context. It is more probable that he is thinking of the right of the apostles to give commands and be respected in a broad sense. While the Greek phrase used cannot mean 'to wield authority' and 'to be a material burden' simultaneously, the latter *thought* could already

be in Paul's mind, and, having dealt with the primary contrast in
vv. 7f., he takes up the secondary point in v. 9.

This right to honour could have been claimed by the missionaries
as apostles of Christ. This phrase denotes those who were regarded
as being sent out by Christ himself as missionaries with the task of
founding churches, and they are to be distinguished from the
apostles of the churches (2 C. 8:23; Phil. 2:25) who were simply
envoys or messengers appointed for specific tasks as the representatives of the churches. The group of missionaries was of course
greater in number and extent than the reconstituted group of the
twelve disciples who had accompanied Jesus during his earthly
ministry. The phrase, however, causes some difficulty in that elsewhere Paul appears to ground his apostleship not merely in his call
to missionary work, which was confirmed by the fact that he could
point to his converts, but also in the fact that he had 'seen Jesus
our Lord' (1 C. 9:1f.; cf. 15:8–10; Gal. 1:15–17); in other words,
apostleship sprang out of a commission received at a resurrection
appearance of Jesus (cf. the collective appearances in Mt. 28:16–20;
Lk. 24:44–49; Jn 20:21–23). The problem then is that Paul seems
to include Silvanus and Timothy as apostles, although no resurrection appearance to the former is known (even if it cannot be ruled
out as impossible) and it is virtually certain that Timothy had not
seen the risen Jesus. Elsewhere Timothy is not called an apostle (see
2 C. 1:1; Phil. 1:1; Col. 1:1). It has, therefore, been suggested that
in the present passage Paul is using the 'we'-form to make statements
which apply in fact only to himself, or that he is saying that he and
his companions could have claimed such honour as the apostles of
Christ were entitled to, without identifying himself and his colleagues as belonging to the group of apostles. Neither of these
solutions is particularly convincing.

Best, p. 100, suggests that Paul's view of apostleship may have
been less fully formulated in this early epistle than it was by the
time of the Corinthian correspondence, but the time-gap is in fact
quite brief. R. Schnackenburg ('Apostles before and during Paul's
Time', in W. W. Gasque and R. P. Martin (ed.), *Apostolic History
and the Gospel*, Exeter, 1970, pp. 287–303) argues that the concept
of an apostle was not clearly defined, that the word means basically
a missionary, and that an appearance of the risen Jesus was not
universally regarded as an essential qualification for being an apostle.
It is difficult, however, to believe that the Paul who so strongly
stressed the connection between seeing the risen Lord and being an
apostle in 1 Corinthians should have had a much broader view of
apostleship only a year or two earlier. Perhaps the best solution is
that offered by W. Schmithals (*The Office of Apostle in the Early*

Church, London, 1971, pp. 23, 65–7): Paul is thinking *only* of Silvanus and himself in this passage and tacitly ignores the junior member of the group of missionaries. Silas, as a Jerusalem Christian (Ac. 15:22), could well have been an apostle. In this way we avoid the difficulty of Timothy being reckoned an apostle here and not recognised as such in Paul's later correspondence. Whatever be the case, the point is that the apostles, as representatives of Christ, occupied a position of leadership as the founders of the churches and were entitled to obedience and respect in virtue of this office. Paul applies the same principle to church workers generally in 5:12f.

7. Despite this legitimate claim to honour and the right to deal authoritatively with the church, Paul and his colleagues had adopted a different method. Paul's own approach was to adopt a spirit of fatherly love and to use discipline only as a last resort (1 C. 4:14–21; see D. R. Hall, 'Pauline Church Discipline', *TynB* 20, 1969, pp. 3–26). The first part of the verse, **But we were gentle among you**, is regarded as the beginning of a new sentence and closely linked with the following phrase 'like a nurse. . .' by *RSV* and other English versions. The majority of commentators, however, regard the phrase as belonging to the previous sentence; v. 7*b* then forms the commencement of a new sentence which extends into v. 8. This latter understanding of the sentence structure is preferable; it links the 'like. . .' phrase to the 'so. . . clause' and avoids a difficult asyndeton at the beginning of v. 8. The word **gentle** (Gk. *ēpioi*), which occurs elsewhere in the *NT* only in 2 Tim. 2:24 and there refers to the gentleness which a pastor must show, is found in a group of MSS of generally inferior quality; the variant reading, attested by a group of earlier MSS, is 'babes' (Gk. *nēpioi*). Because of its superior attestation and because the imagery is bolder this reading has had considerable support from commentators. There can, however, be little doubt that the less well-attested reading is correct; the rarer word was replaced by a more familiar one (Paul uses 'babe' ten times), possibly by scribal accident. The significant fact is that Paul elsewhere compares himself to a father in relation to his converts, and this makes the image of a gentle mother much more probable here than the image of a child, which would in any case destroy the unity of the passage. We therefore side with the minority opinion of the editors of the UBS text (Metzger, pp. 629f.). Paul's claim is then that the missionaries were not harsh or overbearing to the church, but rather showed a kindly disposition. Their aim was the good of the church, not the establishment of their own position or the securing of their own ends.

Paul proceeds to speak of the affection which the missionaries had for the church by drawing a comparison between their attitude and that of **a nurse taking care of her children**. Since the phrase refers to 'her own' children, the picture is of a mother who personally cares for her children instead of entrusting them to someone else's care, and the reason why Paul says 'nurse' instead of 'mother' is to underline this element of loving care for the children. The etymology of the word (it is related to a verb meaning 'to nourish') has suggested to some commentators that Paul is thinking of a 'wet-nurse' who suckles a child; Best, p. 101, translates as 'nursing mother'. It seems doubtful, however, whether we should take the word in this more specific sense. The element of tender loving care for the children is expressed sufficiently in the verb which conveys the idea of taking them in one's arms, fondling them and keeping them warm and safe (Eph. 5:29), just as a mother-bird broods over her young (Dt. 22:6). A. J. Malherbe, art cit., pp. 211–14, again demonstrates how Paul is using a figure of speech employed by philosophers and applying it to the Christian preacher.

8. The comparison now follows. Paul uses a rare word (Gk. *homeiromai*) which means to long for or desire something (Job 3:21 LXX; Ps. 62:1 Sym; H. W. Heidland, *TDNT* v, p. 176). It brings out the deep affection which the missionaries felt for their converts. From this affection sprang the longing of the missionaries **to share with** the Thessalonians **not only the gospel of God but also** their **own selves**. 'To share', as Rigaux, p. 422, notes, is to give something while preserving part of it for oneself. The missionaries who had experienced the blessings brought by the gospel wanted the Thessalonians to have their share of them. No doubt for Paul the gospel itself was the thing of highest value, but, since in general people regard their own lives as their most precious possession, he expresses the depth of his longing to share the highest gifts with the Thessalonians by saying that the missionaries would have given their lives to them as well. This could mean that they were willing to lay down their lives in self-sacrifice for them (Lightfoot, p. 26). But most commentators take 'selves' (Gk. *psychē*, 'soul', hence 'life' or 'self') to mean the inner being of the missionaries. The language is that of love in which a lover wants to share his life with the beloved in an act of self-giving and union, rather than the language of self-sacrifice. The last clause in the verse confirms this interpretation. Paul and his colleagues felt deeply involved with their converts and spoke in terms of love for them; something of the love which they believed God had for the Thessalonians (1:4) was channelled through them.

9. Paul draws attention to a further feature of the missionaries' conduct in Thessalonica. The opening **For** shows that the verse gives a further proof of what he has already said about their humble and loving attitude to the Thessalonians, their desire not to impose upon them or to give the impression that they were looking for some return for their work of evangelism. Again, Paul appeals to the memory of the Thessalonians to substantiate what he says. They themselves could **remember** the **labour and toil** of the missionaries. The two words express respectively the hard, tiring nature of the work (Gk. *kopos*) and its painfulness (Gk. *mochthos*; cf. 2 C. 11:27), which were no doubt accentuated by keeping at it **night and day**; the phrase, however, simply means that the missionaries worked both at night and by day, not continuously throughout the twenty-four hour period. The activity was the tent-making mentioned in Ac. 18:3, where the word used may have the broader sense of leather-work generally. Paul may have learned his trade during his days as a Jewish teacher, since rabbis were supposed to support themselves without taking fees. However, R. F. Hock has argued that Paul's practice reflects that of the philosophers who thought that it was good for their hearers to see them living in the world with all its hardships and putting their teaching into effect (*The Social Context of Paul's Ministry*, Philadelphia, 1980; 'Paul's Tent-making and the Problem of his Social Class', *JBL* 97, 1978, pp. 555–64; 'The Workshop as a Social Setting for Paul's Missionary Preaching', *CBQ* 41, 1979, pp. 438–50; cf. A. J. Malherbe, *Social Aspects of Early Christianity*, Baton Rouge, 1977, p. 24). Paul's own comment, however, is that he and his friends worked in this way in order to avoid laying the **burden** of looking after them on the Thessalonian Christians. They both worked and **preached the gospel of God**. To some extent Paul's needs were met by gifts from the church already established in Philippi (Phil. 4:16), but, if what Paul said later about the extreme poverty of the churches in Macedonia (2 C. 8:1f.) was true at this earlier date, these gifts may not have been very large and were insufficient to support the missionaries. Paul repeats the substance of the present statement in 2 Th. 3:8, where he uses his conduct as an example for the Thessalonians to follow instead of living in idleness and expecting other people to provide for them. From the later passage it seems that even during the missionaries' visit to Thessalonica some members of the church were abstaining from work, and Paul felt it necessary to comment again on this in the present epistle (4:11). It is clear that he is already preparing the ground for his later exhortation.

10. Verses 10–12 form one long sentence which moves on from the character of the missionaries' evangelism to their care for the new converts. Paul again stresses the virtuous and blameless lives of the preachers, and sees a further proof of this in the fatherly admonitions which they gave to the readers to live lives **worthy of**

God. The implications of the sentence are twofold. On the one hand, Paul appears to be saying that the moral content of the preaching is a confirmation that the preachers were themselves living morally; they were unlikely to be living immorally if their message was concerned with morality—and the readers themselves could testify to this. On the other hand, Paul is moving from the thought of how the preachers lived, giving an example to their hearers and urging them to live in the same way, to an expression of thanks that their work had been successful in bringing them to conversion.

The sentence opens abruptly without the usual Greek connection with the preceding one, and this indicates that the same line of thought is being pursued. In a particularly solemn way Paul calls not only on the readers but also on **God** himself as **witnesses** to the lives of the missionaries. The readers are cited because they had to be convinced from their own observation of the truth of Paul's remarks, and God is cited because there was always the possibility that the missionaries could have been guilty of a subtle deception practised upon the human witnesses. The solemnity of the tone suggests strongly that Paul was dealing with real accusations that were being used by the opponents of the church to denigrate the missionaries and their message and so to turn the converts against them. But Paul felt that he could confidently refute any such accusations by an appeal to the **holy, righteous and blameless** lives of the missionaries. The three adjectives (representing three Greek adverbs) are close in meaning and are put together for emphasis. **holy** (Gk. *hosios*, a less common word in the *NT* than its synonym *hagios*) expresses an attitude of piety and reverence towards God which affects a person's conduct (1 Tim. 2:8; Tit. 1:8). **righteous** is used of conduct which accords with justice, a universally recognised standard but one which for Paul was based on God's revelation of how men ought to live. **blameless** refers to conduct which is free from any accusation that it falls below the standard of justice (5:23). The final phrase **to you believers** may simply mean 'among you' or 'for your benefit'; the former rendering is the more likely (Rigaux, pp. 427f.). The addition of **believers** indicates that by this point Paul is thinking of the manner of life of the missionaries among the Christian group which was formed in response to their preaching by those who believed the Christian message; in vv. 11f. he goes on to mention what he taught those who had already responded to the gospel.

11. Confirmation of Paul's statement about the missionaries' personal way of life is given by the Thessalonians' remembrance of the sincere and loving teaching which they were given and of its moral content. The missionaries dealt with their converts as individuals, speaking personally to each one of them and giving them appropriate counsel. Elsewhere Paul speaks of being **like a father** to his converts, no doubt in the sense that he was responsible for bringing them to spiritual birth (Phm. 10; 1 C. 4:14f.). A father can hope that his children will follow his example (1 C. 4:16), but he also has the responsibility of teaching them how to live, and he does this in a spirit of love and concern for their welfare. Protestant Christians may dislike the self-appellation of 'Father' used by Roman Catholic priests (and they have scriptural warrant for their opinion, Mt. 23:9), but there can be no doubt that the title does reflect the kind of attitude which should be shown by the pastor as he cares for the congregation.

The second part of the verse (which is the first part of v. 12 in UBS and other Greek texts) contains three verbs describing the manner of the teaching given by the missionaries to the converts. These verbs are participles in the Greek text and the clause lacks a main verb, probably because Paul has forgotten how the long sentence began and committed an anacolouthon. **exhorted** is the most general word for Christian instruction to converts (3:2, 7; 4:1, 10, 18; 5:11, 14) and its frequency in this epistle indicates how Paul's concern here is not so much instruction as appeal and encouragement to live as true Christians. The verb can also mean to comfort (3:7; 4:18), but here the sense of spiritual and ethical admonition is dominant. **encouraged** is very similar in meaning, and the verb can convey the ideas of admonition (as here) and encouragement (5:14) or consolation (Jn 11:19, 31). If 'exhorted' conveys the sense of a command to the converts, 'encouraged' refers to the way in which the missionaries assured them that they were capable of fulfilling the command. The third verb, **charged**, has the sense of making a solemn and emphatic affirmation or demand, and thus indicates the importance of heeding and obeying the missionaries' commands.

12. Now comes the purpose of the ethical appeal, which is at the same time a statement of its content. The converts are **to lead a life worthy of God**. Paul here employs a verb which literally means 'to walk', but it was used particularly in biblical Greek (and also on occasion in Classical Greek) with the metaphorical sense of living one's life. The Christian life-style is to be one that is **worthy of God** (Col. 1:10). The phrase is found in Greek religion, where priests were expected to conduct themselves in a manner worthy of the gods whom they served. The determinative factor is accordingly the particular character of the god in question. The Christian God expects his worshippers to live in a way that will bring honour to him and that corresponds to his own character: 'you shall be holy,

for I am holy' (Lev. 11:45, cited in 1 Pet. 1:16) is an apt summary
of the point. In the present context, however, Paul stresses that the
Christian God is the one **who calls** men **into his own kingdom and
glory**. God's call is his summons to men through the gospel message
to receive salvation and so to become his people. Paul normally uses
the past tense of the verb to signify God's initial calling of men to
conversion (4:7), but here he uses the present tense (cf. 5:24) to
show that God's call is not a once-for-all affair. The goal of God's
summons is entry to his kingdom in the future, and hence Paul
thinks of believers as not only having been called into their present
relationship to God but also as being continually called by God to
final entry into his kingdom. It follows that the kingdom of which
Paul is speaking here is the future realm in which God will manifest
his full salvation for his people. This is Paul's normal use of the
term (1 C. 6:9f.; Gal. 5:21; 2 Th. 1:5), although he can also speak
of the kingdom as a present reality (Rom. 14:17; 1 C. 4:20). He
thus reflects the tension found in the teaching of Jesus where the
kingdom of God is regarded both as already present (Mt. 11:12; Mk
1:15; Lk. 11:20) and as still to come (Mt. 6:10; Mk 9:1). The
'kingdom' is both God's act of ruling and the area over which he
rules, bringing to men the blessings of salvation by his mighty
power. Paul links the term especially with the final establishment
of God's rule in the future age. This is clear in the present verse
from the association of the kingdom with God's **glory**, a term which
here indicates the visible radiance of God's majesty revealed in
heaven and shared with his people (Rom. 5:2; 8:18; Col. 1:27).
Those who have such a prospect before them must live in a fitting
manner in the present time during which God himself is working
in them to prepare them for their future state (2 C. 3:18).

Paul's discussion of the manner of life of the missionaries was
intended primarily to help the members of the Thessalonian church.
The truth of the gospel was vindicated by the upright lives of the
missionaries, and hence the section is meant to reassure the readers
that the visit of the missionaries was a firm foundation for their
belief. For the modern reader the significance of the passage may
lie more in a secondary application. Paul's description of the life of
the missionaries constitutes an example to be followed by those who
preach the gospel today. It is doubtless the case that false or evil
messages can be put over by attractive personalities. A messenger's
pleasant and sincere manner is not necessarily a proof of the truth
of his word. But it is equally the case that the Christian gospel will
make little or no impression if it cannot be verified in the lives of
its messengers. They cannot be too scrupulous in giving no ground
for insinuations against their honesty and probity, nor can they do

too much in putting themselves entirely at the service of the Lord and of the people to whom they bring the message.

THE RECEPTION OF THE MESSAGE

2:13-16

The Thessalonian converts had recognised that the message preached by the apostles was no merely human word but the Word of God (1:5). The proof of their genuine acceptance of it was seen in the fact that they were prepared to believe despite the suffering in which their response involved them. Although they knew that the missionaries had already suffered before they came to them and had met a hostile reception in Thessalonica itself (2:2), this did not stop them from believing. Their experience was in no way unusual, for already the churches in Judea had suffered in the same way from the Jews who had attacked Jesus and the missionaries in order to prevent the Gentiles from hearing the gospel. Retribution, however, would come upon them, now that their sins had reached a climax, and this could be regarded as a vindication of the gospel and its messengers.

The paragraph forms the climax of the first section of the epistle, and rounds off Paul's account of how the missionaries came to Thessalonica and by their faithful ministry brought their hearers to Christian faith. It also prepares the way for the following section which deals with the very real fears that Paul had for those who had accepted the gospel amid such adversity and were still exposed to opposition. The note of thanksgiving is characteristic of Paul's mood in the epistle (cf. 3:9f.); it is a fitting conclusion to the section and in no sense structurally awkward (see further, pp. 7–9).

13. From the preaching of the message Paul turns to the reception of it, and finds reason to **thank God** for the positive response of the Thessalonians. The opening of the sentence is not absolutely clear. The word **also** is taken by several commentators with **we**, in which case there would appear to be a contrast between the writers of the epistle and some other group of people. Frame's view (originally suggested by Rendel Harris) that Paul is making a contrast with a letter from the Thessalonians in which *they* thanked him for bringing the gospel to them is far from obvious. The view that the contrast is with the people who had told Paul about the conversion of the Thessalonians (1:8f.; Marxsen, p. 47) comes to grief on the fact that there has been no earlier mention of their thanksgiving. Masson, p. 31, suggests that Paul means 'we too for our part' in contrast to the 'you' in v. 1.

A second possibility is to take 'also' with the verb 'thank,' but this again raises problems. Is Paul drawing a contrast with a previous act of thanksgiving (1:2), or is he contrasting thanksgiving with some other activity? The third possibility is to take the 'also' with 'for this' (for this stereotyped phrase, cf. 3:5; Eph. 1:15; Col. 1:9), so that the point is that Paul has a fresh or further reason for thanksgiving, or simply that he wants to emphasise the reason; Moule paraphrases 'That is in fact why we give thanks' (*Idiom-Book*, p. 167).

A further problem is whether **for this** refers backwards to what has just preceded (Masson, p. 31) or forwards to the 'that . . .' clause. It seems likely that the main reference is forwards, but at the same time there is a sense in which Paul is giving thanks for the successful preaching of the gospel despite all difficulties, described in 2:1–12, which led to the response of the Thessalonians. Paul uses a word which became a technical term in early Christianity for the reception of authoritative traditions when he says that the Thessalonians **received** the message (4:1; 2 Th. 3:6). The verb **accepted** is synonymous, but lacks this technical sense, and Paul probably uses it simply for the sake of literary variation. What the Thessalonians heard through the intermediary of the missionaries was **the word of God**, the gospel as a communication from God to men. The Thessalonians could have regarded it simply **as the word of men**, but they accepted it (1:6) as **the word of God**. This is an astonishing claim to make: as the Helvetic Confession recognises, the faithful preaching of the Word of God is itself the Word of God (*Praedicatio verbi Dei est verbum Dei*. See T. H. L. Parker, 'The Word and the Gospel', in T. H. L. Parker (ed.), *Essays in Christology for Karl Barth*, London, 1956, pp. 177–90). Nevertheless Paul insists that this is the nature of Christian preaching, and he saw the proof of it in the effect of the message, **which is at work in . . . believers.** The word is not merely heard by men; it also operates powerfully in their lives, since it is uttered in power and in the Holy Spirit (1:5). *RSV* takes the verb as a middle form ('is at work', Gk. *energeitai*); but it could also be a passive: 'is made operative (*sc.* by God)'; the sense is not greatly affected. It is in **believers** that the word is effective; those who accept it as the word of God experience its transforming power, but where faith is lacking the word is powerless. Paul does not discuss here the relation between the operation of the word and the development of faith and ask why the word does not always engender faith. The relation between the divine cause and the human effect lies beyond human comprehension by its very nature.

14. The proof that the Thessalonians had truly received the word was to be seen in their willingness to undergo affliction for their faith, a response which ranged them alongside other Christians and indeed Jesus himself. The word **imitators** (cf. 1:6) is used either passively to indicate that the Thessalonians were suffering the same fate as other Christians, or actively to imply that they met their sufferings with the same steadfast faith and courage as their fellow-Christians. Paul compares them especially with **the churches of God . . . in Judea**. Here it is interesting to note that Paul can refer to several churches (cf. 2 Th. 1:4; 1 C. 11:16). Although he can think of the church as one entity (Gal. 1:13), he also thinks of the one church as consisting of many churches in different localities. They are churches of God, congregations belonging to him, but Paul adds the qualification **in Christ Jesus**, which is part of his normal description of the church (1:1) and in this case may be intended to distinguish Christian groups from Jewish ones. The churches **in Judea** are singled out for mention. This may be because they were particularly the object of persecution by the Jews, and it was also the Jews who were responsible for the persecution in Thessalonica (Ac. 17:5). It is true that Paul could have referred to other churches in his mission-field where the Jews had also been instrumental in causing trouble; the Judean churches may be singled out because they were the first to be persecuted, or perhaps because they had suffered intensely, or, most probably, because Paul wants to relate the suffering of the Thessalonians to an attitude which stemmed from Palestine and was part of a series of attacks on the prophets, Jesus, and his followers. It has been claimed that Paul's contrast between **your own countrymen** in Thessalonica and the **Jews in Judea** implies that the persecution in Thessalonica was carried on purely by the Gentiles (in contradiction to Ac. 17:5), but this view leaves Paul's outburst against the Jews in vv. 15f. quite unmotivated and tangential to his present theme. 'Your own countrymen' is to be taken in a local rather than a racial sense and does not exclude the Jewish population of Thessalonica. The argument for a racial sense, as presented by von Dobschütz, pp. 109f., amounts to the claim that the Thessalonian church was composed of Gentile Christians (cf. 1:9) and that therefore their 'own countrymen' would be understood as also being Gentiles. Von Dobschütz does not question the statement that Jews instigated the persecution in Thessalonica (Ac. 17:5), but thinks that Paul here ignores this point. However, E. Haenchen (*Die Apostelgeschichte*, Göttingen, 1959, pp. 452f.) argues that nobody would think Jews were in Paul's mind in this verse were it not for the evidence of Acts, and proceeds to question the historicity of the account in Acts. Such scepticism is unwarranted, and Haenchen himself has finally

to admit that he has no compelling evidence for his view. Granted
that the church consisted mainly of Gentiles, and that Paul is here
thinking primarily of Gentile opposition, nothing hinders the view
that Acts is correct in reporting the conversion of some Jews, that
Paul's choice of word here can include fellow-citizens who were
Jews, and that in the section as a whole he is thinking of the
opposition towards himself incited by Jews (cf. Masson, p. 33 n. 2).

15. The persecuting activity of the Jews is seen as forming part
of a series of attacks on God's messengers for which they stand
under divine judgment. (For this tradition in Judaism and its use
in the *NT*, see O. H. Steck, *Israel und das gewaltsame Geschick der
Propheten*, Neukirchen, 1967.) The height of their sin was that they
killed the Lord Jesus, but this is linked with the earlier murders
of **the prophets.** ('Prophets' should be taken as the object of 'killed'
and not of 'drove out', *pace* Neil, p. 51). What happened to Jesus
should have been no surprise to those who knew what happened to
the prophets before him. For the same line of thought, see Mt.
23:29-36 par. Lk. 11:47-51; it is likely that Jesus was using a Jewish
tradition, and that Paul follows the same line of thought.

The fate of the followers of Jesus is the same. The Jews **drove us
out**, says Paul (or, perhaps, 'persecuted us'). The reference is probably to the experience of the missionaries (so in v. 16) rather than
of Christians in general. Since this verb (unlike the following ones)
is an aorist participle, a definite event may be in mind, and this
could well be the ejection of the missionaries from Thessalonica,
which was instigated by the Jews; this would give the necessary link
with v. 17 which otherwise is unprepared for. It is true that Paul
was attacked in this way more than once by the Jews, but in the
context this would seem to be the obvious allusion for the readers
to pick up. The real nature of this action becomes obvious in the
three following phrases. First, such an action is part of an attitude
which **displeases God.** This is not a description of the intention of
the Jews but rather of how their attitude appeared to God, since it
was directed against his messengers. Second, it was an act of hostility
against **all men**, i.e. all other peoples than themselves. Again, it
would not have appeared so to the Jews, who were willing for
Gentiles to become proselytes and thus part of God's family—on
their own terms. But the strict separation which the Jews practised
between themselves and Gentiles in general inevitably appeared as
hostility to the latter, and Tacitus, the Roman historian, summed
it up: 'toward every other people they feel only hate and enmity'
(*Hist.* 5:5).

16. The Greek construction shows that the third phrase explains
how the Jews manifest their attitude to God and the Gentiles; it is

by hindering the Christian missionaries **from speaking to the Gentiles that they may be saved**. The missionaries were sent out by God (2:4) and their field was the Gentile world. Their method was to speak, i.e. to make known the gospel by word of mouth, and their goal was to save their hearers. This latter verb is found only here in the epistle (cf. 2 Th. 2:10, and the noun 'salvation', 5:8f.; 2 Th. 2:13), but the concept is a central one to express the benefits announced in the gospel. It is linked with the idea of healing the sick (including those in danger of death) and rescuing from danger. Hence it can have the negative nuance of deliverance from a state of sinfulness and its ultimate judgment (cf. 1:10, where a synonymous verb is used) and the positive nuance of entry into a state of happiness and blessedness. In Paul the thought is often 'eschatological,' i.e. it is future deliverance from the wrath of God and entry into heavenly bliss which is in mind (e.g. Rom. 5:9f.); but here the thought is more general, and probably present deliverance is meant.

Such conduct on the part of the Jews is **always to fill up the measure of their sins**. It is not clear whether the construction expresses (God's) purpose or the actual result of the Jews' action, but probably the former is in mind. The thought is that there is a fixed measure or amount of sin to be committed in order to bring about judgment; it is like filling up one pan on an old-fashioned pair of scales until eventually it counterbalances the weight in the other pan and begins to fall. The idea is found in Gen. 15:16; Dan. 8:23; 2 Mac. 6:14; Mt. 23:32, and there is a related thought in Rev. 6:11, where the full number of martyrs must die before the End can come. This latter notion is found in apocalyptic writings (2 Esd. 2:41; 4:36f.). Paul, then, is using an idea which was current in apocalyptic thinking and in early Christianity. It is strange that the verb **to fill up** (aorist, of a punctiliar action or of a series of actions regarded as a whole) is qualified by **always** which suggests a continuous action. Paul seems to be saying that the various hostile actions of the Jews which they are continually performing against the missionaries are all going to fill up the total number of their sins; in other words, the total is not yet complete. Von Dobschütz, p. 114, eases the sentence by taking the adverb to mean 'completely', but he gives no evidence for this meaning.

The final clause, **God's wrath has come upon them**, is very difficult. The verb is in the past tense and in no way can it be turned into a future; the possibility of a 'prophetic' aorist (von Dobschütz, p. 116) is excluded, since no motive for its use can be seen. It is possible, however, that 'has come' (Gk. *ephthasen*) means not 'has arrived' but 'has drawn near, even to the very point of contact' (Thomas, p. 260; see K. W. Clark, 'Realised Eschatology',

JBL 59, 1940, pp. 367–83). The phraseology is very similar to that in Mt. 12:28 par. Lk. 11:20 where Jesus says that the kingly power of God has drawn near to his hearers and is there for them to grasp (I. H. Marshall, *The Gospel of Luke*, Exeter, 1978, p. 476). So the sense could be that the divine **wrath** has drawn very near to the Jews and will fall upon them once the measure of their sins is complete. The divine wrath is operative in the world as God gives up sinners to further acts of sin for which they will experience his coming judgment (Rom. 1:18–2:11). It has been suggested that here too Paul sees God's wrath already at work in the hardening of the hearts of the Jews to commit further acts of hostility to the gospel and to reject it. Following Lightfoot, pp. 35f., C. E. B. Cranfield, 'A Study of 1 Thessalonians 2', *IBS* 1, 1979, pp. 215–26, holds that Paul is looking back to the crucifixion of Jesus as the event in which the disobedience of the Jews reached a climax and God displayed his judgment upon them. This is over-subtle. The wrath of which Paul speaks here is more likely to be God's final judgment upon sin.

The qualifying phrase (Gk. *eis telos*), translated in *RSV* as **at last**, is ambiguous, and several possibilities have been suggested. (1). The *RSV* rendering has the force of 'at long last' or 'finally' (*GNB*; *NIV*; Milligan, p. 32; Frame, pp. 114f.; Rigaux, p. 453; Best, p. 121). This translation lacks firm attestation in biblical Greek, but gives a good temporal contrast to balance 'always' in the previous clause. (2). The phrase can mean 'completely', 'to the uttermost' (*RSV* mg 1; von Dobschütz, p. 115 n. 3; Thomas, p. 260; Moule, *Idiom-Book*, p. 70; G. Delling, *TDNT* VIII, p. 56). For this possibility, see Jos. 8:24; 2 Ch. 12:12; Jn. 13:1. (3). The phrase can mean 'for ever,' 'to the end,' i.e. 'lasting for ever' (*RSV* mg 2; *NEB*; AG; G. Stählin, *TDNT* v, p. 434). This translation has strong biblical support (Ps. 76:8 LXX; 78:5 LXX; 102:9 LXX; Mt. 10:22), but it requires that the verb has an extended sense: 'has come (so as to last) for ever.' (4). The phrase might mean 'until the end' (Mt. 10:22) and qualify 'wrath': 'the wrath (that leads up) to the End has come upon them' (I owe this suggestion to D. Wenham).

A choice between these possibilities is difficult, particularly since the underlying Hebrew phrase is also ambiguous. We are tempted to seek refuge in a combination of nuances and suggest that 'fully and finally' gives the sense (see P. R. Ackroyd, 'נ ע ה — εἰς τέλος', *ExpT* 80, 1968–9, p. 126).

The problem is not solved by recourse to the almost identical occurrence of the clause in T. Levi 6:11, where historically it refers to the coming of the wrath of God on the inhabitants of Shechem for their sins. Here the verb clearly refers to an actual, past act of judgment; but the sense of the adverbial phrase remains ambiguous. The closeness of wording between the two documents suggests some kind of literary dependence, but in the present state of uncertainty regarding the composition of T. Levi and the possibility of Christian editing, no satisfactory solution to this problem is possible. The actual usage of the clause in both documents is so different that conscious quotation by either author is unlikely, and it seems more likely that a form of words used in apocalyptic circles has been used by both authors.

The question arises whether some specific event led Paul to see the wrath of God descending upon the Jews. We have already mentioned the possibility that the crucifixion of Jesus could be seen in this way. Much more popular is the view that the passage refers to the decisive manifestation of God's judgment at the fall of Jerusalem in AD 70. If the passage is not prophetic, it would follow that it was composed after the event, and this is one of the reasons for concluding that this section is an interpolation into the epistle (see pp. 11–2). Yet another view is that the expulsion of the Jews from Rome by Claudius in AD 49 (shortly before the date of the letter) could have suggested that judgment was about to break out on the Jews, and with it would come the End (E. Bammel, 'Judenverfolgung und Naherwartung', ZTK 56, 1959, pp. 249–315). An event such as this could have been regarded as a pointer to coming judgment and so sharpened expectations, but on the whole it seems more probable that Paul is writing about an imminent judgment rather than a past one, that he is inspired by the prophecies in the Jesus-tradition (see D. Wenham, as cited at 4:15 note), and that we should not look for a specific *past* event which could be regarded as the full and final coming of God's wrath.

Paul has been thought to condemn the Jews indiscriminately in this passage (and thus to be guilty of anti-Semitism) and also to hold out no hope for them, whereas in Rom. 9–11 he prophesies that 'all Israel will be saved'. The problem is treated well by Marxsen, pp. 48–51, who takes up suggestions by earlier writers. He argues that Paul is writing here about particular Jews, those who have shown hostility to God's messengers, and not about the Jews in general. Further, what Paul says about them is valid only so long as they persist in their hostility to God and the gospel. If this view is correct, Paul is not guilty of anti-Semitism. What he says here about the nearness of God's wrath is true for those Jews who persist in ungodliness, but does not contradict the hope that he holds out in Romans that the present time of Jewish opposition to the gospel will be followed by a turning of the people to God. Marxsen also comments that Paul is not concerned specifically with the Jews but with the general issue of persecution by the 'fellow countrymen' of Christians; from what Paul says about the Jews, the Thessalonians can be sure that God will vindicate the gospel by acting against its opponents.

Paul always holds open the possibility of salvation to those who respond to the gospel, whether Jews or Gentiles, and he expects that God will judge those who persecute the church or are enemies of the cross (Phil. 3:18f.; 2 Th. 1:5–9). The prophecy that all Israel will be saved means that Paul expected a different response from the Jews than was presently the case, but does not exclude the need for their faith in Jesus Christ in order to be saved; nor obviously does it mean that individual Israelites may not be converted during the present time. The man who wrote Rom. 9:1–5; 10:1 is hardly likely to have been guilty of anti-Semitism at any time.

Marxsen's view thus interprets Paul by Paul. Its weak point is its claim that Paul is thinking merely of individual Jews who persecute the missionaries. More probably Paul is thinking collectively of the Jews as a people who by and large were opposed to the gospel and had turned against God during their history. He also seems to have regarded the parousia, with its attendant tribulations, as being divine judgment in full measure upon the last generation of Jews, those in whom the sin of the nation reached its height in the crucifixion of Jesus and the persecution of the church. If, however, we grant the points made in the previous paragraph, then the substance of Marxsen's interpretation can still stand despite this important modification. The view of Best, p. 122, that '1 Th. 2:16c shows Paul holding an unacceptable anti-Semitic position' does less than justice to Paul.

One final comment by Marxsen is important. Nothing in what Paul writes suggests that the Thessalonians should hate their persecutors or react violently against them. Their task is to live the new life of the Christian in love even to their enemies and to leave vengeance to God himself.

See further, Friedrich, pp. 228–30; W. D. Davies, 'Paul and the People of Israel', *NTS* 24, 1977–8, pp. 4–39; G. E. Okeke, '1 Thessalonians 2:13–16: The Fate of the Unbelieving Jews', *NTS* 27, 1980–1, pp. 127–36.

PAUL'S CONTINUING CONCERN FOR THE CHURCH

2:17 – 3:13

Throughout the first half of the epistle Paul is demonstrating his loving concern for the Thessalonian Christians in their difficult situation. He has described the initial visit of the missionaries and the response of the Thessalonians in such a way as to reassure them of the truth of the gospel and the reality of their conversion, and to encourage them to continue to live as true Christians. This same concern for his converts is the continuing theme in this concluding section in which Paul turns from the visit of the missionaries to describe his continuing concern for the church. The section breaks up naturally into four subdivisions (2:17–20; 3:1–5; 3:6–10; 3:11–13).

Paul begins by taking up the thought of his enforced separation from the Thessalonians as a result of his expulsion from the city at the instigation of the Jews, and states how he had made more than one unsuccessful attempt to return to Thessalonica and visit the church which meant so much to him. When these attempts were frustrated, he had to be content with sending Timothy instead to bring back news about the church and to encourage the Christians not to fall away, as Paul feared they might, through their tribulations. The good news brought by Timothy on his return to Paul had encouraged him in the midst of his own difficulties at the time and moved him to thank God and also to long all the more to see the Thessalonians for himself. Finally, he puts into words his own prayers to God that he might be able to visit the Thessalonians and that they might grow in love so as to be fit to stand before God at the return of Jesus. This thought of the moral and spiritual progress of the Thessalonian Christians leads into the theme of the second half of the epistle.

This section of the letter is relatively straightforward to understand and poses no serious problems. Marxsen, p. 52, draws attention to the way in which Paul here speaks of the help and encouragement which he himself has received from the Thessalonian church; their progress has been of spiritual help to him in the midst of his own afflictions. The relationship between the pastor and his congregation is a two-way one, and each can help, or hinder, the other.

17. The opening address, **brethren**, indicates that a fresh section is beginning. In this first sub-section (2:17–20) Paul returns to the main theme of the relationship between the missionaries and the Thessalonian church after the brief comment on their persecutors and the fate in store for them. At the same time there is a double shift in emphasis from the initial visit of the missionaries to their more recent concern for the church, and from the situation of the church to that of the missionaries themselves. This transition is further seen in the **But . . . we** which is not meant to contrast Paul and his colleagues with some other group (whether the Thessalonian

Christians or the Gentile and Jewish opponents of the gospel) but rather to resume the main theme. The phrase in fact is resumptive of 'us' in v. 16 and leads into a description of what the missionaries felt and did after they had been prevented from continuing their evangelism in Thessalonica by the Jews. Their feeling was one of being **bereft** of their friends. The Greek word (*aporphanizō*) could be used of children deprived of their parents or of parents who had lost their children, or more generally in a metaphorical sense. Since Paul has already used the father/children metaphor to express his relationship with the Thessalonians, it is the thought of parents losing their children which is conveyed here, and the metaphor has been continued in the present phrase because the word is expressive not merely of the fact of separation but also of the feeling of loss and deprivation which accompanies it. The phrase **for a short time** (Gk. *pros kairon hōras*, a combination of *pros kairon*, 1 C. 7:5, and *pros hōran*, 2 C. 7:8) would seem to refer most naturally to the time that elapsed between the departure of the missionaries from Thessalonica and Paul's attempts to return, and is used here to indicate that Paul's concern for his friends was so great that only a very short time passed before he made concrete efforts to go back to Thessalonica. The fact that the separation did not mean that he had abandoned his concern for them—an accusation that might well have been made behind his back in Thessalonica—is further countered by his comment that the separation had been merely **in person not in heart**. Though there could be no face-to-face encounter with his friends, yet they were very close to him in his thoughts and feelings: out of sight, but not out of mind. As in Hebrew thought, **heart** is here the centre of the personality, the seat of thinking, feeling and willing. The missionaries were filled **with great desire** (Gk. *epithymia*, here used, as often, in a good sense; cf. Phil. 1:23) **to see** their friends and made strenuous efforts to do so; the verb **endeavoured** implies not merely longing to do something but positive attempts to achieve it (Gal. 2:10). The force of **the more eagerly** is uncertain. It can be taken as having an elative force 'very eagerly' (*NEB*) or as a comparative. In the latter case one looks for an object of comparison, and the thought may be that Paul was more eager to return than he would have been if he had not been forced to leave Thessalonica against his will and earlier than he had intended.

18. If v. 17 refers to the efforts which the missionaries made to see their friends again, v. 18 gives the reason for them in the determination which they had felt to return to Thessalonica. The verb **we wanted** is expressive not merely of desire but of a positive and deliberate plan. Although Paul has been writing up to this point—and will continue to do so—in the names of all three missionaries, he interjects an **I, Paul** which makes it clear that he is thinking very much of his own feelings (although these were no doubt shared by his colleagues) and is bearing in mind that it did prove possible for one of the group, but not himself, to pay the longed-for visit to the church. Again, as if to ward off possible accusations or suspicions, Paul states that he and his colleagues made several attempts to visit Thessalonica. **again and again** is literally 'once and twice' and refers to an indefinite number of occasions (not just two occasions; Dt. 9:13 LXX; Phil. 4:16; Frame, pp. 120f.; L. Morris, 'ΚΑΙ ΑΠΑΞ ΚΑΙ ΔΙΣ', *NovT* 1, 1956, pp. 205–8) on which Paul personally had tried to come to Thessalonica. But all efforts, whether of Paul or his companions, had proved futile, for **Satan hindered us**. With this phrase Paul indicates that he recognised the existence of a malignant spiritual force behind whatever circumstances were at work to prevent their visit. **Satan** (2 Th. 2:9; Rom. 16:20; 2 C. 12:7) is the one who opposes the progress of the gospel and who tempts believers to give up their faith (3:5) or fall into sin (1 C. 7:5). Paul uses a variety of designations for him (see 3:5; 2 Th. 3:3; 2 C. 4:4), but 'Satan' is the most common one.

Best, p. 127, warns against the misuse of the concept of Satan in Christian thinking as a means of avoiding the careful examination of the proximate causes of evil and sin. Paul himself, however, is careful to recognise that Satan is only half the story, and that sin results when people respond to the temptations which come from him. At the same time Paul recognises that behind the opposition to the gospel there can be traced some superhuman principle of evil.

It is this principle which he sees at work here in the factors which thwarted the missionaries, but unfortunately he says nothing about what these factors were. One possibility is that there was an official embargo at Thessalonica on the missionaries returning (Ac. 17:9), but this does not explain how it became possible for Timothy rather than Paul himself to return in due course. It is more likely that the cause or causes must be sought in the circumstances of the missionaries. If 2 C. 12:7 refers to some physical weakness or illness which Paul attributed to the influence of Satan, this would strengthen the case that bouts of illness are in mind here. Although this possibility is generally denied, Paul's statements in 3:1f. may help to establish it; originally, it would seem, the intention was that Paul himself should be one of the party to revisit Thessalonica, and it was only when it became obvious that he himself could not go that he acquiesced in being left on his own while Timothy made the trip. However, it must be confessed that we do not know the precise circumstances (or combination of circumstances) to which Paul is alluding; no doubt the Thessalonians were told orally by Timothy.

19. The opening **For** links the verse not with the immediately preceding clause at the end of v. 18 but with the main theme in vv. 17–18, the longing of Paul and his companions to revisit their Thessalonica. This longing was due to the fact that they regarded the Thessalonian church as the source of their hope and happiness at the future coming of Jesus. To say that the church was their **hope** means that it was the ground of their hope and the basis of their confidence. Paul and his fellow-missionaries were conscious of a task laid upon them by the risen Jesus, namely, to preach about him to the Gentiles and so to create communities of believers in him (Gal. 1:16). Such newly-founded churches were the evidence of the reality of Paul's apostolic calling (1 C. 9:1f.), and they would also be the evidence that he had fulfilled his commission when he stood before Jesus at his coming to give an account of his stewardship. It was Paul's fear that his work might prove to be in vain (3:5) in that he had nothing to show for his labours, and this possibility could arise if the churches which he founded came to nothing. Thus it mattered greatly to Paul that he should have done a work of church-planting which would stand the test of time, and he therefore claimed that, if the Thessalonian church remained loyal to Jesus, this would give him confidence at the day of judgment. The confidence is both present and future, but Paul is thinking primarily of the feelings with which he will come before Jesus at the judgment.

The Thessalonians would also, along with other churches, be the source of **joy** at that time. Best, p. 128, takes this to mean that Paul will derive joy from thinking of the Thessalonian Christians and what they mean to him (as a mother may say of a child, 'He is my joy'), but the thought is rather that the existence of the church constitutes the basis on which Paul knows that he can be joyful in the presence of Jesus rather than sad because he has not achieved any lasting missionary work.

The third element in Paul's expectation is that the church will be a **crown of boasting**. This Hebraism (Prov. 16:31) means 'a crown to boast of', or rather 'a crown to exult in'; from what Paul says elsewhere about the impossibility of men boasting of their own achievements before God (Rom. 3:27; 1 C. 1:29) it may be taken for granted that Paul is not looking forward here to any sort of proud display of his apostolic achievements before the Lord Jesus, but is rather thinking of the joyful exultation which he will be able to feel when the work which God has done through him (1 C. 15:10) is recognised. The **crown** in question is the laurel wreath which was given to a victor in a Greek atheltic contest, and Paul applies the

metaphor to the Thessalonian church itself which will be the sign
that he has successfully accomplished his apostolic labours. The
same thought recurs in Phil. 4:1 in an eschatological context (Phil.
3:20f.).

That Paul is also thinking in terms of the future here is evident
from his reference to the **coming** of Jesus. This is the earliest use
in the *NT* of the Gk. word *parousia*, which means 'presence' (2 C.
10:10) or 'arrival'. The latter sense is the one usually adopted here
in view of Paul's usage when he is talking about Jesus (4:15; 1 C.
15:23). However, the concept of 'arrival' can pass over easily into
that of the 'presence' which is consequent upon a person's arrival,
and here the thought may well be of the abiding presence of Jesus
which follows on from his coming. The word was used of visits by
Hellenistic rulers to cities under their rule, where they were cere-
monially welcomed, and of the coming of gods to help those in
need. Such associations would naturally be present for Gentile readers, but the roots of the idea, as used by Paul, lie in the *OT* and
Judaism. The word is used by Matthew as a synonym for the Day
when the Son of man will appear (Mt. 24:27, 37, 39; par. Lk.
17:24, 26, 30), and this latter expression is connected with the *OT*
idea of the Day of the Lord, which was the Day when he would
come in judgment upon evil and for the salvation of his people (Isa.
13:6; Ezek. 30:3; Jl 3:14; Am. 5:18). Paul himself refers to the Day
of the Lord in 5:2 (cf. 2 Th. 2:1f.) in a context which shows that
this Day is associated with the coming of Jesus; indeed the 'Lord'
in this context is probably Jesus himself. The belief that Jesus would
return rests upon passages in the Gospels which refer to the future
manifestation or coming of the Son of man (Mk 8:38; 13:26; 14:62;
Lk. 12:40; par. Mt. 24:44; Lk. 17:30; 18:8) which were understood
as references to a return of Jesus himself (Ac. 3:20). Scholarly
opinion is sharply divided as to whether the Son of man sayings in
question are creations by the church or authentic utterances of
Jesus, and, if the latter, whether or not he was referring in a cryptic
way to himself. While the view that Jesus was speaking about
himself is not without its difficulties, it remains the most probable
explanation of the nucleus of the sayings (I. H. Marshall, *The Origins
of New Testament Christology*, Downers Grove/Leicester, 1976, ch.
4).

The expectation of the return of Jesus was part of Paul's missionary preaching (1:10), and it occupies a significant position in this
epistle not only as an essential structural element in Pauline theology
but also because of the problems which it raised in the minds of the
Thessalonian Christians. Paul could have referred here to the judgment seat of God (Rom. 2:5; 14:10–12) or of Christ (2 C. 5:10), but

it was natural for him to refer to the presence of the **Lord Jesus** (cf. 1 C. 4:4f.) since the coming of Jesus initiates the judgment, and since he is thinking here of the joy that will attend his coming rather than the possibility of condemnation. (On the parousia see further, Best, pp. 349–54; A. L. Moore, *The Parousia in the New Testament*, Leiden, 1966; and C. Brown's survey-article, 'The Parousia and Eschatology in the NT', *NIDNTT* II, pp. 901–35.)

20. The rhetorical question **Is it not you?** which comes at the end of v. 19 in *RSV* is actually interpolated earlier in the sentence in the Greek text, so that there is less appearance of repetition and redundancy in the words of v. 20 which simply underline what Paul has already said. Paul is in effect giving a firm '*Yes*' to his question and confirming the answer by assuring the Thessalonians that they are already his **glory and joy** (and hence will also be at the parousia). It is the Thessalonian church which is the cause of any glory or praise that can accrue to the missionaries, and also of the joy that they can feel in regard to their work. Once again, as Best, p. 129, rightly emphasises, there is no thought of self-glorification or pride here, still less of any selfish seeking after reward. The reward of the missionaries is simply the work that they have been able, by God's grace, to do and the feelings of joy and satisfaction which it produces. Such feelings are not wrong. It is a false kind of altruism which insists that the person who helps somebody else should feel no satisfaction or joy at the thought of the other person's happiness but simply act out of a disinterested sense of duty. Some people find it hard to believe that God can want Christians to be happy, and thereby completely misunderstand his nature and his purpose.

3:1. Because of the affection and concern which the missionaries felt for the Thessalonian church there came a point when they could bear the situation no longer and so resolved to do something about it. The opening **Therefore** (which marks the transition to the second sub-section, 3:1–5) draws the consequence from the fact expressed in the closing verses of ch. 2, the increasing feeling of frustration at being unable to revisit Thessalonica and the worry that all might not be well with the church. The verb translated **bear** (3:5; 1 C. 9:12; 13:7) originally meant to cover, hence to ward off or protect, and from this there developed the sense of supporting or bearing something in the sense of enduring or putting up with it (W. Kasch, *TDNT* VII, pp. 585–7). A difficulty is caused by Paul's use of the plural form **we** here. In. v. 5 he repeats the substance of the verse in the first person singular form, and this fact, together with the use of the adjective **alone** here, would suggest at first sight that this is an editorial plural which really refers to Paul alone. It can hardly refer to all three missionaries, since it is the

sending of Timothy (v. 2) which causes the writer(s) of v. 1 to be
alone. The reference could then be to Paul and Silas, but it is hard
to see why they should feel themselves to be alone if Timothy were
to leave them. It is possible that Silvanus was not present at the
time (Masson, p. 39, refers to Calvin's view that he had stayed in
Beroea), or that he too went away at the same time as Timothy.
This would certainly seem to follow from the information in Acts
where both Timothy and Silas rejoin Paul in Corinth (Ac. 18:5).
The best solution may be to assume that the thought is expressed
loosely and that Paul means 'We (all three of us, or Timothy and
myself) resolved that I should be left at Athens alone and that
Timothy should be sent to you.' From the account in Ac. 17 we
may draw the conclusion that Paul's work in Athens was not particularly successful; only a handful of people responded to his message (Ac. 17:34), and Paul may have felt a certain loneliness and
depression as a result. But Paul's main thought here in this letter
is of the concern which he felt for his friends in Thessalonica.

2. As the leader of the missionary group Paul had the authority
to send Timothy to Thessalonica, but the point of the verb is
probably to emphasise the way in which Timothy was **sent** as his
representative. If Paul himself could not come (2:18), the next best
thing was to send a person who could fully represent him and take
his place. Paul emphasises the status of **Timothy**, possibly because
he had played only a minor role in the mission (Masson, p. 40). He
is a **brother**, a word which Paul often uses of his colleagues in
missionary work and which underlines the closeness of the relationship between them. The view that **brother** was a technical term for
such church leaders (E. E. Ellis, *Prophecy and Hermeneutic*, Grand
Rapids/Tübingen, 1978, pp. 13–22) goes beyond the evidence,
which shows merely that Paul used a word which normally applies
to fellow-Christians to refer to his colleagues in the work. Timothy
is also **God's servant**, according to *RSV*, which here follows strong
external evidence. Other translations have 'God's fellow-worker'
(*NEB*). This reading has limited textual support, but it is indirectly
attested by various MSS which conflate the two readings in one way
or another, and also by B which simply has 'fellow-worker'. It is
probable that the idea of a person being *God's* fellow-worker proved
difficult to scribes and they substituted the easier expression. On
the other hand, it is hard to see why the *RSV* text, if original, gave
rise to changes. Further, the thought is Pauline, since he writes of
himself and Apollos as 'God's fellow-workers' in 1 C. 3:9. The
textual problem suggests that scribes understood the phrase to mean
a fellow-worker with God (so Henneken, pp. 23f.), but various
scholars argue that the sense is that Timothy is Paul's fellow-worker

in the same work to which God has called him (W.-H. Ollrog, *Paulus und seine Mitarbeiter*, Neukirchen, 1979, pp. 68–71). The former sense is Pauline (2 C. 6:1; cf. Mk 16:20; 3 Jn 8; Heb. 2:4) and should be adopted here. The sphere of Timothy's work is **the gospel of Christ**. The genitive phrase is loosely added and should not be resolved to mean that Christ is *either* the object of the gospel message *or* its source and originator, since both can be implied. The context indicates that the work of the gospel is more than evangelism; it includes the task of sustaining faith in God through Jesus. Timothy's task is to **establish** in the faith and to **exhort**. This combination is found in 2 Th. 2:17. The former verb means to strengthen and expresses a characteristic aspect of pastoral care in the *NT* churches (Lk. 22:32; Ac. 18:23; Rom. 1:11; Jas 5:8; 1 Pet. 5:10), which depends ultimately on the working of God (Rom. 16:25; 1 Pet. 5:10; 1 Th. 3:13). The latter verb (2:11 note) is difficult to translate; 'exhort' is archaic. The sense is to encourage by means of Christian teaching. The phrase **in your faith** goes with both verbs and expresses the thought of continuing trust and loyalty, the state of being a believer.

3. If the positive purpose of Timothy's visit indicated in the previous verse is achieved, a second, negative result will also be secured, namely, **that no one** will **be moved by these afflictions**. The Gk. verb used here (*sainomai*) is a rare one and its interpretation caused difficulty to earlier commentators. It was used from the time of Homer to refer to the wagging of a dog's tail, and hence arose the metaphorical sense 'to fawn, flatter, cajole'. In the present context this would refer to Christians being talked out of their faith, perhaps by the Jews. However, this sense does not fit easily into the context of affliction. Another possibility is that the verb means 'to disturb, agitate', and this is how it was interpreted in the early church. The difficulty with this view (stressed by Lightfoot, p. 42) was the lack of evidence for it in Greek literature. However, the ambiguous earlier-known evidence was strengthened by a papyrus discovery in 1941 where the verb has the required meaning (see. H. Chadwick, 'I Th. 3:3: σαίνεσθαι', *JTS* 1, 1950, pp. 156–8; F. Lang, *TDNT* VII, pp. 54–6, gives an excellent summary of the position).

The thought, then, is of being disturbed by persecution (cf. 2 Th. 2:2). But who is being persecuted? Von Dobschütz, pp. 134f., argues that **these afflictions** must be those of Paul himself, those of which he has just been writing (so, many early commentators). Paul fears that the Thessalonians will be tempted to give up their faith if they know that he is being persecuted. But this is unlikely, since the Thessalonians and Paul had already suffered in Thessalonica. It is more probable that Paul is thinking of the continuation of troubles, both theirs and his, but with the emphasis on the former.

The encouragement which he gives them in their afflictions so as to prevent them being moved by them is the reminder that persecution is the **lot** of Christians; literally, they were appointed for this fate (cf. Phil. 1:16). If a person knows that something unpleasant is part of his destiny, something that is inevitable, then he will brace himself to meet it and will not think that it is a sign that he is on the wrong track or be taken by surprise by it. The belief that the Christian way inevitably involves suffering and persecution was common *NT* teaching, by both Jesus (Mt. 5:11f., 44; 10:17–23; 23:34; 24:9f.) and the apostles (Ac. 9:16; 14:22; 1 Pet. 1:6; 3:13–17; Rev. 2:10). It was seen as part of the increasing evil in the world which would precede the parousia and the winding up of history. Christians could regard suffering with Christ as the essential preliminary to sharing in his heavenly reign (Rom. 8:17), and indeed the fact of suffering as a Christian was some guarantee that one was truly a member of God's people and destined for heavenly glory (Rom. 8:36–39; 2 Tim. 2:11–13). Understood in this way, tribulation should not put faith in danger, but rather strengthen it (Rom. 8:35).

4. So fundamental was this thought for Paul that he had already spoken of it during his mission in Thessalonica, **when we were with you** (2 Th. 3:10; for repetition in Paul's letters of facts taught orally, cf. 1 C. 11:23; 15:1). The tense of the verb (imperfect) indicates that Paul had repeated the lesson several times, which would not be surprising in view of the constant attacks made during his visit. The fact that Paul said 'we are going to suffer affliction' indicates that he spoke prophetically of what was certain to happen and could indeed be regarded as part of God's plan for his people. Paul may have said this before persecution actually happened, and then made it clear after any given outburst of it that more could be expected. His words were confirmed by what happened, as the readers themselves could testify.

5. In the preceding verses Paul has wandered away from his main intention, which was to describe the events leading up to Timothy's visit to Thessalonica and so to move on to the good news which he brought on his return. He found himself carried away briefly by his comments on the certainty of persecution for Christians. Now he returns to the original train of thought in a verse which recapitulates vv. 1f. but at the same time takes into account the apparent digression, and moves on to a new thought which prepares for the next verse. **For this reason** repeats the 'therefore' of v. 1. There the thought was of Paul's separation from the Thessalonians which he found it increasingly hard to bear, but here the thought is strengthened by the reference to the sufferings and trial of faith which the Thessalonians were undergoing in Paul's absence. The later part of the verse will tie in closely with this thought. Paul switches from 'we' to **I**, since he is thinking particularly of his own reaction to the situation, and no doubt since he himself was the one who remained alone in Athens while Timothy and Silvanus were away. The words **could bear it no longer** again repeat the content of v. 1, but in the light of what follows it seems that the thought is not just of the separation from the Thessalonians but also of the lack of news about their spiritual welfare. The verb **sent** has no object expressed, but it is obvious that Timothy is in mind.

But now a new purpose for the visit is mentioned. Timothy's coming was not only to strengthen the Thessalonians but also to provide Paul with news about them on his return. He wanted to **know** their **faith**, that is, the reality of their Christian existence. For Paul **faith** was the fundamental Christian activity and characteristic, out of which grew everything else. He wanted, therefore, to be sure that their faith in God was still real and active. He knew that there was a possibility of defection. His **fear** (the word is not present in the Greek, but is most naturally supplied) was that **the tempter had tempted** them and made the **labour** of the missionaries come to nothing. There is a significant difference between the moods of **tempted** (indicative) and **would be in vain** (subjunctive). Paul's fear that the tempter had been active is concerned with what could have already happened by the time of writing, while his fear of futile missionary work refers to the possible future result of the tempter's activity. Satan is here characterised as the **tempter** (1 C. 7:5; for the noun, cf. Mt. 4:3). The Greek verb can mean simply to test or prove, but here the thought is clearly of encouraging somebody to do what is evil and contrary to the will of God. The 'testing' is to see whether the person will do what is wrong. What is intended by Satan as 'testing' in the sense of enticing to do what is sinful can also be seen as part of God's purpose in which he allows people to be tested in order to prove the reality and staying-power of their faith and obedience. The effect of temptation would be that the Thessalonians would give up their faith, so that the work of the missionaries would turn out to have been **in vain** (Gal. 2:2; Phil. 2:16) and they would have no 'crown' to wear (1 Th. 2:19). But the verb **tempted** indicates merely an attempt, not necessarily successful. Temptation can be resisted! Hence Paul speaks of his fear that the missionaries' labour might be in vain as merely a possibility and not yet a reality. Although the danger was a real one, his fears proved to be ungrounded. The Christian pastor needs to have a real concern for his flock lest they should fall away from the faith, even though he also trusts firmly in the gracious power of God to keep them faithful to himself.

6. The third sub-section (3:6–10) describes the return of Timothy after his visit to Thessalonica. His good news brought comfort to Paul, and he expresses his feelings in an outburst of joy. The opening **But now** indicates that Paul's joy and relief were so great that he lost no time in writing this letter to express his feelings and to make up for the fact that he himself still could not visit them. When Timothy returned (with Silas: cf. Ac. 18:5), he **brought good news** to Paul. This verb is used everywhere else in the *NT* with the technical sense of proclaiming the gospel, the good news about Jesus. It could have simply the non-technical sense 'to announce' good news here, but Masson, p. 41, raises the possibility that information about successful missionary work could be part of the Christian gospel in the broadest sense, so that Timothy's news was a real proclamation of the good news to Paul himself. This is an attractive suggestion which should be accepted (see also J. Jervell, as in 1:8 note; Best, pp. 139f.). The preaching of the gospel includes the news that Jesus Christ is proved to be a mighty Saviour in the experience of those who respond to the Christian message; knowledge of this can lead non-believers to faith and believers to thanksgiving and deeper faith.

Timothy's good news contained two elements. First, he spoke of the **faith and love** of the Thessalonian Christians. These two qualities are frequently linked by Paul, whether as a pair (Eph. 1:15; Phm. 5) or as part of a fuller listing of Christian qualities (1 Th. 1:3; 5:8; 2 C. 8:7). They might easily be regarded as conventional and formal, but there is no doubt that for Paul they were living and vital and summed up the essence of Christianity. Both qualities are essential. For Paul **faith** was the attitude which brought people within the sphere of God's saving activity in Jesus, and **love** was the new relationship to God and other people which springs from it. Paul's formula 'faith working through love' (Gal. 5 : 6) expresses the intimate relationship between the two qualities. The lack of mention of hope (contrast 1 : 3; 5 : 8) has no significance; despite the fact that it forms part of an early Christian triad, it is not on the same plane as faith and love, but can be regarded as one aspect of faith. The presence, then, of faith and love proved to Paul that his doubts about the Thessalonians were groundless.

But the second part of Timothy's report was also calculated to increase his confidence. He **reported that you always remember us kindly and long to see us**. The Christian message is closely associated with the missionary, so that a joyful acceptance of the gospel will be associated with a warm and positive relationship to the missionary. This relationship took the form of a continually present memory of Paul. *RSV* **kindly** translates the Greek adjective 'good' which qualifies 'memory' (literally the Greek is 'always have a good memory of us'). The thought, as contrasted with a bad recollection of somebody, is of approval and hence of affectionate feeling towards the person remembered. This note of affection is more clearly expressed in the comment that the Thessalonians were longing to see Paul again, a feeling which, he assured them, was mutual. In view of their desire to have the missionary revisit them, there could be no question of their having turned away from his message. Here, rather, we have the evidence which enabled Paul to write about them in such confident tones in the opening verses of the letter. Here was proof that God had chosen them (1 Th. 1:4).

7. After the lengthy description of Timothy's return and news in v. 6, Paul sums up the first part of his sentence with **for this reason**. What began as a temporal clause is thus turned into a causal one, giving the reason for Paul's being **comforted**, or better, 'encouraged' (cf. 3:2). The verb is qualified by three further prepositional phrases. **about you** indicates that Paul was encouraged so far as concerned his fears about the Thessalonians and their spiritual state. The phrase, however, could also mean 'because of you' (Frame, p. 133; Best, p. 141), giving the thought that Paul's general distress in his present situation of affliction caused by other factors was relieved by the fact of the Thessalonians (who were standing firm in the faith). This second interpretation seems to be preferable, but the distinction is a subtle one. **in all our distress and affliction** describes the continuing difficulties which Paul was facing; the news from Thessalonica gave him better heart to stand up to them. **distress** is virtually synonymous with **affliction**, and both words appear to indicate outward calamities (cf. 2 C. 6:4; the combination is found in the LXX, PS. 24:17 LXX; 118:143 LXX). **through your faith** sums up the news which Paul had about the Thessalonians and forms a transition to the thought expressed in the next verse. **faith** is singled out for mention because it is the steadfastness of the Thessalonians' faith which is primarily in Paul's mind as the cause of thanksgiving.

8. Paul proceeds to explain why it is that the news about the Thessalonians has been such a source of encouragement to him. **we live**, he writes, **if you stand fast in the Lord**. The **now** should be taken temporally to indicate the contrast with the period before Paul heard the good news. Before this news came he was not experiencing 'life' in the proper way. Paul was aware of the paradoxical juxtaposition in Christian experience of what he calls dying and living.

Throughout his ministry he was conscious of a daily process of 'dying' (Rom. 8:36; 1 C. 15:31; 2 C. 4:10–12) which was related to his missionary work as well as to his personal Christian existence. The Christian life involves the gradual dying of the old, physical and sinful nature of the believer. The physical body wastes away by natural decay, but it is weakened by temptation and persecution and other afflictions. The believer also needs to put his old nature to death, since it is the source of sinful desires.

Among the factors which contributed to this process were Paul's missionary labours, both physical and also spiritual. He speaks of the 'daily pressure upon me of my anxiety for all the churches' (2 C. 11:28). He felt that his life was so bound up with that of his converts that when they showed signs of spiritual weakness he himself felt involved and weakened: 'Who is weak, and I am not weak? Who is made to fall, and I am not indignant?' (2 C. 11:29). But at the same time the presence of the Spirit in Paul meant that a new life was being communicated to him. If he 'always carried in the body the death of Jesus', this was 'so that the life of Jesus may also be manifested in our bodies' (2 C. 4:10). If 'our outer nature is wasting away, our inner nature is being renewed every day' (2 C. 4:16). And among the means by which this spiritual life was nurtured there was the growth in life and spiritual strength of Paul's converts. If their weakness made him weak, so too their strength made him strong (2 C. 7:3), and he was invigorated by their spiritual growth (Rom. 15:32; 1 C. 16:18; 2 C. 7:13; Phm. 7, 20). Thus we can see how Paul felt that his spiritual life was experiencing renewal despite the continuing afflictions which surrounded him.

For Paul, then, it was of vital importance that his friends should **stand fast**. The use of a conditional clause (the somewhat irregular use of *ean* with the indicative) does not call in question the reality of the news about the Thessalonians but rather emphasises its factuality and at the same time contains as implicit admonition to them to continue to stand fast and not be moved by their afflictions (3:3). The appeal to stand fast is common in Pauline exhortations (2 Th. 2:15; 1 C. 16:13; Phil. 1:27). The phrase **in the Lord** (cf. 1:1) is rightly explained by von Dobschütz, p. 143, as referring not simply to holding fast to fellowship with the Lord and confession of him, but more broadly to standing fast in every respect which is related to the Lord. They are to continue faithfully in every aspect of their life which comes under the jurisdiction of Jesus as their Lord. They stand fast 'because of what the Lord has done for them (in his death, etc) and because their response to this has brought them into a relationship with him' (Best, p. 143).

9. The joy which Paul felt as a result of his encouragement by the good news from Thessalonica leads him to a rhetorical expression of the inadequacy of the thanksgiving which he feels to God. The opening **For** is an over-literal translation of a Greek conjunction which can mean no more than a logical 'then' when used with a question (cf. Ac. 19:35). Although Paul asks rhetorically how he can thank God sufficiently for what has happened, the 'surface grammar' of the sentence conceals a real expression of **thanksgiving** to God. Paul means 'I am tremendously grateful to God – and yet I realise that am incapable of giving him the gratitude which he deserves.' The verb **render** conveys the idea of giving somebody what is due to him (Rom. 12:19; 2 Th. 1:6). Here the thought is implicit that the good Christian standing of the Thessalonians which has encouraged Paul is due not to themselves but to the gracious action of God.

We see here something of the paradox of Christian faith and growth which is both due to the working of God by his Spirit and also due to the activity of the believer. Christian growth is not produced 'automatically' by divine grace, so that the believer needs to make no effort, but rather the believer must be encouraged to show faith and love. Hence Paul can both pray to God for his converts and thank him for their spiritual progress and also urge them to grow in their faith and express his delight when they respond to his urging (or rebuke them when they fail to do so). Here, then, the grace of God leads to thanksgiving, an activity which results in the increase of God's glory as more and more people recognise his goodness (cf. 2 C. 1:11; 4:15; 9:11f.).

If **for you** expresses the ultimate circumstance for which Paul gives thanks, the phrase **for all the joy which we feel** indicates the immediate emotion produced by the news about the readers which moved Paul to give thanks. Joy and thanksgiving are not necessarily identical. A child may be filled with happiness by a birthday present but needs reminding to say thank-you to the donor. Paul's new situation of joyfulness stands in contrast to the situation of distress and affliction in v. 7, and demonstrates the way in which the Christian can be filled with a superlative joy despite circumstances that could reduce him to misery. The **all** brings out this superlative quality of Paul's intense joy, a joy which, as he reminds his readers, is due to them (cf. Phil. 2:2). Finally, Paul speaks of expressing his joy **before our God**. This is a phrase drawn from the *OT* (Dt. 12:12, 18; Lev. 23:40; Isa. 9:3) where it indicates a joy which is conscious of the divine origin of the good things of life and expresses itself in thanks to God instead of becoming selfish and secular.

When Paul speaks of **our** God, this is a further way of acknowledging the way in which God acts for the good of his people.

10. From the thought of the joy which finds expression in his prayer of thanksgiving to God Paul moves on quite naturally to the petitions which also form part of his prayer and further express the depth of feeling which he has for his friends. It is natural for a prayer of thanksgiving to lead to further petitions to the God who has already shown that he cares for his people and answers their prayers. Paul thus adds loosely to his previous sentence the participle **praying** (Rom. 1:10) which conveys the thought of petition to God (Mt. 9:38; Lk. 21:36; 22:32). The two additions **earnestly** and **night and day** express the intensity of Paul's prayer. The latter (2:9) indicates that the Thessalonians were always in Paul's thoughts. His prayers for them even made inroads into the time he might have spent in sleep, prayer by **night** being a sign of deep concern (Ps. 42:8; 63:6; 77:2; 2 Mac. 13:10; IQS 6:6–8). The former phrase is a very strong adverb, 'hyper-exceedingly' (5:13; Eph. 3:20), of a type that is characteristic of Paul; it implies that Paul's concern goes beyond all due measure.

The content of Paul's prayer (expressed in the form of a purpose-clause in Greek, but the purpose and content of a prayer are usually the same) is twofold. First of all, he expresses his longing to God to **see** his friends again **face to face** (2:17). Despite sending Timothy and receiving good news from him Paul's heart still aches to actually be with the Thessalonians, to rejoice with them and to encourage them. Paul still hopes that the Satanic hindrances to revisiting Thessalonica will be removed and falls back on the only weapon which can deal with them, namely, prayer.

Second, Paul indicates that the ultimate aim of his visit, the thing that he is really concerned about, is to **supply what is lacking in their faith**. The phrase **what is lacking** means 'shortcomings', both physical (Lk. 21:4; 2 C. 8:13f.) and spiritual (Phil. 2:30), and the verb signifies the completion of something that is imperfect or requires repair (it is used of repairing broken nets, Mk 1:19; cf. 2 C. 13:11; Gal. 6:1; 1 Pet. 5:10). This part of Paul's prayer shows that for all his exuberant joy in the spiritual stability of the Thessalonian Christians he was still sufficient of a realist to recognise that their present spiritual resources could be improved and perfected. The language does not suggest any blame or reproach cast upon them, but rather that the Thessalonians should be encouraged to make further progress. **faith** must thus be taken in a broad sense to refer to the whole of their Christian experience.

Paul does not make it clear whether the need of the Thessalonians arose from their own slowness to make spiritual growth or from the

inadequacy of the teaching which he had given to them before his
visit was cut short. Probably both factors are in view, since Paul
recognised that Christian faith was something that grew and developed and did not come to full fruition in a moment (Phil. 1:9; Col.
1:10; 2 Th. 1:3). But the accent may well lie on the latter thought
of the need of the Thessalonians for further teaching. In that case
the present phrase marks the beginning of the transition to the
second part of the letter in which Paul will proceed to give the
Thessalonians some of the instruction which he would have preferred to give them by word of mouth. The prayer thus serves as a
reminder to the Thessalonians of their need for further spiritual
growth and prepares them for the remaining part of the letter.

11. The fourth sub-section (3:11–13) closes the first part of the
letter with a prayer. From telling his readers about his prayers to
God for them (1:3; 3:10) Paul turns to express his thoughts in an
actual prayer. Instead, however, of addressing God in the second
person ('O God,. . .'), Paul expresses his prayer in the form of a
wish put in the third person and using the Greek optative mood (a
mood of the verb expressing a wish; it was falling into disuse by
NT times). For this type of prayer, see 5:23; 2 Th. 2:1f.; 3:5, 16;
Rom. 15:5f., 13; 2 Tim. 1:16–18; Heb. 13:20f. The form has been
studied by R. Jewett ('The Form and Function of the Homiletic
Benediction', *Anglican Theological Review* 51, 1969, pp. 18–34),
who thinks that such prayers were used in early Christian preaching,
perhaps as a prayer at the end of a sermon: 'God was seen to be
imparting himself and his blessings as the word was set forth and
related to the situation of the believers' (ibid., p. 34). For a more
detailed study of such passages, see G. P. Wiles, *Paul's Intercessory
Prayers*, Cambridge, 1974, who traces a broad background in the
OT and Judaism (Num. 6:24–26; Ps. 20:1–5; 2 Mac. 1:2–6).

The present prayer takes up the themes mentioned in v. 10,
Paul's desire to visit Thessalonica (v. 11) and the Thessalonians'
need of spiritual growth (vv. 12f.), here defined more closely in
terms of love and holiness and placed in the context of readiness to
meet the Lord at the parousia. These same themes will recur in the
second main part of the letter (holiness: 4:1–8; love: 4:9–12; the
parousia: 4:13 – 5:11).

In Greek Paul's wish begins with the word **himself** (also found in
his other prayers composed in this form). This does not express any
contrast with what precedes, but rather underlines the earnestness
of the petition to God personally to hear and respond powerfully to
prayer. The description of God as **our God and Father** is a familiar
one in the *NT* (1:3; 3:13). The use of **and** in the phrase appears to
be Jewish but is sparsely attested (3 Mac. 5:7; Sir. 23:1, 4; G.

Schrenk, *TDNT* v, p. 1007 n. 371). What is distinctive here is the addition **and our Lord Jesus.** Whether or not the opening 'himself' is meant to cover both God and Jesus, and whether or not the singular form of the verb 'may direct' is deliberately used with a plural subject are matters of debate. It is arguable that the singular verb is used in agreement with the nearer subject when two subjects are coupled by 'and' (Mt. 5:18; 6:19; Jn 12:22). However, the combination of the use of 'himself' and the singular verb and the repetition of essentially the same phrase in reverse order in 2 Th. 2:16 strongly suggest that Paul closely couples God and Jesus together as the common subject of the verb.

Whatever our verdict on these syntactical points, the close collocation of God and Jesus in the prayer indicates that for Paul they are thought of as working together in unity, and this has undoubted implications for the supreme position which Paul ascribes to the Son of God (1:10) alongside the Father. To say that 'this does not imply that Paul held a Trinitarian or Binitarian theology' (Best, p. 147) is as much an overstatement as is the claim of Morris, p. 111, that 'Full divinity is ascribed to him'. It would be more exact to say that Paul *assumes* the divinity of Jesus—to call him 'Son of God' in the way in which Paul uses the phrase cannot mean anything else.

It is, then, to the Father and Jesus that Paul directs his prayer that they will **direct** his **way** to Thessalonica. The thought may be of the removing of Satanic obstacles or (less probably) of divine guidance to go to Thessalonica in the course of his journeyings. That the prayer was eventually answered may be deduced from Ac. 20:1.

12. Even if his prayer for himself should not be fulfilled as he hopes, Paul nevertheless longs and prays for the spiritual growth of his readers, and the word **you** (the first word in the verse in Greek) emphasises this contrast between himself and them. Having already mentioned the need for growth in faith in v. 10, he goes on to speak of the need for further growth in **love** in this verse. The giver of the gift is named as **the Lord,** a title which in its context here ('the Lord Jesus', 3:11, 13) and in view of Paul's normal usage must refer to Jesus and not to the Father (cf. 2 Th. 3:5, 16; Ac. 7:59f.; 1 C. 16:22; 2 C. 12:8; 2 Tim. 1:16, 18). Since the commandment to love one another is particularly linked with the teaching of Jesus (Jn 13:34), it is appropriate that he should be asked to **make you increase and abound in love**; but this may be over-subtle. The two verbs used are synonymous and their combination simply strengthens the idea: 'make you greatly abound' is the thought. Such love is in the first instance towards one's fellow-believers. The

Thessalonians were already showing it (4:9f.), but Paul wishes that
it may increase (Phil. 1:9) and its circle be broadened to include **all**
people (cf. 5:15). For Paul Christian love is not confined to the
members of the church, although within this limited circle one may
begin to know the full meaning of Christian love for the first time,
but must spread outwards to embrace people of all kinds, even
including one's enemies (Gal. 6:10; Mt. 5:43–48; Lk. 6:32–36;
10:25–37). Finally, Paul refers to his own example, an indication
that the verse is not only a prayer to the Lord but at the same time
an exhortation to the readers to let the Lord fulfil his purpose in
their lives. That Paul and his fellow-missionaries could present
themselves as examples of abundant love may seem embarrassingly
bold, but it is not uncommon in his letters (cf. 1:6; 2 Th. 3:7–9;
Ac. 20:35; 1 C. 4:16; 11:1; Phil. 3:17; 4:9).

13. The purpose or ultimate goal of Paul's prayer is that his
converts may be seen as holy at the parousia. The connection of
thought makes it clear that this is achieved through growth in love.
The verse may be regarded as broadly dealing with Christian hope,
thus completing the triad of faith, love and hope which is at the
back of Paul's mind here. The verse offers not so much a further
petition by Paul as rather the aim or purpose which he sees as being
fulfilled through the growth of the Thessalonians in love. The effect
of growth in love is to **establish the hearts** of the Thessalonians.
The verb is that already used in 3:2, and the association with the
heart, i.e. the inner, spiritual being, reflects *OT* phraseology (Jg.
19:5, 8; Ps. 104:15; 112:8; cf. Sir. 6:37; 22:16). The suggestion is
of the establishing of a firm and steady Christian character. As the
Christian grows in faith and love, so these become increasingly the
normal characteristics which he shows. The result of such a settled
character is that when it is tested the person is found to be **unblam-
able** (2:10); there is nothing to condemn him. Paul particularly
associates this quality with the final judgment (5:23; 1 C. 1:8). But
since he believed that this could happen at any time, his prayer was
that his converts would be blameless here and now (cf. 2:10), ready
at any time to face their judge.

Associated with blamelessness is the concept of **holiness** (Rom.
1:4; 2 C. 7:1), one of Paul's favourite themes in the Thessalonian
correspondence (2:10; 4:3, 7; 5:23; 2 Th. 2:13). Holiness is a quality
of God himself. It can signify his majesty and unapproachableness,
that which makes him different from man, but at its heart it refers
to his moral righteousness and purity as opposed to anything which
is unclean and immoral. The word is then used to refer to a quality
of objects and persons which are set aside from ordinary use for the
service of God. Religious objects take on this same characteristic of

separateness from ordinary things, but when the concept is used of holy people, the thought is much more that those who are separated to serve God must show the same righteousness and purity which characterise him. It is this idea of moral perfection which is expressed here. This can be understood in a negative manner of freedom from sin—which is undoubtedly a dominant element in the concept—but it would be wrong not to see also the thought of positive virtue. In the present context this is clear from the close connection between love and holiness (on the concept, see H. Seebass and C. Brown, *NIDNTT* II, pp. 223–38; A. S. Wood, *ZPEB* III, pp. 173–83; O. E. Evans, *Saints in Christ Jesus*, Swansea, 1975).

The qualities required here are to be demonstrated **before our God and Father**, a phrase which, as the following words show, refers not so much to the fact that the hearts of men always lie open to the Lord (2:4), but much rather to the activity of God as the judge (Rom. 2:5–8; 14:10). The judge is described as **our Father**, not to suggest that the judgment will be a partial one, showing favour to God's children, but rather to stress that as God's children believers are under obligation to obey him and do his will. The judgment takes place **at the coming of our Lord Jesus**, which is the occasion both for reward and for condemnation (2:19; 2 C. 5:10).

Jesus is thus associated with the Father in the act of final judgment (Jn 5:27; Ac. 10:42; 17:31; 2 C. 5:10). The unity of the Father and Son in judgment is important. It means that we do not have to face any other God than the One who has revealed himself in Jesus. Equally it underlines the importance of Jesus Christ as the One authorised by the Father to bestow life and salvation. Whiteley, p. 58, stresses that Paul has substituted 'Jesus' for 'the Lord my God' in the underlying *OT* text, Zech. 14:5.

The solemnity of the occasion is finally marked by the allusion to the coming of Jesus as taking place **with all his saints**. The *RSV* translation (lit. 'holy ones') interprets the underlying Greek term, in accordance with its universal use in the *NT*, to be a reference to believers (see especially 2 Th. 1:10; cf. Did. 16:7; Asc. Isa. 4:14; Const. Apos. 7:32). This fits in with the expectation that the dead in Christ will rise first and then along with those believers who are still alive they will meet the Lord (1 Th. 4:16f.; cf. Col. 3:4). The difficulty with this view is that this union of believers with the Lord appears to take place after his coming rather than before it; 4:16f. hardly means that he comes with *all* his saints.

Now the present phrase undoubtedly contains an echo of Zech. 14:5, which speaks of the final coming of God 'and all the holy ones with him'. Here the 'holy ones' are the angels who attend God in his heavenly dwelling (Ps. 89:5, 7; Isa. 6:2f.; Dan. 7:10) and accompany him, especially at the judgment (1 En. 1:9; cf. Jude 14); they also accompany the Son of man (Mk 8:38; 13:27; Mt. 13:41; 25:31; 2 Th. 1:7). It is true that Zech. 14:5 was taken to refer to the saints in Did. 16:7, but it is doubtful whether Paul so understood it here. Since there are no real grounds for rejecting this interpretation here (other than the uniqueness of the word-usage in the *NT*), and since there are difficulties in taking the reference to be believers, the reference to angels should be accepted (von Dobschütz, pp. 152f.; and most scholars; *contra*: Rigaux, pp. 491f., O. E. Evans, op. cit., pp. 89f.). A reference to both angels and departed saints is suggested by Lightfoot, p. 50; but nothing in the linguistic usage suggests that the latter are included with the former. Paul will deal with the problems that the Thessalonian church had about dead believers in the next chapter; it is unlikely that they are already in mind here.

EXHORTATION TO ETHICAL PROGRESS

4:1–12

In the first main part of the letter Paul has explained the circumstances which prevented him from returning to the church at Thessalonica in order that he might encourage and instruct the members to become strong and mature in the Christian faith. Now in the second main part he proceeds to write the kind of instructions that he would have liked to pass on to them orally. He deals first with ethical and practical problems of the Christian life (4:1–12). The opening section is concerned with the need for a life that is pleasing to God who has called his people to be holy; in particular Paul raises the question of sexual morality (4:1–8). A further section deals with love within the community, and linked with this is an encouragement to live in such a way that they will command the respect of outsiders and so be the less liable to persecution (4:9–12). It is noteworthy how Paul commends the church for already living the kind of life that he wishes them to practise. His injunctions are an encouragement to make further progress and do not contain any censure for their lack of Christian growth. Nevertheless, the solemn responsibility of avoiding immorality is placed before the readers, as they are reminded that God's will for them is holiness and that immorality stands under his judgment.

1. The first two verses constitute an introduction to the section, but they also stand as a preface to the whole of the remainder of the letter with its predominantly ethical and hortatory tone. The beginning of a new section in the letter is marked by the use of **brethren**

(1:4 note) and also by the inclusion of a 'therefore' (not translated in *RSV*,) which Paul uses when moving from a more doctrinal section to its ethical and practical consequences (Rom. 12:1; Eph. 4:1; Col. 3:1,5). The adverb **Finally** may seem strange when there is still a substantial portion of the letter to come, but in fact Paul has reached the last major section of the letter. However, there is evidence that the word (Gk. *loipon*) was used in Hellenistic Greek simply as a transitional particle with the meaning 'therefore', to introduce practical instruction (R. Bultmann, *Der Stil der paulinischen Predigt und die kynisch-stoische Diatribe*, Göttingen, 1910, pp. 54, 101; cf. M. E. Thrall, *Greek Particles in the New Testament*, Leiden, 1962, pp. 25-30); *NEB* 'and now' is correct.

The friendly and encouraging tone which is evident in the use of **brethren** is continued in the verbs **we beseech and exhort**. These two words are essentially synonymous. The former simply means to ask or request (5:12; 2 Th. 2:1; Phil. 4:3). The latter is the verb already used in 2:11 and 3:2. C. J. Bjerkelund, *Parakalô*, Oslo, 1967 (helpfully summarised in Best, pp. 154f.), has detected a stereotyped use of this (or a synonymous) verb with a form of address, an optional prepositional phrase, and a request or command. It is found in Hellenistic Greek documents and in the *NT* (5:14; Rom. 12:1f.; 15:30–32; 16:17; 1 C. 1:10; 4:16; 16:15f.; 2 C. 10:1f.; see also 1 Th. 5:12f.,27; 2 Th. 2:1f.; 2 C. 2:8; 6:1; Gal. 4:12; Phil; 4:2f.; Phm. 9–12), and could be used on a personal or more official 'diplomatic' level. Bjerkelund argues that Paul uses the formula in the latter way, where his authority is not in question and he can make a request in the confidence that it will be accepted. The prepositional phrase **in the Lord Jesus** conveys the thoughts both that Paul is issuing instructions which have the authority of the Lord behind them and also that the readers are people whose life is determined by their acceptance of Jesus as Lord and their entry into fellowship with him (cf. 1:1 note). It would be attractive to find that Paul uses 'in Christ' when he is thinking primarily of the new situation of salvation achieved by Jesus and 'in the Lord' when he is thinking primarily of the new situation in which Jesus demands the obedience of his people, but his usage is less tidy than this. The content of the request is expressed in a complicated manner. We may presume that Paul wanted to say something like 'we exhort you that, just as you learned how to live, so you may live'. However, Paul was so eager to express the fact that the Thessalonians were already living in the way that they should (**just as you are doing**) that by the time he reached the actual content of the command he inserted a further unnecessary 'that' (rightly dropped in translation) and altered the originally intended wording to the rather vague **you do so more and more**. Thus instead of giving a concrete instruction, Paul simply tells the readers to continue more fervently in what they are already doing. It becomes clear that ethical instruction had formed part of Paul's original ministry to the church: **as you learned from us** refers back to this occasion and not to the earlier part of the letter. The verb which is used (2:13 note) expresses the reception of an authoritative tradition, here of an ethical character (2 Th. 3:6; Rom. 6:17; 1 C. 11:2; Phil. 4:9; Col. 2:6). For the verb 'live', see 2:12 note, and for the concept of pleasing God, see 2:4. The commendatory clause **just as you are doing** is omitted by some late MSS, but is undoubtedly what Paul wrote (for a similarly overloaded construction, see Col. 1:6). The phrase **do so more and more** is literally 'abound more and more' and repeats the verb used in 3:12. Paul wants a superabundance of behaviour that wins God's approval.

2. Before proceeding to explain which commands he wants his readers to fulfil all the more zealously, Paul pauses to underline the fact that they already know what he is going to say to them. Von Dobschütz, p. 158, notes that Paul does this elsewhere with ethical instructions (4:6; 1 C. 6:9; Gal. 5:21); the same style is followed by other ancient moralists (see A. J. Malherbe's article in *ANRW*, cited in 2:1–12 note). The **you know** formula has already appeared in the letter (1:5; 2:1 note). The conjunction **For** here introduces a parallel statement to what precedes. It serves to underline the importance of abounding in goodness and stresses that the Thessalonians should have no difficulty in knowing and doing their Christian duty since they have already been clearly instructed about it. The term **instructions** (1 Tim. 1:5, 18; for the verb, see 1 Th. 4:11) has a military flavour, and refers to the specific individual ethical commands that Paul associated with the gospel. These commands were given **through the Lord Jesus**. The meaning of this phrase (cf. 4:14) is obscure and disputed. The difficulty may arise from the fact that Paul wished to avoid repeating 'in the Lord Jesus' from the previous verse and substituted what is simply a literary variation. The phrases are certainly close in meaning as may be seen from comparison of 1 C. 1:10 with 2 Th. 3:6 and Col. 3:17 with Eph. 5:20. Among the possibilities suggested are: (1). the phrase is equivalent to 'in the name of Jesus' (Moule, *Idiom-Book*, p. 57). (2). The source of the commandments is God who gave them through Jesus. (3). The inspiration to Paul to give the commandments came from Jesus. (4). Best adopts the suggestion of W. Thüsing (*Per Christum in Deum*, Münster, 1969) that the phrase has a mystical sense and means 'through the activity of Christ in whom we are'. Von Dobschütz, p. 159, points out the variety of ways in which commandments could be given by Jesus—by his words, whether as the earthly teacher or as the exalted Lord speaking through prophets, by his example, and by his spirit. However we take the phrase, the point is clearly that the commands are to be thought of as the commands of Jesus to his church and Paul is merely his agent in passing them on to his readers.

3. Paul proceeds to explain the instructions about how the Thessalonians are to please God. The opening **For** introduces explanation rather than a reason or cause. We should probably regard **this** as the predicate and **the will of God** as the subject of the sentence, with **your sanctification** being in apposition to the predicate. The inverted order of words and the omission of the article with 'will of God' in the Greek may be due to the fact that Paul is giving only one aspect of the will of God which has a much broader and fuller content, and also because Paul's emphasis is on the content ('*this*'; cf. '*what* instructions', v. 2) of God's will. Paul, in other words, can assume that his readers accept the fact that they must fulfil God's will; the problem is what this will requires of them. God's **will** is his intended purpose, sometimes what he plans to do and will himself carry out (his so-called 'primary' will), at other times what God wishes to happen but may not happen (his so-called 'secondary' will). It can thus refer to God's saving purpose for the world (1 Tim. 2:4) and to the means which he employs to bring it about (Rom. 1:10), but above all to what he wishes his people to do (5:18; Rom. 2:18; 12:2).

This rather formal and abstract term needs to be given content, and Paul explains it as **your sanctification**, thus taking up and underlining the ethical injunction which is implicit in 3:13. The word used, here, however, refers to an active process which leads to the state of holiness which is the goal of Christian living in 3:13 (*hagiasmos*, 4:4,7; 2 Th. 2:13; Rom. 6:19,22; 1 C. 1:30; 1 Tim. 2:15; Heb. 12:14; 1 Pet. 1:2). As with other expressions used to describe the nature of Christian character, so too this one refers to qualities which are due both to the action of God in the believer (5:23) and to the action of the believer himself. Holiness, as we have seen, is to be understood both negatively of freedom from sin and positively in terms of love. It is arguable that these are two sides of the same coin since for Paul 'love does no wrong to a neighbour' (Rom. 13:10). If in the present context Paul expounds holiness in terms of its negative element, the ultimate roots of this lie in the fact that love forbids certain attitudes and acts.

Paul goes on to expound what holiness involves with a series of infinitives, expressed in *RSV* as noun clauses; they are tantamount to imperatives. The logical relation of these to one another is de-

batable and a final verdict depends on the interpretation of v. 6*a*;
but at the outset we can say that the first clause (v. 3*b*) is explanatory
of 'your sanctification' and the second (v. 4) is virtually in apposition
to the first. The first clause states one aspect of holiness, namely,
abstention from (sexual) **immorality**. It should scarcely need comment that this is not the sum-total of holiness, although critics of
Christianity sometimes try to suggest that Christians are obsessed
with this aspect of ethics (often, one may dare to say, because such
critics dislike the Christian standard). The word **abstain** (*apechomai*)
seems to have been common in early Christian ethical teaching (Ac.
15:20,29; I Th. 5:22; I Pet. 2:11). It implies complete abstinence
from evil, and it is worth commenting that where things are evil the
Christian attitude is necessarily one of abstention and not of mod-
eration. **immorality** should be understood to refer to all kinds of
sexual immorality. This understanding of the term has been questioned by B. Malina ('Does *Porneia* mean Fornication?', *NovT* 14,
1972, pp. 10–17), who argues that it does not include pre-marital
sexual relationships. But his view has been refuted by J. Jensen
('Does *Porneia* mean Fornication? A Critique of Bruce Malina',
NovT 20, 1978, pp. 161–84). The term refers to all sexual intercourse other than that which takes place within the marriage relationship. How far this sin was prevalent in the Thessalonian church,
we cannot tell. The strong terms in which Paul continues his exhortation (vv. 6, 8) suggest that there were some cases of it, and
this would not be surprising in a Christian group converted from
first-century paganism with its low level of practice, though not
necessarily of ideal (cf. I C. 5:1–5; 6:12–20; Rom. 1:24–27).

4. In the second 'that'-clause (vv. 4–5) Paul explains more positively what is meant by abstaining from immorality in terms of the
action which his readers should take in order to avoid this sin. *RSV*
interprets the Greek as **that each one of you know how to take a
wife for himself**, on the assumption that the Greek word *skeuos*,
literally 'vessel, container', should be understood metaphorically
with reference to a **wife**. It is surprising that there is no marginal
reference in *RSV* to the literal meaning of the word and to the
alternative interpretation of it as a reference to one's own body
(*NEB*; *NIV*). There is a complicated exegetical problem here.

(1). The word in question is used literally of household utensils
and containers (Mk 11:16; Lk. 8:16; Rev. 2:27; 18:12). It can then
be used metaphorically of persons who are instruments for somebody's purpose (Ac. 9:15). In Rom. 9:22f. the literal and metaphorical uses are closely related. The human body can be thought
of as like a piece of earthenware, a fragile container (2 C. 4:7); this
metaphor is present in I Pet. 3:7 where the wife is 'the weaker sex,'

literally 'the weaker vessel,' a phrase which implies that the husband is also a weak vessel and shows that the word does not automatically mean a woman as opposed to a man. A different metaphorical use is found in some rabbinic sources (well presented by C. Maurer, *TDNT* VII, pp. 361f.) where a woman can be described as a 'vessel' in a sexual sense and 'to take' is a euphemism for sexual intercourse. The present verse can then be understood in this way. Paul is urging his readers to maintain an honourable and pure sexual relationship with their wives and not to act in passion and lust. He writes in terms of the attitudes of husbands, possibly because they were the more liable to temptation; but his instructions can easily be applied to wives. This interpretation finds considerable favour among commentators (von Dobschütz, pp. 163–5; Frame, pp. 149f.; Best, pp. 161–3; C. Maurer, *TDNT* VII, pp. 365–7, gives the best exposition of it; cf. *GNB*).

(2). This interpretation is not without difficulty. It is open to the suggestion that it implies a low, even contemptuous view of the wife as nothing more than an instrument for the gratification of the husband. The objection is not wholly valid, since Paul is speaking specifically about the problem of physical sexual relationships and not about other aspects of marriage, and also since he insists on a holy and honourable relationship. A second objection is that the parallel drawn between this verse and 1 Pet. 3:7 is invalid. Although Maurer still claims support from this verse, Frame rightly recognised long ago that it is not a true parallel (see above). Nevertheless, this is not a decisive objection. A third objection is that the rabbinic evidence is ambiguous. This objection has now been refuted by Maurer; but it is significant that some of the evidence which he considers is expressive of a low attitude to women and that none of it is early. A fourth objection is that on this view the qualifying phrase in vv. 4*b* and 5 relate to an honourable approach to intercourse with one's own wife (the avoidance of lustful and indecent practices), whereas the logic of the passage leads one to expect a reference to the avoidance of sexual relationships with other partners. This is a decisive reason for exploring the second possibility of interpretation, namely, that the word 'vessel' refers to the man's own body in its sexual aspects (Rigaux, pp. 504–6; Morris, pp. 123f.; Whiteley, pp. 60f.). The thought is not of the body as the container of the soul, but rather Paul may be using a euphemistic expression for the male genital organ (Ellingworth and Nida, p. 79, draw attention to the parallel in 1 Sam. 21:5, where the Hebrew word has this sense; LXX has a garbled rendering). On this view the reference is to sexual self-control, and this gives the required sense for the passage. In favour of this view is the fact that the word can have this meaning in Greek (LSJ, *s.v.*) and that it does not require that Greek readers should appreciate a somewhat uncertain background in rabbinic usage. But there are objections. First, it has been claimed that the adjective 'his own' (concealed in *RSV* **for himself**) is inappropriate with 'body' but appropriate with 'wife' (1 C. 7:2); this objection seems to be irrelevant, since the form 'his own' was becoming weak in force in Hellenistic Greek and Paul uses it elsewhere of a person's own body (Rom. 4:19; Eph. 5:28f.). Second, a more important difficulty lies in the use of the phrase translated to **know how to take**. On either view of the passage this should be taken as one phrase with 'know' meaning 'learn how to' (Frame's separation of the verbs, 'that each of you respect his own wife; that each of you get his own wife . . .', has not found any support and should be dropped from consideration). The problem is the verb **take**, literally 'to gain, acquire'. This is hardly an appropriate verb to use in relation to one's own body. Supporters of the first interpretation of the verse are quick to point out that it can be used of 'taking' a wife (Sir. 36:24; Ru. 4:10) and have a durative sense. C. Maurer draws attention to a corresponding Hebrew phrase which is used of sexual intercourse as the basis of marriage (Dt. 21:13; 24:1; Isa. 54:1). The possibility is to be granted, but it need not be an argument against the second interpretation, unless the use of the verb with regard to one's own body is impossible. In fact, however, the verb can be used in the sense 'to gain mastery over' (MM, *s.v.*), and there is evidence that the present can have the force of a perfect, 'to possess'. (Yet another view is that the verb means 'to win over', and is used here of making one's partner favourably inclined to sexual intercourse; W. Vogel, 'εἰδέναι τὸ ἑαυτοῦ σκεῦος κτᾶσθαι. Zur Deutung von 1 Thess 4, 3ff. im Zusammenhang der paulinischen Eheauffassung', *ThBl* 13, 1934, pp. 83–5. But this view of the passage is open to the same objections as the first view.) Rigaux claims that if we adopt this view we obtain a parallel with 1 C. 6:12–20, where the same thoughts of avoiding immorality and glorifying God in one's body instead of sinning against one's own body are found. (Those who adopt the first interpretation find a parallel with 1 C. 7:2, where Paul's remedy for immorality is that each person has his own wife.)

The sexual side of life is to be conducted **in holiness and honour**. **holiness** extends to the physical aspects of life; it does not exclude sexual activity (as a long ascetic tradition within Christianity has tended to suggest) but controls its character. The thought is of conduct pleasing to God, and hence in accordance with his commandments. **honour** must refer to the attitude to other people, not only one's wife but also other people whom one refrains from dishonouring by immoral acts; it is here that we see the motive of love expressing itself in respect for other people. This qualification will fit both interpretations of the verse. On the first view, it requires that a man's choice of wife should not be dictated simply by physical desire but should be based on honour for his wife as a person. On the second interpretation, the man is to control his sexual impulses by respect for other people as people.

5. Paul's point is underlined by a contrast with the life-style of the **heathen**. The word used is that normally translated 'Gentiles', and the *RSV* rendering brings out the characteristic which Paul wants to emphasise: they **do not know God**. The Greek construction shows that this is the chief characteristic of the Gentiles and warrants the narrower definition of them as heathen or pagan. The language is drawn from the *OT* (Ps. 79:6; Jer. 10:25); Paul uses it elsewhere (2 Th. 1:8; cf. 1 C. 1:21; Gal, 4:8), and regards ignorance of God, or refusal to recognise him when the truth of the gospel has been proclaimed (2 Th. 1:8; 2:10), as the root of sinful and unrighteous behaviour (Rom. 1:18–32). Such people are controlled by **the passion of lust**. The former word expresses an overpowering feeling, and can be used of sexual passion in a bad sense (Rom. 1:26; Col. 3:5), and the latter word reinforces the thought of sinful desire (Rom. 6:12; Gal. 5:16; it is used in a good sense in 1 Th. 2:17). The point then is that Christians must not follow physical desire wherever it leads them in sexual relationships. This makes good sense with either of the possible interpretations of the previous verse, but it is more appropriate of control of the sexual impulse in general than of married life in particular. The criticism of the pagan world expressed by Paul is of course very general and would not apply to every single person. Nevertheless, the moral reputation of the Roman Empire was low, and Paul's characterisation of its typical way of life was justified. It would be possible to offer a similar verdict on modern western civilisation, as represented by its films, TV and novels, and as reflected in the statistics for marital breakdown, and yet to recognise that there are still many people who maintain high moral standards and have stable marriages.

6. A third infinitival phrase, rendered as a 'that'-clause, follows; but the relation to what precedes is not clear and depends partly on how we interpret the wording. Three main possibilities have been suggested. (1). First, there is the view that Paul introduces a new subject here. The way in which the infinitive is introduced (by the neuter article *to* in Greek) could suggest that Paul is introducing a new theme in apposition to 'your sanctification' in v. 3. The language can be understood to refer to business affairs – **that no man transgress, and defraud his brother in business** (*RSV* mg).

On this view the verb translated 'transgress' in *RSV* should be regarded as transitive with the meaning 'to over-reach, defraud' or 'to disregard'; the second verb is used of taking advantage of somebody (2 C. 2:11; 7:2; 12:17f.). The prepositional phrase must refer to an item of business. On this view, then, Paul turns from sexual morality to honesty in business, and it is claimed that the language supports this, since it is hard to see how one's brother is involved if v. 4 refers to married life — a point which loses its force if we adopt the other interpretation of v. 4 which makes it refer to sexual self-control in general. The problems with this view of the verse are that the change of subject from sexual immorality is abrupt, especially when Paul returns to this theme in v. 7, and that the translation of the prepositional phrase (*en tō pragmati*) as 'in business' gives it a difficult and unparalleled meaning. (2). It is preferable, then, to link the verse with what precedes, as is done by *RSV* txt, which takes the prepositional phrase to mean **in this matter**. This may simply mean 'in the matter we are discussing', but there are good grounds for taking it as a euphemism for a sexual 'affair'. The verbs will then refer to disregarding and taking advantage of somebody else by adulterous behaviour. The enormity of the sin is expressed in the fact that it is against a brother, by which Paul undoubtedly means a fellow-Christian (*pace* Whiteley, pp. 62f.; 1 C. 6:8). This does not mean that Paul was unconcerned about wronging a pagan neighbour, but rather that he was primarily concerned with sinful actions within the Christian community. This interpretation of the verse is free from difficulty (the problem of the initial articular infinitive is solved by taking the phrase in apposition to v. 4 and regarding it as bringing out what is involved in not keeping the precept expressed there). (3). Nevertheless, a third view has been suggested, which affects the interpretation of the earlier verses. H. Baltensweiler ('Erwägungen zu 1 Thess 4.3–8', *TZ* 19, 1963, pp. 1–13) argues that the passage is concerned with whether Christians should follow the Greek marriage law which required the marriage of a daughter to somebody of near kin who would be regarded as a 'son' for purposes of inheritance. Such a marriage might not only be contrary to Jewish law with its forbidden degrees of union, but the possibility of it could lead to legal squabbles between different relatives who wished to marry the heiress. Paul counsels that Christians must avoid incest (vv. 4f.) and legal disputes. This view requires that **in this matter** be taken to mean 'in the lawsuit' (cf. 1 C. 6:1), but nothing in the context suggests that it has this special meaning, and the whole passage appears to refer to a more general situation. Best's criticisms of the theory are cogent.

We accept, then, the second interpretation (cf. C. Maurer, *TDNT* VI, pp. 639f.).

In the second part of the verse Paul commences a general justification of the commands which he has just been giving. He warns those who disregard the claims of their brothers that **the Lord is an avenger in all these things**. The **Lord** is Jesus, as is normal in Paul's terminology (3:12), especially since in the following verses Paul refers explicitly to 'God' and ascribes a different function to him. If Paul is citing the wording of Ps. 94:1 here, he has deliberately omitted the word 'God' to obtain a reference to Jesus—and incidentally applied an *OT* passage about God the Father to Jesus. Jesus is, then, the avenger of wrongs done to men. Christians are not to seek vengeance on those who wrong them, but to leave the matter to the Lord (Rom. 12:19, citing Dt. 32:35). This suggests that **in all these things** refers primarily to acts involving other people, but the phrase is wide enough to cover acts of immorality in general. The concept that such judgment is administered by Jesus, who thus shares in the activity characteristic of God himself, is common *NT* teaching (2 Th. 1:7f.; Jn 5:27; 2 C. 5:10). It is not clear whether the reference is to the future judgment only or also includes a reference to present acts of judgment (1 C. 11:30) which are intended to warn believers to repent lest worse things befall them. This warning was nothing new for Paul's readers; in his preaching and instruction he had spoken beforehand of what would happen to sinners and solemnly testified to it.

The first of the two verbs in this hendiadys, rendered in *RSV* as **we solemnly forewarned**, conveys the thought of telling about something before it happens (3:4; not 'telling on an earlier occasion than the present one', as Best p. 167, takes it; cf. 2 C. 13:2; Gal. 5:21). The second verb emphasises the element of warning and exhortation implicit in the prediction: if the Lord will avenge such conduct, see that you do not practise it. The thought of divine vengeance is common in the Bible. It is not popular with some people who argue that if God commands Christians to return good for evil and love their enemies, he himself ought to follow the same principles. The difficulty is probably that in contemporary English the words 'avenge' and 'vengeance' have taken on the sense of acting out of personal vindictiveness, whereas in the Bible the thought is rather that God takes the side of the victims of crime and wickedness and secures justice for them, and that he acts as the upholder of the moral order against those who think that they can break it with impunity.

7. Paul gives a second reason why Christians should obey the commands which he has been giving; the opening **For** thus refers

back to vv. 3–6a, so that the verse is parallel to v. 6b. The reason
lies in the nature of the calling experienced by Paul and his readers
(who are linked together as **us**). God's call has already been mentioned in 2:12, where it was linked with the need to live a life
worthy of God, and in 5:24 it is associated with the promise of
God's faithfulness and his power to make his people holy. This
thought is implicit in the present verse: what God calls his people
to be, he will do for them, and sanctification in particular is his
work in the believer (1 C. 1:30; 6:11). There is a certain stress in
the Greek on God; it is he who calls people to be Christians, and
such a divine call obviously has serious implications, as v. 8 makes
clear (von Dobschütz, p. 170). But the main stress is on the contrast
not . . . for uncleanness, but in holiness. The two prepositions are
often taken as synonymous and expressive of the goal or result of
God's call: he did not call us to be unclean but so as to be holy
(Rigaux, pp. 512f.) This is a possible understanding of the sentence,
but another view may be preferable. On this view the first preposition (*epi*) expresses the ground or condition of God's call and the
second (*en*) expresses the mode. The thought then is that God did
not call us on the basis of our uncleanness, as if this was something
to be maintained (contrast 1 C. 7:20), but he called us in a way that
involves sanctification. **uncleanness** expresses the state of the un-
converted and is wider in application than the sexual area of life
(2:3), and **holiness** must be understood here passively as God's
activity in sanctifying his people (1 C. 1:30). 'If God is working in
them in this way they ought not to fall back into the old ways, and
the realization that God is so working should itself be a motive
leading to their self-sanctification' (Best, p. 168, following von Dobschütz, p. 171).

8. Paul draws a conclusion from what he has just said, but its
wording is such that it also contains a further reason why his readers
must follow his instructions. The conclusion is expressed by the
unusual conjunction **Therefore** (*toigaroun*, found elsewhere in the
NT only in Heb. 12:1), which introduces the logical conclusion
from what has been said. If it is God who has called us so that we
may be sanctified, it follows that to regard what has been said as of
no account is not to disregard man but God himself. The phrase
who disregards has no object in the Greek, but *RSV* supplies **this**,
sc. the preceding instructions. The verb means to disregard a person
(Mk 6:26) or a thing Mk 7:9; 1 C. 1:19; Gal. 2:21; 3:15); here it
signifies not merely the despising of instructions but refusal to obey
them. Such a person is not despising a **man**, i.e. the one who
conveys the instructions; here Paul himself is implicitly meant (*pace*
Best, p. 169). He is despising **God** himself, the real author of the

instructions which express his purpose of holiness for his people
(4:3). The form of the saying resembles 1 Sam. 8:7; but the nearest
parallel is the saying of Jesus in Lk. 10:16 (with its positive counterpart in Mk 9:37; cf. also Jn 5:23). There may be an echo of Isa.
21: 2 LXX, but it is also possible that Paul is echoing the saying of
Jesus.

The solemnity of the saying is heightened by the description of
God which Paul appends to it. Not only is God the one who calls
to holiness. He is also the one **who gives his Holy Spirit to you**.
The use of the present form has been thought to indicate a continuous supply of the Spirit by God, but more probably the Greek
participle is timeless and serves to characterise God simply as the
giver of the Spirit. The Greek word-order lays stress on the two
facts that the Spirit is God's Spirit and that the Spirit is **holy**. There
can be no doubt that the stress is on the Spirit as the power to make
believers holy; it is through the Spirit that God's work of sanctification (5:23) is carried out. Thus the *OT* promise (Ezek. 36:27;
37:6, 14) which Paul here echoes (whether consciously or unconsciously) finds fulfilment in the sanctification of God's people as
individuals (the **to you** rather than 'to us', as might have been
expected after v. 7 tends to personalise the gift). If the sign and
power of the New Age has come upon God's people in this way,
then it is out of character for them to persist in their old, sinful way
of life.

9. Having dealt with what we may regard as the negative aspect
of God's will for his people, Paul now turns to the positive aspect,
and takes up the theme of **love** which was adumbrated in 3:12.
(This and other motifs in vv. 9–12 were themes (*topoi*) in the writings of the philosophers; see A. J. Malherbe's article in *ANRW*,
cited in 2:9 note.). He has found it necessary to give careful instructions about sexual immorality, **but concerning love** (i.e. in effect
God's command to love) he does not need to do so, since the readers
have already been taught to do so. This explanation of the connection of thought makes it unnecessary to suppose that the present
section is loosely appended to the previous one, or that Paul is
taking up a theme about which the Thessalonians had specifically
sought advice (whether by a written letter [so Frame, p. 157; Masson, pp. 51f.] or orally through Timothy). **love of the brethren** is
Greek *philadelphia*, a word which originally meant quite literally
love for one's physical brothers and sisters but came to be used in
Christian circles for love within the Christian fellowship (Rom.
12:10; Heb. 13:1; 1 Pet. 1:22; 2 Pet. 1:7; cf. 1 Pet. 3:8). The
thought is of mutual love, as contrasted with the usual word for
love, *agapē*, which can signify unrequited love. Paul has no need

to write in order to explain the idea or to encourage the practice. His readers have been **taught by God to love one another**. The word 'taught-by-God' (*theodidaktos*) is used here for the first time in Greek literature (for the thought, see Isa. 54:13; Jn 6:45). Commentators have been puzzled as to what exactly Paul has in mind. Brotherly love is taught in the *OT* (Lev. 19:18) and was part of the tradition of the teaching of Jesus handed down in the church (Mk 12:29–31; Jn 13:34). We may be sure that it had formed part of Paul's elementary instruction to the church (1:3; 3:6, 12). Since none of these channels of instruction appear to require special characterisation as divine teaching, recourse is had to the suggestion that inward instruction by the Spirit is meant, such as was expected in the messianic era (Jer. 31:33f.). Best, pp. 172f., thinks that Paul may have been influenced by Isa. 54:13, and that the language is fairly general. But a more satisfactory interpretation is that Paul is thinking not just of being taught the need to love but rather of being taught how to love. The readers have been divinely empowered so as **to love one another** (for this phrase, see Jn 13:34; 15:12, 17; 1 Jn 3:11, 23; 4:7, 11). Exhortation is not needed because the readers have experienced an inward, divine compulsion to love one another. In other words, Paul ascribes their growth in love (1:3) to the sanctifying power of the Spirit (cf. 4:8). One may be tempted to ask cynically why the Spirit had taught them brotherly love but not apparently sexual purity. There is no answer to such a question, beyond the fact of common observation and experience that people may follow the Spirit's promptings in one area of Christian living and ignore them in another.

10. The praiseworthy sentiment in v. 9 is confirmed (*RSV* **and indeed** renders Greek 'for indeed') by the fact that the Thessalonians' love extends beyond the bounds of their own fellowship. Paul had evidence that they loved **all the brethren throughout Macedonia**, and from this he rightly deduced that the same spirit prevailed among the members of the church. By this time there were Christian groups in Philippi and Beroea, and doubtless in other centres also. Since Thessalonica was an important commercial centre and port, it is very likely that Christians from other towns in Macedonia would visit it. They would be glad of hospitality from the local Christians, since in the ancient world it was difficult for travellers to get decent accommodation except from their friends. The writer of 3 John could praise Gaius for welcoming Christian brothers, even though they were strangers to him (3 Jn 5), and hospitality was a much-commended virtue in the early Church. The Thessalonian Christians may also have given material gifts to help the poor

or to support the Christian mission, as was done by the church at
Philippi (Phil. 4:14–18).

Having thus implicitly praised the readers, Paul can nevertheless
exhort them **to do so more and more**. The reference can only be
to increasing in the brotherly love of which he has just been speaking. For the 'form' of the exhortation, see 4:1 note, and for the
thought of increasing in Christian behaviour, see 3:12 and 4:1. No
matter how far one has progressed in faith and love, there is always
the possibility of further advance. Paul in fact will go on immediately
to spell out one particular area where their present Christian activity
needs augmenting.

11. Paul's further exhortation is expressed in a series of infinitives,
followed by a parenthetic comment that he is telling them nothing
new, and concluding in v. 12 with an expression of the purpose of
his injunctions. The second infinitive, **to live quietly**, is dependent
on the first, **to aspire** (Calvin wrongly separated them and took the
first to refer to being zealous in showing brotherly love; this is an
unnatural rendering, and Pauline usage [Rom. 15:20; 2 C. 5:9] is
against it). The verb **to aspire** can mean to be ambitious or to be
eager. Commentators generally prefer the former rendering in the
sense 'consider it a matter of honour' (German common language
translation, cited by Ellingworth and Nida, p. 89). **to live quietly**
is here the opposite of 'to be a busybody' (2 Th. 3:11). It was used
in Classical Greek of looking after one's own business and keeping
out of public life, and the same meaning is found for the phrase **to
mind your own affairs**. Older commentators found this sense here
and assumed that Paul was concerned with members of the church
who were getting involved in local politics; Frame, p. 161, however,
objected rightly that the members of the church were working
people who did not spend their time in the market place talking
politics. The two phrases should be taken in a more general sense.
As the next phrase indicates, the people in question were not getting
on with their work, and had to be exhorted **to work with** their
hands. Behind this command may lie the Greek attitude which
despised manual labour, an attitude which Paul rejected both in his
own way of life (1 C. 4:12) and in his teaching (Eph. 4:28).

But there may be more to the matter than this. Clearly at least
some of the members were living in idleness and needed to be
exhorted to work. Since they could not live without the necessities
of life, it looks as though they were taking advantage of the kindness
of the other members of the church who were known for their
brotherly love. This will explain why Paul brings in this exhortation
at this point in the letter in connection with the theme of brotherly
love. He commends the church for its love; but, while encouraging

this virtue, he warns against the attitude of idleness which was thriving in this environment. It was evidently a continuing attitude. Paul comments that he had already given a command to this effect, and later in 2 Th. 3:6–15 the same problem is discussed again at greater length and the church is urged to take action against slackers who will not work. Although Paul does not say so explicitly, commentators generally assume that some members of the church felt that because of the imminence of the parousia and the end of normal life there was no need for them to work and to provide for their future. In their idleness they had nothing better to do than to make a nuisance of themselves to their Christian friends and probably their pagan neighbours as well; in this way their failure to live quietly and to mind their own business is explained.

Although the connection between expectation of the parousia and idleness is not made in so many words, the way in which instruction about the parousia follows this section (4:13–5:11) and is then itself followed by a further comment about the idle (5:14) may suggest that the two themes are connected. The imminence of the parousia is not an excuse for idleness and so being a nuisance and a burden to other people. On the contrary, the exhortations in the Gospels are to the effect that servants should be found going about their duties when the Master returns unexpectedly (Mt. 24:45–51; Mk 13:34–37). However, Moore, p. 66, urges caution in associating idleness with expectation of the parousia. It arose rather, he argues, from misunderstanding of brotherly love.

12. Paul concludes with a purpose-clause which expresses part of the reason for his exhortation. Christians must live in such a way as to **command the respect of outsiders**. Literally, they must walk (2:12; 4:1) in a seemly manner (Rom. 13:13; 1 C. 14:40) taking account of (i.e. with an eye to the verdict of) those outside (*sc.* the fellowship; cf. 1 C. 5:12f.; Col. 4:5). This motive of avoiding giving offence to people who were not yet Christians and hence of giving the church a bad reputation is not uncommon in the *NT* (1 C. 10:32f.; Col. 4:5; 1 Tim. 3:7; 1 Pet. 2:12). Best, p. 177, rightly observes that Christians will never please everybody, but at least they can avoid bringing themselves into disrepute by failing to live up to the accepted standards of the society in which they live. In particular, Paul concludes, Christians must aim not to be dependent on anybody, especially those outside the church who will take a poor view of them if their religion makes them a public nuisance and burden. The Greek phrase could also be translated *to have need of nothing*, but the context supports the former rendering: Paul's worry is not that the members of the church will go hungry but that they will be parasites on society.

The second main subject in the instructional and hortatory section of the letter is the parousia of Jesus. This topic has already been mentioned comparatively frequently in the first part of the letter (1:10; 2:19; 3:13), and it must have formed an integral part of Paul's missionary preaching (cf. Ac. 17:31). Two problems raised by it had been conveyed to Paul from the Thessalonians. The first (4:13–18) was concerned with members of the church who had died before the parousia. Did their death mean that they were excluded from the glorious events associated with it? Commentators differ as to whether the problem was fear that they would be totally excluded from future salvation or merely be at a disadvantage compared with those still alive at the parousia. In either case, Paul's basic answer is that belief in the death and resurrection of Jesus entails the belief that the dead will come with Jesus at his parousia. This basic deduction is backed up by a 'word of the Lord' which confirms that the dead will rise first and then the living will be taken up with them to meet the Lord. There is, therefore, no need to sorrow about the dead.

The second problem (5:1–11) was about the timing of the parousia. Behind it lay the fear that the parousia might take the living unawares and so they would not participate in salvation. (Fear of dying before the parousia (Marxsen, p. 65) is not present.) Paul's reply is that it is true that the parousia will happen unexpectedly and bring sudden destruction to those who are not prepared for it. But this fate should not overtake the readers, for God has destined them for salvation. They belong to the new world, so let them live accordingly, always ready and watchful for their Lord. Here, again, there is comfort for the readers, but it is closely associated with exhortation. The paradox of predestination and the need for human spiritual progress is clearly expressed.

13–14. The introduction of a new topic with no direct connection with what has just preceded is signalled by three phrases, the conjunction **But**, the address to the readers as **brethren** (1:4) and the statement **we would not have you ignorant**, which serves both to introduce a new topic and to convey fresh (though not necessarily previously unknown) information (Rom. 1:13; 11:25; I C. 10:1; 12:1; 2 C. 1:8); it is equivalent to the positive 'I want you to understand' (I C. 11:3; Phil. 1:12; Col. 2:1). This information is **concerning those who are asleep**. The prepositional phrase (cf. 4:9; 5:1) is used to introduce a fresh topic, often one raised by

Paul's correspondents (1 C. 7:1; cf. 8:1; 12:1; 16:1, 12), although not necessarily in writing (*pace* Frame, p. 166); an oral report from Timothy may be all that is meant.

The word 'sleep' was common in the ancient world as a euphemism for death and is found in both the *OT* and the *NT* (Gen. 47:30; Dt. 31:16; 1 Ki. 22:40; Jn 11:11–13; Ac. 7:60; 13:36; 1 C. 7:39; 11:30). Since the term was used in cultures which did not believe in any kind of afterlife but simply drew the obvious analogy between the states of sleep and death, the verb in itself does not convey the sense of a state out of which one may be 'awakened', nor does it say anything specific about the present condition of the dead. It is true that the metaphor could be extended to take account of a belief in resurrection, as in Dan. 12:2 (cf. 2 Esd. 7:32; 1 En. 100:5) and Mk 5:39), but this does not necessitate that in Christian usage the word had taken on an extended meaning. Elsewhere Paul uses the word where the thought of resurrection is not in view (1 C. 7:39; 11:30; 15:6, 18, 51; cf. Ac. 13:36; 2 Pet. 3:4). Here Paul is simply describing the dead from the point of view of his readers. They were in danger of grieving over them **as others do who have no hope**. The **others** are clearly pagans (Eph. 2:3), who lacked the certainty of a life after death that was worthy to be called such and hence of a reunion between the living and the dead. It is true that a belief in immortality of the soul was found in various mystery religions, and Paul can hardly have been ignorant of this; some of the philosophers too, such as Plato, taught an afterlife. But these ideas were not universally held and probably did not affect the majority of the population. The grave inscriptions of the time tell a different tale of hopefulness in the face of death, and the picture of an afterlife painted by those who hoped for it was generally far from satisfying. Paul's characterisation of the situation is realistic. All that the average pagan could do was to mourn, as a well-known papyrus letter indicates: 'Irene to Taonnophris and Philo, good comfort. I am as sorry and weep over the departed one, as I wept for Didymas. And all things, whatsoever were fitting, I have done, and all mine, Epaphroditus and Thermuthion and Philion and Apollonius and Plantas. But, nevertheless, against such things one can do nothing. Therefore comfort ye one another' (Frame, p. 167).

The Christian **hope**, as Paul understood it, however, went beyond mere survival or immortality to the continuation of life with Christ. It was thus a hope based on faith in God, and Eph. 2:12 brings out the connection: 'having no hope, and without God in the world'. Christians, who have this hope, do not grieve like those who do not know God (4:5). Despite this categorical denial elsewhere the fact of mourning by Christians is taken for granted (Mt. 5:4; Rom.

12:15). We should distinguish between mourning which laments the sad fate of a person who has been cut off from the enjoyment of life and the mourning which is due to the rupture caused in one's own life by the loss of a loved one. The former is overcome by the Christian belief that to be with Jesus is 'far better' (Phil. 1:23). The latter is a natural psychological reaction to the gap created in one's own life, although this too can be overcome not only by the lapse of time and adjustment to a new way of life but also by the reality of spiritual comfort from God and other Christians (Mt. 5:4; Rom. 12:15; 1 Pet. 5:10).

The question of the cause of the grief of the Thessalonians is much debated:

(1). It has been argued that because of the nearness of the parousia and its prominence in his thinking and his message Paul had given no instruction about the resurrection of the dead at Thessalonica (even though he must have spoken about the resurrection of Jesus). In the early days of the church the problem of death before the parousia had simply not arisen (Marxsen, p. 65; *id.*, 'Auslegung von 1 Thess 4, 14-18', *ZTK* 66, 1969, pp 22-37; J. Becker, *Auferstehung der Toten im Urchristentum*, Stuttgart, 1976, pp. 46-54; cf. Dibelius, p. 23). The weakness of this view is that, so far as Paul was concerned, by the time of the mission to Thessalonica the question of the fate of dead Christians must have arisen and been given an answer. G. Lüdemann, *Paulus, der Heidenapostel*, Göttingen, 1980, I, pp. 220-30, seeks to overcome this objection by dating the mission (and the epistle) extremely early within nine to fourteen years of the death of Jesus. This radical proposal confessedly involves a rejection of the chronological structure of the Pauline mission in Acts which in our opinion is completely unjustified. Furthermore, the fact that Paul is able to cite an already existing 'saying' about the resurrection of the dead in vv. 16f. shows that the question had already arisen and been answered in the church. It is, therefore, highly unlikely that Paul himself had not yet formulated his teaching about the resurrection of the dead.

(2). It remains possible, however, that the Thessalonian Christians had not yet fully understood this doctrine. In view of his belief that the parousia was imminent and as a result of the brevity of his visit to Thessalonica it is possible that Paul had not mentioned, or at least had said little about, the resurrection of the dead. What he did say may not have been fully understood by the Thessalonian Christians, and it is quite possible that their emotional response to the death of some of their number had blunted their apprehension of the doctrine of the resurrection. It is, after all, one thing to have a theoretical belief in resurrection and quite another to maintain that belief in the actual presence of death and physical decay (P. Siber, *Mit Christus Leben*, Zürich, 1971, pp. 13–22). Morris, p. 136, suggests that the Thessalonians may have regarded death before the parousia as a judgment upon sin (cf. 1 C. 11:30) which would involve exclusion from final salvation. But if this were the case, it is strange that Paul writes about the dead in general and says nothing at all about whether death before the parousia is a judgment.

(3). Another possibility is that, instead of the dead being absolutely at a disadvantage compared with the living in that they had no hope at all of future salvation (view 2.), the Thessalonians regarded them as being only relatively at a disadvantage. This view is generally expressed in the form that the Thessalonians believed in the resurrection but held that it would not take place until after the parousia, with the result that the dead would be excluded from the joyful reunion with the Lord at his retun. (A variant of this view is that the Thessalonians thought that the dead would be excluded from the millennial reign of the Lord which would immediately follow the parousia and precede the resurrection. But there is no evidence that Paul (or his converts) believed in the millennium. See H.-A. Wilcke, *Das Problem eines messianischen Zwischenreiches bei Paulus*, Zürich/Stuttgart, 1967, pp. 109–50.) U. Luz, *Das Geschichtsverständnis des Paulus*, München, 1968, pp. 318–31, suggests that the formerly pagan Thessalonians had not been able to bring together the concept of the resurrection and the apocalyptic hope of the parousia in a systematic manner. In favour of this view is Paul's comment that the living will not precede the dead at the parousia (v. 15b). However, it faces the decisive objection that, if the dead were ultimately to be raised, it is impossible to see why the Thessalonians had such a feeling of utter hopelessness about their fate.

(4). A reaction to the difficulties facing views (1) and (3) can be found in the view of Schmithals, pp. 160–7, and Harnisch, pp. 16–51. They argue that something had happened to disturb the Thessalonians' belief in the resurrection. The church had been infected by Gnostic teachers who insisted that the resurrection was a spiritual experience which had already taken place in the lives of Gnostics (2 Tim. 2:8; 1 C. 15:12 and 2 Th. 2:2 are taken in the same sense). Paul's concern is to point out polemically the implications of such a view: if it is correct that there is no future resurrection, then the readers' departed relatives and friends are obviously excluded from salvation. The same viewpoint is detected in 5:1–10 where, it is claimed (Harnisch, 52–158), Paul is attacking Gnostics who denied the parousia and who thought that they had been once and for all delivered out of darkness into light and hence had no need to be spiritually awake and sober in expectation of the parousia. This view is rejected by Best, 182, on the grounds that Paul would have reacted more sharply to the presence of such heretics if there had been any in the church, and that the whole case for Gnosticism at Thessalonica is without foundation. Harnisch's view also requires interpreting 4:13 and 18 in an unnatural manner in terms of warning rather than of comfort (see further G. Lüdemann, *op. cit.*, 221–224).

(5). N. Hyldahl, 'Auferstehung Christi – Auferstehung der Toten (1 Thess. 4:13–18)', in S. Pedersen (ed.), *Die Paulinische Literatur und Theologie*, Århus/Göttingen, 1980, pp. 119–35, has proposed that the problem which Paul was dealing with in 1 Th. 4:13–18 was not primarily concerned with the resurrection of the dead. Rather, the Thessalonian Christians' hope that Christ would come and take them while still alive to be with him had been shattered by the deaths of some of their members; from these deaths they concluded that the hope of the parousia was a delusion. Paul responded to this loss of hope by showing that at the parousia the dead would be in no way disadvantaged but would participate along with the living; consequently, there was no need to abandon hope in the parousia. This novel hypothesis is well argued, but it faces the difficulty that nowhere in the letter does Paul suggest that his readers (or some of them) had lost hope in the parousia or assure them that the parousia will take place; rather, he is able to assume that they share his belief in the parousia.

It thus emerges that none of these views is free from difficulty. The most satisfactory is some form of view (2), according to which Paul's message of the resurrection of the dead had not become part of the thinking of the Thessalonians; the death of some members of the church had accordingly led to grief because they feared that they were excluded from the future salvation associated with the parousia.

14. Paul's answer to the problem of his readers is that there is no need for those who believe in the resurrection of Jesus to grieve over the dead for **God will bring with Jesus those who have fallen asleep**. In essence Paul is stressing that the character of *Christian* belief in God carries the implication that he will raise the dead. This point is perhaps not immediately clear for the opening clause refers to belief that **Jesus died and rose again**. Elsewhere, however, Paul usually speaks of God raising Jesus rather than of Jesus rising; he refers to 'the God who raised Jesus from the dead' (Rom. 4:24; cf. 8:11; 10:9; 1 C. 15:15; 2 C. 4:14; Gal. 1:1; Col. 2:12; 1 Th. 1:10). The adoption of a slightly different form of words here may indicate that he is dependent on a traditional formula (W. Kramer, *Christ, Lord, Son of God*, London, 1966, p. 29 [§5c]; Harnisch, pp. 32f., argues that we have an allusion rather than a citation), and probably Paul has so worded it to emphasise that Jesus died, just as the dead Thessalonians had died. In any case, for Paul the action of raising the dead is God's act, so that in the second clause **God will bring with him** 'God' means 'the God who raised Jesus' and who is thus 'the God who raises the dead' (2 C. 1:9). For Paul this understanding of God thus rested on the historical fact of the resurrection of Jesus in which both he and his readers believed. The conditional form 'if (*RSV* **since**) we believe' does not place the reality of the readers' belief in any doubt. It is sometimes suggested that the line of Paul's thought is: 'Since we believe that Jesus died and rose again, even so *we also believe that* God will bring with him those who have fallen asleep', but in fact Paul omits the italicised words. Paul is not making a declaration of what God will do provided that we believe, as has also been suggested (H.-A. Wilcke, *op. cit.*, pp. 125f.), but rather saying, 'If this is what we believe about Jesus, this is what follows from it'; he is drawing out the implication of belief in the resurrection of Jesus (Harnisch, pp. 33, 36). It is at first sight surprising that Paul does not speak here about God raising the dead but about his bringing them with Jesus. The thought of the resurrection of the dead is implicit in the Christian concept of God, and it is logically presupposed by the reference to bringing the dead with Jesus, since obviously this could not happen to people who were still dead. The accent lies rather on the parousia and the fact that the dead are going to share in it by being **with him**. Hence there is no need to argue with Marxsen, pp. 67f., that Paul has made a secondary link between the resurrection and the parousia here. Marxsen finds the lack of parallelism between the conditional clause and the main clause odd, and he concludes that the reference to the resurrection is a Pauline addition to a sentence that origianlly referred only to the parousia. The reference to the resurrection, however, is essential in the context, since otherwise the bringing of the dead with Jesus would be inexplicable.

This emphasis on the parousia rather than the resurrection retains its significance for present-day readers. Resurrection of the dead has replaced the hope of the parousia in much popular Christian thinking. But resurrection from the dead is an empty concept if the prospect that lies before those who are resurrected is left undefined. The thought of unending existence is not particularly attractive or comforting if it is no improvement on the present life. For the Christian, however, life here and now is life in fellowship with Jesus, and the future hope is of a life that is even more closely joined to him. Thus the fact that God will bring the dead with Jesus (or 'so as to be with Jesus', as Harnisch, p. 35 n. 33, suggests, following E. Lohmeyer) is the central aspect in the Christian hope, and the resurrection of the dead is a means to this end.

The phrase **through Jesus** is linked with the verb **will bring** by *RSV* and most recent writers. However, the sentence structure decidedly favours linking it with **those who have fallen asleep** (*NEB*; W. Marxsen, art. cit., pp. 34f., attempts to take the phrase with the whole clause, but it is not clear what he means by this). The basic reason for rejecting this view is that 'dying through Jesus' is held to be a meaningless idea. The phrase would have to mean something like 'those who died as Christians'. Von Dobschütz, p. 191, took the phrase as a kind of statement of attendant circumstances, equivalent to 'in Christ': they died in a situation where there was a relationship to Jesus. There would appear to be a new and unparalleled conception of Christian dying in which Jesus brings believers into the state of death. Just as Jesus committed himself to God at his death (Lk. 23:46), so Stephen prayed, 'Lord Jesus, receive my spirit' (Ac. 7:59). If God could be regarded as involved in the death of Jesus, so for Christians Jesus took the place of God as the One to whom they committed themselves in dying. This would give a possible meaning to Paul's phrase. On this view, the death of believers does not take place apart from Jesus, and hence Paul can conclude that God will raise them up and bring them into the presence of Jesus at the parousia. God will treat those who died trusting in Jesus in the same way as he treated Jesus himself, namely, by resurrecting them.

Those who find this explanation difficult argue that the phrase goes with the verb and precedes it in order to avoid a clash with the following phrase with him. Jesus is then the means of the resurrection of believers. In this case the reference of the phrase is somewhat vague. Marxsen, p. 62, takes it to mean 'on account of the salvation given in Jesus' (i.e. causally). But it can also mean 'through the action of Jesus (i.e. instrumentally; Best, p. 189), in which case we have an anticipation of the thought in 1 C. 15:21 (cf. Rom. 5:9). Both explanations, then, are possible, and we have a slight preference for the former.

Finally, God will bring the dead to the place where Jesus will meet with living believers at the parousia. Ellingworth and Nida, p. 97, hold that the dead are brought to heaven, on the grounds that God does not come from heaven to earth, the dead are not already in heaven, and v. 16 fills out the picture (cf. P. Ellingworth, 'Which way are we going?. . . 1 Thes. 4:14b', *Bible Translator* 25, 1974, pp. 426–31). This view is unlikely. Paul believed that the parousia would be the coming of Jesus from heaven to earth, to a world that has been freed from corruption (Rom. 8:21; cf. 2 Pet.

3:13; Rev. 21:1f., 10, for the same expectation that the future destiny of God's people is not in heaven, as is commonly but wrongly assumed, but in a renewed earth); consequently it was natural for him to believe that the dead must be brought with Jesus to this new world. (The text need not imply of course that God himself will come with the dead and lead them to the earth; 'will bring' means 'will cause to come'.)

15. Having stated his basic response to the anxious fears of his readers, Paul confirms and elaborates it by referring to a word of the Lord. **this** refers forwards to the second half of the verse. A **word of the Lord** is at first sight a saying of Jesus uttered during his earthly ministry. Elsewhere Paul appeals to the teaching of Jesus (Rom. 14:14; 1 C. 7:10; 9:14; cf. 11:23–25). When he does so, he always refers to Jesus as **the Lord** (for clear examples of this term as a means of referring to the earthly Jesus see 1 C. 9:4; 11:23), he refers to sayings preserved in the Gospel tradition, and he alludes to the teaching of Jesus instead of citing it word for word (1 C. 11:23–25 is an exception; Paul is here citing an authoritative church tradition, but even so the wording does not agree exactly with any of the other accounts of what Jesus said at the Last Supper). These facts make it quite possible, if not indeed probable, that here too Paul is alluding to teaching of the earthly Jesus.

There are two difficulties. First, there is no exact parallel in the Gospels to Paul's teaching here. The nearest parallel is Mt. 24:31: 'And he will send out his angels with a loud trumpet call, and they will gather his elect from the four winds, from one end of heaven to the other.' Second, the wording of vv. 15–17 ('*we who are alive* . . .') is hardly compatible with the style of a saying by Jesus about his followers.

Some scholars get round the first of these difficulties by claiming that Paul is not alluding to a particular text in the Gospels; either he sums up the apocalyptic teaching of Jesus (Rigaux, pp. 538f.; D. Hill, *New Testament Prophecy*, London, 1979, pp. 130f., 166), or he is citing an 'agraphon', a saying of Jesus preserved outside the Gospels (Frame, p. 171; Morris, p. 141; J. Jeremias, *Unknown Sayings of Jesus*, London, 1964). Most recent scholars, placing more emphasis on the second difficulty, argue that what Paul is citing or alluding to here is a statement of the risen Lord, i.e. a saying by an early Christian prophet speaking in his name; or, less probably, a revelation directly to Paul himself (von Dobschütz, p. 194; Best, p. 193; U. Luz, op. cit., pp. 327f.; Harnisch, pp. 39–41; Henneken, pp. 73–98). The existence of such prophecies, given in quite concrete terms, is attested in Ac. 21:11, and Paul himself claimed to be the recipient of divine 'mysteries'. In this connection we cannot overlook the 'mystery' in 1 C. 15:51f. which has close parallels to the present passage.

However, the two difficulties surrounding the first view are capable of resolution. If Paul's practice is not to quote sayings of the Lord exactly, then the lack of precise parallelism between the present passage and the teaching of Jesus in the Gospels is not a real problem. In fact there is a considerable amount of dependence in 1 and 2 Th. on the apocalyptic teaching of Jesus (D. Wenham, 'Paul and the Synoptic Apocalypse', in R. T. France and D. Wenham [ed.], *Gospel Perspectives*, Sheffield, 1981, II, pp. 345–75), and this strengthens the case that Paul is dependent on the same source here. Again, the form and content of Paul's wording represents his application of the teaching of Jesus to the situation of his readers and is no argument against a basis for this wording in the sayings of Jesus. (On the problem see also L. Hartman, *Prophecy Interpreted*, Lund, 1966, pp. 178–205).

What, then is the wording of the saying? Nearly all scholars are agreed that v. 15 contains a declaration which Paul makes on the basis of the teaching of Jesus, and vv. 16f. give the essence of the saying. The basic elements in the saying are: (*a*). the descent of the Lord; (*b*). the resurrection of the dead; (*c*). the rapture of those who are still alive. It is the conjunction of (*a*) and (*b*) which is essential for Paul's argument. Now we find essentially these same elements in 1 C. 15: 52 (cf. von Dobschütz, p. 194; Henneken, pp. 95–8): (*a*). the last trumpet (which accompanies the Lord's descent); (*b*). the raising of the dead; (*c*). the 'changing' of those who are still alive. Here, then, we have a direct parallel to Paul's wording here and a demonstration of the freedom in quotation which he could employ. Attempts have indeed been made to establish a common source or wording which may lie behind both passages (G. Löhr, '1 Thess. 4:15–17: Das "Herrenwort" ', *ZNW* 71, 1980, pp. 269–73; for other reconstructions of the saying see, e.g., Harnisch, pp. 39–46; G. Lüdemann, op. cit., pp. 242–7; P. Siber, op. cit., pp. 35–9). As for Mt. 24:30f., here we have elements (*a*) and (*c*), but there is no explicit mention of element (*b*), the resurrection of the dead. But this element is probably implicit in the saying, since the gathering of the 'elect' must have included both the dead and the living; the resurrection of the dead formed part of the expectation of Jesus (Mt. 8:11; 22:23–33), and earlier in the apocalyptic discourse and elsewhere Jesus reckoned with the certainty of death before the parousia for some of his followers (Mt. 24:9; Mk 13:12; cf. Mk 9:1).

It can thus be maintained that there is an adequate basis in the teaching of Jesus—or at least in the Gospel tradition (since the authenticity of all these sayings of Jesus is disputed)—for Paul's statement here, and that this, rather than a special revelation or 'a miniature Jewish apocalypse' (G. Lüdemann, op. cit., pp. 247–54), lies behind the present passage. I C. 15:51f. will represent another paraphrase of the same tradition (the fact that Paul calls it a 'mystery' does not compel us to believe that it was a personal revelation to himself; rather it is a divine secret which men would not have known had God not revealed it). The possibility that the tradition had undergone some development before it reached Paul cannot be excluded.

In v. 15 Paul draws a conclusion in advance from this saying of the Lord. Those **who are alive shall not precede those who have fallen asleep.** To **precede** translates a Greek verb (*phthanō*; cf. 2:16) which contains the idea of doing something before somebody else and so of gaining an advantage over him. Paul uses an emphatic negative construction (Gk. *ou mē*, also used by other *NT* writers with a weaker sense) to underline the fact that the dead will in no way be at a disadvantage compared with the living. He thus deliberately contradicts a view which was current in Judaism that those who were alive at the end of the world would fare better than the dead (Dan. 12:12; Ps. Sol. 17:50; 2 Esd. 13:24). **we who are alive** naturally includes Paul himself; it is the so-called 'preacher's "we"', by which he makes a statement applicable both to himself and to his hearers. The phrase has raised difficulties because it suggests that Paul expected that he would be living at the time of the parousia, whereas in fact he died without experiencing it. Either, then, Paul was mistaken in his statement, or else it must be taken in a different sense. Certainly in his later writings Paul reckoned with the possibility and even the likelihood of his own death before the parousia (1 C. 6:14; 2 C; 4:14; 5:1; Phil. 1:20). Here in the present passage there is really no difficulty in taking his words to mean 'those of us who are alive'. (We may well ask how Paul could have said 'those of us who are living then' shortly and succinctly without using the actual wording employed here.) Scholars who insist that Paul's wording *must* mean that he expected to be alive at the parousia misinterpret him.

It is significant that Paul qualifies his phrase with the words **who are left until the coming of the Lord.** The verb, used only here and in the repetition of the phrase in v. 17, suggests the idea of survival and thus implies that those who are still alive at the parousia will constitute an exception to the vast group of those who will have fallen asleep (including God's people from *OT* times). We should also note that in 5:10 Paul clearly implies that 'we'—he himself and his readers—may be awake or asleep at the time of the parousia. (See especially Lightfoot, pp. 65–7, for a balanced discussion.)

16. For introduces the 'word of the Lord' which substantiates what Paul has just said. A sign of editing can be seen in the use of **the Lord**, since Jesus is more likely to have referred to the coming One as the Son of man. Paul continues to refer to Jesus as the Lord partly under the influence of the wording in v. 15. He uses 'Jesus' for the earthly figure who died and rose from the dead, but 'Lord' for his status as the coming One. There is quite probably an echo of Mic. 1:3 which describes a theophany: 'For behold, the Lord is coming forth out of his place, and will come down and tread upon the high places of the earth' (cf. Exod. 19:11). The concept of the parousia of the Lord is based ultimately on the *OT* portrayal of the coming of God to the world and of the coming of the Son of man to exercise rule and judgment (Dan. 7:13, using imagery which in part rests on the description of the theophany in Ezek. 1).

As with the texts which speak of the ascension of the Lord and the end of his bodily presence with his disciples, so too the texts about the parousia must be taken symbolically. A real event is being described, but it is one which cannot be described literally since the direct activity of God cannot be fully comprehended in human language. The biblical writers have therefore to resort to analogy and metaphor, the language of symbol, in order to convey their message. They use phrases like 'come down' which, if pressed literally, lead to antinomies and contradictions. Thus the ascension of Jesus can be regarded as an acted parable of his 'departure' to be with God, his transfer from one mode of existence to another. In his helpful discussion of the present passage Whiteley, p. 72, appeals to Calvin, who commented on the last trumpet, 'I prefer to regard it as a metaphor', and who said of the present verse, 'It is quite certain that the sole purpose of the apostle in the present passage was to give a brief glimpse of the magnificent and venerable appearance of the Judge' (Calvin, p. 283). Such a view of the passage must be emphatically distinguished from a demythologising interpretation which sees here the mythical presentation of timeless truths, or which regards Paul's statements as antiquated mumbo-jumbo which must be jettisoned by modern Christians. Paul's statements must be taken seriously, though not necessarily literally.

It is with this principle in mind that we must approach the remainder of the saying with its description of the accompaniments of the Lord's coming. First, there is **a cry of command**. This is not a call to Christ to begin to act but the call of the Lord that initiates the resurrection of the dead. Apart from Jn 5:24 there is little in the way of background to the idea, although Burkeen, pp. 180–96, has related it to the word of rebuke addressed to the demons and evil powers and thus finds an element of judgment in the cry. **the archangel's call** is also a somewhat unparalleled concept. Archangels are not mentioned elsewhere in the Bible, except in Jude 9, but in Judaism they formed part of the heavenly entourage of God. Since angels are associated elsewhere with the coming of God to judgment (Jude 14; 1 En. 1:9) and with the parousia (Mk 8:38), mention here of the topmost grade of angels is not surprising. It is not clear whether the archangel's voice is to be identified with the 'cry of command'. Some scholars would in fact identify both of these events and the sounding of the trumpet of God; this is quite possible since Rev. 1:10; 4:1 contains the idea of a voice which sounds like a trumpet. Paul is simply using standard apocalyptic imagery in which the commands of God can be given through the intermediary of angels (e.g. Rev. 7:2).

the trumpet of God adds vigour to the picture. The blowing of trumpets is associated with theophanies in the *OT* (Exod. 19:16; Isa. 27:13; Jl 2:1; Zech. 9:14) and in particular with God's final appearing (in addition to the references just given, with the exception of Exod. 19:16, see Zeph. 1:14–16). A broader usage is found in Rev. 8:2–10:7; 11:15–19 where seven trumpet blasts by angels introduce a series of divine judgments. The resurrection of the dead is accompanied by the sounding of the last trumpet in 1 C. 15:52, and the Son of man sends out his angels with a loud trumpet call to gather his elect in Mt. 24:31. These references (together with 2 Esd. 6:23; Sib. Orac. 4:174) suggest that the blowing of a trumpet was a stereotyped feature in descriptions of the end. The sound acts as a summons and alert, a warning of action about to commence, and a call to readiness. Here the thought seems to be that the sound will rouse those who are asleep and summon them to meet with the Lord. The coming of the Lord is preceded by a call to his people to prepare for his coming, and this call is addressed to the dead and awakens them.

Hence Paul can go on to say that **the dead in Christ will rise**. *RSV* rightly links the phrase 'in Christ' with 'the dead', although Jeremias would like to link it with the verb on the analogy of 1 C. 15:22. The phrase refers to the dead who stand in relationship to Jesus (cf. 1:1). If their earthly life was essentially determined by their relationship to the crucified and risen Lord, so too is their existence in death, and it is in virtue of this relationship that they hear the summons of the Lord to be with him. They rise **first**, in contrast to living Christians who meet Jesus at the next stage (as v. 17 makes clear), and not in contrast to the rest of the dead, who do not come within Paul's view here. It remains unclear whether the reference to the dead rising first comes directly from the word of the Lord on which Paul bases his exposition. The thought is found in Jn 5:25f., 28f., and this strongly suggests that there was a tradition which regarded the voice of the Lord as being primarily a summons to the dead to awake. Paul follows this tradition, but whether this understanding was spelled out in the original word of the Lord is not certain. At the very least, however, we must say that the association of the call and the rousing of the dead must have been so firmly made that Paul could use it as a basis for argument. Since the call was simultaneous with the descent of the Lord and was heraldic of his coming Paul could draw the conclusion for himself that the resurrection of the dead would precede the gathering of the saints which follows the descent of the Lord. A further problem which remains unsolved is that the trumpet figures only in Matthew's account of the teaching of Jesus (Mt. 24:31) which is generally regarded as secondary to Mark's account (Mk 13:27); probably Matthew was influenced by a continuing oral tradition which in this case preserved the saying in the form in which it was known to Paul.

17. After the raising of the Christian dead to life, there **then** follows the next stage in the denouement. Paul returns to those **who are alive, who are left**, and he links them with the newly-resurrected dead. Both groups are treated together, and it now becomes clear that, so far from the living having any precedence over those who had fallen asleep (v. 15) or vice versa, they all share together as one group in what happens. Evidently Paul thinks of the dead as being resurrected out of their graves to join the living, and then they are **all caught up in the clouds to meet the Lord in the air**. These last words probably constitute the final part of the word of the Lord which Paul is paraphrasing, but it is also possible that they represent a deduction by Paul from the fact that the Lord is said to come on the clouds rather than down to the earth itself. The thought of being caught up and transported through the air is found in Acts 8:39, and that of being caught up to heaven in 2 C. 12:2, 4; Rev. 12:5. This, however, is the only place where a 'rapture' of God's people is associated with the parousia. The nearest parallel to the idea is the taking up of Enoch to be with God (Gen. 5:24 and Wis. 4:11, where the same Greek word is used as here). **in the clouds**, literally 'in clouds', appears to refer to the mode of transport rather than to the destination; the phrase comes from Dan. 7:13, where it is used of the coming of the Son of man (cf. Mk 13:26; 14:62; Rev. 1:7; Ac. 1 ; 9). Believers use the same symbolical means of transport as the Son of man.

The destination is **in the air**, the space between earth and heaven.

It is here that his people go **to meet the Lord**. Although this rests on a common *OT* phrase, the Greek word used here probably carries an allusion to the way in which a visiting dignitary might be met on the way to a city by a representative group of citizens who would then escort him back to the city. We may compare how Paul was met by the Roman Christians some miles from the city (Ac. 28:15, where the same phrase is used). A further occurrence of the same idea in the context of the parousia is to be found in Mt. 25:6. If this is a correct interpretation, then we may well take the further step of deducing that the Lord's people go to meet him in order to escort him back to the earth and that this is where they shall always **be with the Lord**. It is improbable that this permanent union takes place in the air or in heaven (4:14 note).

What matters, however, is not the place of meeting, in which Paul is not interested, but the fact of being **with the Lord**. It has been observed that whenever Paul speaks about future existence with the Lord he uses the less common Greek preposition *syn* instead of the more common synonym *meta* (5:10; 2 Th. 2:1; 2 C. 5:8; Phil. 1:23; Col. 3:4). Best notes that the same preposition is used by Paul in a series of compound verbs referring to dying and living with Christ in this life (Rom. 6:3–11; 8:17; Gal. 2:20; Col. 2:12–3:4) and draws the correct conclusion that the two types of expression are linked; dying and rising with Christ leads to the fullness of life with him at the parousia, so that the future life with Christ is the consummation of a relationship which has already begun. Moreover, this relationship is one which involves Christ and his people as a whole and is not simply between Christ and the individual Christian. It follows that the parousia leads to the reunion of dead and living Christians in the one people of the Lord.

18. The consequence which follows is that the Thessalonians have indeed no need to sorrow about those who have already died. Rather they can **comfort one another with these words**. Here the word translated **comfort** has the sense of consolation (contrast 4:1) and encouragement (5:11 note). The consolation given by Paul through the word (here **words**) of the Lord is to be passed on by the Thessalonians to one another. They can rest on the firm assurance provided by an appeal to the authority of the Lord himself.

5:1 Verse 18 brought Paul's discussion of the fate of those who had fallen asleep to a clear conclusion. The opening phraseology of this verse (cf. the use of **brethren**) is equally clearly the introduction of a new topic, which is, however, directly related to what has just preceded and is a further aspect of the general problem raised by the parousia. Paul's wording strongly suggests that he is taking up a further question which the Thessalonians had asked him to answer. It is expressed in rather general terms as a concern **about the times and seasons**. Although some commentators attempt to distinguish the meanings of these two words, taking the former in the sense of chronological periods and the latter in the sense of significant moments (so Morris, pp. 149f.), it was recognised rightly by von Dobschütz, p. 204, that the two terms are synonyms and that Paul is writing pleonastically under the influence of *OT* usage (Est. 10:3; Dan. 2:21; 7:12; Wis. 8:8; cf. Mk 13:32; Acts 1:7) which loves such redundancy. What is meant is clearly the timing of the parousia: when is it going to take place?

Behind the question we can probably detect (with Frame, p. 178) a concern about their own participation in the meeting with the Lord: since they did not know when it was to happen, how could they be sure to be prepared and ready for it, so that they would not be left out of it? The question was thus not one that arose out of uncertainty or a fear that nothing was going to happen (perhaps because the period of waiting seemed unduly long and was giving rise to the fear that the parousia was an empty delusion), but rather out of an exaggerated worry that perhaps they might be morally and spiritually unworthy to be summoned to meet the Lord. Hence arose their anxiety to know when it would happen so that they could adequately prepare themselves. It may be that they wished to know if there were any signs which would give advance warning that the parousia was about to happen. But Paul refuses to give them any information. He tells them that they **have no need to have anything written to** them (for the wording cf. 4:9). Indeed, as will shortly appear, there is nothing that can be written to answer their question.

2. Paul has no need to expound the theme because he has already given the Thessalonians oral instruction on the matter and so he could say that they themselves **know well** all that can be said about it. The word **well** is found only here and in Eph. 5:15 in Paul's writings, and Findlay (cited by Frame, p. 180) conjectured that Paul perhaps took it from the Thessalonians' question: 'Tell us *precisely* when the parousia is going to happen.' The word means 'accurately' or 'in detail'. It is worth observing that many people today crave detailed information about both the time and the course of the last events, and there are writers who are prepared to answer the question in minute detail and with not a little imagination. Some advocates of 'dispensational' teaching about the second coming of Jesus are particularly prone to offering exhaustive and elaborate timetables of future events. Not so Paul. When he was asked for detailed information, he had nothing more to say than he says in this passage. Christian teachers today would do well to follow his example and so avoid 'going beyond what is written' (1 C. 4:6, literal rendering).

All that Paul does, therefore, is to remind his readers that they know **that the day of the Lord will come like a thief in the night. the day of the Lord** is an *OT* phrase which, whatever its origins, had come to be used to signify that future date on which God would act in power to establish his will (Burkeen, pp. 209–22). It is above all the day of his judgment (Am. 5:18–20; Isa. 13:6–16; Jl 1:15); but it also brings salvation (Ob. 15–21; Zech. 14). It was taken over in *NT* use to refer broadly to the time of the End (Rev. 16:14), which can be simply called 'that day' (Lk. 10:12; 2 Th. 1:10). Jesus altered the phrase by speaking of the day of the Son of man (Lk. 17:24,30; the plural 'days' is also used in this context), which Matthew understands as the parousia (Mt. 24:27,37,39). The early church naturally understood the 'Lord' in the *OT* phrase to be Jesus. Sometimes the phrase was altered accordingly (1 C. 1:8; 2 C. 1:14; Phil. 1:6,10; 2:16); at other times, as here, 'Lord' clearly means Jesus (2 Th. 2:2; 1 C. 5:5). The arrival of the day will be like the arrival of a burglar (Harnisch, pp. 84–116). Ancient burglars, like modern ones, operated under the cover of darkness. The comparison used here goes back to the Gospels. In Lk. 12:39f. par. Mt. 24:43 we have the little parable: 'But know this, that if the householder had known at what hour the thief was coming, he would have been awake and would not have left his house to be broken into. You also must be ready; for the Son of man is coming at an hour you do not expect.' The parable provides the source of the metaphor used here and also of the simile in 2 Pet. 3:10; Rev. 3:3; 16:15.

The point of comparison is twofold. First, it expresses the unexpectedness of the event. The burglar comes when he is not expected and takes the household by surprise. Second, we should probably also see an element of unwelcomeness. Paul is looking at the matter from the point of view of those who will find that the day is one of judgment, and therefore he says that it will be as sudden and unwelcome as the visit of a burglar. The presence of this negative element, which is perhaps not what might have been expected in a positive admonition (cf. v. 4), indicates that Paul is taking over an existing figure of speech. The other echoes of the apocalyptic teaching in the Gospels confirm the case that Paul is here dependent on the Gospel tradition (D. Wenham, cited at 4:15 note, p. 347), and indeed there is every reason to believe that the tradition here contains an authentic saying of Jesus (*pace* Harnish, ibid.). And this is all the information that Paul has about the time of the parousia; he can only say that it will come at an unpredictable time. While Paul certainly envisaged that it could happen within the lifetime of his readers and perhaps indeed within a very short time, he did not delimit the time of its arrival within a definite period but left it quite open as to when it would happen, as A. L. Moore has rightly emphasised (Moore, p. 73; id., *The Parousia in the New Testament*, Leiden, 1966).

3. The introduction of this somewhat negative metaphor to indicate the unexpectedness of the day of the Lord leads Paul to develop the thought slightly further in the same direction before turning to positive encouragement in v. 4. He thus first of all fills out the picture slightly, and in so doing introduces a shift in the metaphorical comparison. Coming back from the metaphorical picture to the real world, he paints a picture of people at large saying **'There is peace and security'**. The wording echoes such *OT* passages as Jer. 6:14; 8:11; Ezk. 13:10 and Mic. 3:5, which speak of the activity of false prophets who assured the people that they had nothing to fear despite the moral rot which characterised society. Here in Paul, however, the thought may be more of the sinful world which comforts itself by thinking that nothing can happen to it (cf. 2 Pet. 3:3f.). It will be just when this is being said that **sudden destruction will come upon them**. The wording here (except for the addition of **destruction**, which is a familiar term for the ultimate fate of sinners, 2 Th. 1:9; 1 C. 5:5; 1 Tim. 6:9) is parallel to that of Lk. 21:34, where it comes at the end of Luke's version of the Marcan apocalyptic discourse and in the context of an exhortation to watchfulness. It again seems very likely that Paul is dependent on the Gospel tradition. (It has been argued that Lk. 21:34–36 is a late, Hellenistic passage, possibly even composed by Luke himself, but it seems much more likely that it is a pre-Lucan tradition. Best, p. 207, suggests that Luke may have composed the passage on the basis of Isa. 24:17 and the Pauline tradition; if by the 'Pauline tradition' he means a gospel tradition known to Paul and also to Luke, this would amount to the same as our own view.)

It has been argued by Best, p. 207, that **When people say** is iterative and means 'as often as people say', so that Paul has taken a general, perhaps proverbial statement and reapplied it to the parousia. But the Greek word used here (*hotan*) need not have this general sense (even with a present subjunctive; see, for example, Mk 13:4; Jn 7:27,31; and contrariwise Mk 14:25; Lk. 12:54). The unexpectedness of the parousia is emphasised by Paul's second comparison, **as travail comes upon a woman with child**. This is a common biblical metaphor (Ps. 48:6; Isa. 13:8; 26:17f.; Jer. 6:24; 22:23; Mic. 4:9; cf. 1 En. 62:4; Harnisch, pp. 62–77), used to express the sheer pain and agony of unpleasant experiences. It is probably this sense which is uppermost in Mk 13:8 where the metaphor is applied to the catastrophic events which will precede the parousia. The unpleasantness of judgment is present in the use of the metaphor here, but the emphasis is much more upon the way in which the birth pangs come upon the expectant mother more or less without warning, and, as Paul's final comment makes clear, as something that is inevitable: **there will be no escape**. Here again there may be an echo of Luke's version of the teaching of Jesus (Lk. 21:36). The point of the verse, then, is to emphasise the inevitability and inescapability of this unexpected judgment. To those who are unprepared the day of the Lord will have the character of certain judgment.

4. What Paul has said about the day of the Lord was drawn from a saying of Jesus which expressed both its unexpectedness and its character of inescapable judgment. But Paul is writing not to un-believers but to his Christian friends, and therefore what he has said needs some qualification. So he draws a contrast with **But you** between his readers and the rest of mankind, the unbelievers (not Gnostics, *pace* Harnisch, pp. 77–82) whom he has vaguely charac-terised in v. 3 as 'people' (Greek, literally 'they'). He reminds them of their Christian status by addressing them as **brethren**, and takes up the metaphor of the burglar and extends it by commenting that for them the present time is not one of **darkness**, the time when burglars come and take people unawares.

Although the extension of the metaphor is obvious enough, the reason for Paul's development of thought lies not so much in the metaphor itself as in the happy way in which it could be merged with another important piece of Christian imagery, that of day and night, which is developed in the next verse. In early Christian literature the association of light with divine revelation, righteous-ness and salvation and of darkness with ignorance of God, sinfulness and judgment is very common. It is a very natural metaphor, and it has its antecedents in the *OT* and Judaism (see, for example, Ps. 27:1; 112:4; Prov. 4:18f.; Isa. 9:2; 5:20; 1QS 3:13–4:26). God's revelation is associated with light (Lk. 2:32; Jn 1:4–9; 8:12; 1 Jn 2:8). Righteous behaviour is naturally linked with light (Mt. 5:14–16; Rom. 13:12; 2 C. 6:14), and so God's people can be called 'sons of light' (v. 5; Lk. 16:8; Eph. 5:8). They live in the light of divine revelation and do what is pleasing to God. Thus they no longer live in the darkness of sin which leads to ignorance of God and his ways (Col. 1:12f.). When the day of the Lord comes, therefore, it should not come as a dreadful surprise to them, as it will to those who live in darkness. It will not have the character of a thief but of a friend. (The Greek text is uncertain here. *RSV* rightly follows the large group of MSS which have **like a thief** [nominative]; a few important authorities have 'like thieves' [accusative] which compares the readers to thieves caught red-handed by the dawn, but this extension and allegorisation of the metaphor is unlikely to be original.) It is then, the character of the day of the Lord as judgment which Paul qualifies decisively for his readers: for them it should mean salvation. But the unexpectedness and unpredictability remain unaffected, since otherwise Paul would not have introduced the metaphor only to withdraw it completely. Unpredictable events have different effects on those who are unprepared for them and those who are ready for them. Paul wants to assure his readers that they are ready for the parousia, whenever it may happen.

5. So Paul continues by spelling out more fully the theological motif which was already in his mind when he used the word 'darkness' in v. 4. **For you are all**, he writes, **sons of light and sons of the day; we**, i.e. we who are Christians, writer and readers alike, **are not of the night or of darkness**. The use of **all** is common in Paul (1:2; 2 Th. 1:3; Rom. 1:8; Gal. 3:26,28; Phil. 1:4), but this does not mean that it has no force here (*pace* Best, p. 210). Paul uses it to assure his readers that each one of them who believes in Jesus is a son of the light (Frame, p. 184). This is a Semitic type of construction, and indeed the actual phrase is found in the Dead Sea Scrolls (1QS 1:9f.; 1QM 1:1). It signifies people who have a particular quality or belong to a particular sphere, here probably the latter: the force is that the readers belong to the sphere of righteousness and salvation (Eph. 5:8; cf. Lk. 16:8).

Paul extends the thought by describing them as **sons of the day**. The **day** in question is the day of the Lord, but the association of 'day' with light lies behind his thinking. The day of the Lord brings salvation to those who are in the darkness, just as the dawn takes away the darkness of night (Rom. 13:11f.). Here, however, Paul emphasises that the readers are not in darkness. They are not only destined for the Age to come, the age of light, but they already share in that Age and live in the light of the gospel. Here we have that mixture of future expectation and present experience which is characteristic of the Christian life. God's salvation is still to come in all its fullness and replace the present age of sin; but already it has come and God's people can enjoy its benefits through faith. The Age to come overlaps the present evil age for the believer. The Christ who will come has already come.

6. What began as the answer to a question slides over into exhortation. The question regarding the time of the parousia cannot be answered by the provision of information; what matters is readiness for an event that may happen at any time. Although Paul has

assured his readers that as children of light they are in a state of
readiness for the parousia whenever it may happen, nevertheless he
finds it necessary to urge them to 'be what they are'. **So then** is his
formula for introducing the inescapable moral consequence of a
piece of teaching (2 Th. 2:15; Gal. 6:10) or for drawing a logical
conclusion. Those who are sons of the day must obviously not fall
into the state of **sleep** which is appropriate at night-time and is
characteristic of **others**, i.e. those who are sons of the night. It is
obvious that here **sleep** is being used in a different sense from 4:13–
15 where it referred to physical death. Here the reference is to a
moral sleep (cf. Eph. 5:18), the state where a person is spiritually
unconscious and insensitive to the call of God. If the day has already
dawned, sleep is inappropriate. Christians are those for whom the
new day has already come, and they must not fall back into the state
out of which they were awakened. On the contrary they must **keep
awake** (Mt. 25:13; Mk 13:35; 1 Pet. 5:8), a phrase which is used of
spiritual alertness and watchfulness. The picture is perhaps that of
the watchman who must keep awake in order not to miss the coming
of the enemy. Christian wakefulness includes being ready for the
parousia whenever it may happen, so that it does not catch the
believer unawares, living the kind of life which would disqualify
him from sharing in the final revelation of salvation.

Paul adds that the Christian must also **be sober** (v. 8; 1 C. 15:34;
2 Tim. 4:5; 1 Pet. 1:13; 4:7; 5:8). The verb literally refers to the
opposite of being drunk, a state which some commentators regard
as one of undue elation and hence lack of self-control, while others
take it of stupor and unconsciousness. Either way, the drunk person
has lost control of his faculties and is out of touch with reality. It
stands to reason that Paul would have regarded literal sobriety as an
essential aspect of the Christian life (Rom. 13:13f.; cf. 1 Pet. 4:3f.),
but probably this idea is contained within the more general one of
a spiritual sobriety which avoids any kind of excess that would stifle
sensitivity to God's revelation and purpose.

7. The admonition is reinforced by the reminder, taken from
observation of ordinary life, that sleep and drunkenness are both
associated with the **night** and not the day; they are states which
belong to the situation from which Christians have already been
delivered. Paul is drawing on the observation that, in normal circumstances, one sleeps during the hours of darkness, and also that
drunkenness tends to be associated with night-time (drunkenness
during the day is regarded as even more reprehensible than drunkenness during the night; Isa. 5:11; Ac. 2:15; 2 Pet. 2:13; pagan
examples in von Dobschütz, p. 209 n. 5). The two words are used
here in their literal sense as a basis for the metaphorical application

in the previous verse. Since, however, Paul is using the information metaphorically, we should not press it too far, for example, by arguing that sleep is a good and necessary activity for mankind during night-time. This thought is not in Paul's mind, and he is thinking simply of night as the spiritual antithesis of the coming of the light symbolised by day.

8. Having given a basis for the exhortation in v. 6, Paul goes on partly to repeat the exhortation before adding a fresh, related thought. It is because Christians **belong to the day** (cf. v. 5) that it is appropriate for them to **be sober**. The new thought is that spiritually they are like soldiers who must wear the appropriate armour for the battle in which they are engaged. Best, p. 213, thinks that Paul is using **sober** in the sense of 'vigilant' (one might have expected Paul to repeat the word 'awake'), and he adopts the view that Paul's thought moved from the thought of vigilance to that of being on sentry-duty and so to that of the armour worn by the soldier on duty. It is interesting that the same association of putting on the appropriate clothing with spiritual wakefulness is found in Rom. 13:11–14. This suggested train of thought seems quite plausible. The metaphors of putting on clothing and of military service are not uncommon in Paul. For the former, see Gal. 3:27; Eph. 4:24; Col. 3:10, 12; the first of these passages is associated with conversion and baptism as the event in which the person 'puts on' Jesus (cf. Rom. 13:14), and the same association may be present in the other passages. For the latter metaphor, see Rom. 6:13; 7:23; 1 C. 9:7; 1 Tim. 1:18; 2 Tim. 2:3f.; 4:7. The two metaphors come together in the concept of the Christian's armour (Rom. 13:12f.; 2 C. 6:7; 10:4; Eph. 6:13–17). Behind the *NT* use lies Isa. 59:17 (which is also developed in Wis. 5:17–20). The *OT* passage speaks of God's armour, but it was an easy step to apply it to a man's.

The verb **put on** (aorist participle in Greek) is generally taken to refer to an act coincident with the adoption of a sober attitude. One might take it to refer back to the putting on of spiritual armour at conversion (cf. Gal. 3:27); but Rom. 13:12, 14 offers strong support for the former interpretation. It is common for the *NT* to urge believers to do what they have already started to do at conversion or to be what they have already become. Isa. 59:17 speaks of righteousness as a breastplate and a helmet of salvation. Paul alters the picture by associating **the breastplate** with **faith and love** and the **helmet** with **the hope of salvation**. He is not quoting the *OT* passage but making a flexible use of its language, and in so doing he brings in the Christian triad of faith, love and hope (1:3). No intrinsic reason for associating the particular virtues mentioned with

the two items of armour can be detected, any more than in Eph.
6:13–17, and one should not attempt to produce artificial links. **faith
and love** are the essential qualities which the Christian must show
in relation to God and men, and the **hope of** final **salvation** is the
assurance that enables him to persevere despite every difficulty.

The wording makes the **hope of salvation** the climax of the
thought. It is interesting that the thought of battle is not present;
elsewhere it is clearly expressed, but here it is merely implicit. It
looks as though Paul has been led on to mention a motif which was
associated with spiritual wakefulness in Christian tradition, but since
it went beyond his immediate purpose to develop the latent thought
he made no attempt to do so. The point which was uppermost in
his mind was that Christians have the hope of salvation to encourage
them in watchfulness, and so he now proceeds to develop this idea
briefly.

9. Paul assumes that the Christian is entitled to wear the helmet
which is the hope of salvation because (*RSV*, **For**), as he now goes
on to explain, **God has destined us . . . to obtain salvation.** The
hope which should sustain the Thessalonian Christians and which
they should therefore joyfully appropriate depends ultimately on the
action of God in destining them to be saved. Already in 1:4 he had
reminded them of God's election of them, and in 3:3 he referred to
the way in which their experience of affliction was part of the destiny
which was appointed for them within the plan of God. Now he
emphasises again that their destiny depends on the fact that God
has a purpose for them. Negatively, this consists in deliverance from
the fear of God's **wrath** (1:10), the experience of his reaction to sin
at the last judgment.

Positively, it is to **obtain salvation.** The verb **obtain** translates a
Greek noun-phrase 'for the possession of', which should be understood actively to mean 'for the acquiring of salvation'. More commonly the word means 'possession' or the thing possessed (Eph.
1:14; 1 Pet. 2:9), but this sense is inappropriate here. Paul does not
simply say 'God has destined us for salvation', because he wants to
bring out the need for Christians to play their part in receiving
salvation. One might say that God's plan is that the readers should
do what is necessary to acquire salvation. Yet this emphasis on the
process of being saved does not prevent Paul from encouraging the
readers to do what is necessary by being watchful and sober. He
does not suggest that God's plan is fulfilled independently of the
action of man. There is paradox here as we try to relate the plan of
God to the action of man, and it is a paradox which is incapable of
resolution, for example, by arguing that God's plan is carried
through independently of man, or that man acts like an automaton

in believing and persevering because God has willed that he must do so. Rather, Paul speaks of God's plan when he is addressing Christians to assure them that their salvation depends upon God and not on any merit of their own, and to encourage them to persevere because of God's intention for them is salvation. Paul's exhortations to vigilance would be nonsensical if vigilance was the product of some inward causation in the believer by God or if there was no possibility of disobeying the exhortation.

Furthermore, Paul does not suggest that the appointing of certain people to salvation means that others are appointed to wrath (not even in Rom. 9:22f., *pace* von Dobschütz, p. 212). A predestination to wrath that operated independently of the responsible action of mankind in sinning and rejecting the gospel is as unthinkable as a predestination to salvation that overrules human responsibility or makes it ultimately of no account by operating through it. The fact that God has appointed the Thessalonian Christians to obtain final salvation (the future state of salvation as opposed to condemnation at the last judgment is meant, Rom. 13:11; Phil. 1:28; cf. Rom. 5:9f.) is the basis for their living in confident hope that will not be disappointed. The obtaining of salvation takes place **through our Lord Jesus Christ**; it rests on what he has done, and not on anything that we may do. From start to finish salvation depends on God's act in Jesus.

10. This action is explained by the descriptive phrase which Paul uses of Jesus as the one **who died for us** (cf. Rom. 14:9). The reason why believers may look forward to salvation and not to wrath lies in the person of Jesus who died for them. The implication is inescapable that through the death of Jesus something happened which transformed the destiny of believers. Had Jesus not died, they would have been destined for wrath. Paul does not explain how this change has taken place, beyond stating that Jesus died for them. The Greek MSS here vary between *hyper* and *peri*, but these prepositions were virtually synonymous in Hellenistic Greek and convey the thought of an action done with reference to somebody; the death of Jesus took place with reference to us, a phrase which can only mean that it accomplished something for us or was done for our benefit. Its effect was to deliver us from the divine wrath. Paul is not concerned here with the way in which this happened, but rather with the hope that results from a knowledge that Jesus **dies for us**.

To unfold the theology of the cross which is latent here, we have to turn to other passages, such as Rom. 3:24–26 and 2 C. 5:19–21, which makes it clear that Jesus' death had the force of an atoning sacrifice for sin and that in dying he became at one with us in our sinfulness in order that we might be at one with him in his righteousness. Paul's thought in the present passage is that Jesus **died** *for us* in order that **we might live with him**, and this suggests that an interchange takes place: Jesus shares our death (and indeed takes it over from us) so that we might share his risen life. (This verse can thus be cited as evidence for M. D. Hooker's thesis of 'Interchange in Christ', *JTS* 22, 1971, pp. 349–61.) The content of future salvation is life with Jesus (cf. 4:14, 17). Best, p. 219, argues that sharing future life with Jesus implies 'some kind of unity between Christ and believers so that his actions (e.g. death, renewal of life) are reproduced in their lives'. The theology expressed in Rom. 6; 2 C. 4–5 and Gal. 2:20 is thus implicit in the present verse; but Paul does not develop it here since his primary aim is to emphasise the certainty of future life with Jesus which arises out of his death for believers.

Paul also says nothing here about the resurrection of Jesus (he has already brought out its importance in 1:10; 4:14); but it is plainly presupposed in the reference to Christians living with him. It implicitly forms the foundation for his comment that the hope of life with Christ is for all believers **whether** they **wake or sleep**. Here Paul reverts to the problem discussed in 4:13–18 and makes his final comment on it. It is obvious that **wake** and **sleep** are used here in the same sense as in 4:13 where sleep means death, and not in the metaphorical sense of spiritual life and death which is found in the intervening passage 5:6f. (*pace* Thomas, p. 286). If there is to be life with Christ for those who sleep, their resurrection is presupposed, just as Jesus himself died and rose from the dead (4:14).

11. The section thus concludes on a note of strong confidence. While Paul has warned of the need to live as sons of light, to be sober and watchful, his predominant thought has been of the certainty that his converts will in fact be watchful and will not be taken unawares by the parousia; they can look forward with confidence to life wth Christ. **Therefore**, they can **encourage one another**. The wording of the first part of the verse repeats that of 4:18, although this is disguised in the *RSV* translation which translates the same Greek word by 'comfort' and 'encourage'. The *RSV* translators doubtless thought that the 'encouragement' had a more pronounced nuance of comforting mourners in 4:18, but the basic sense in both verses is the same one of strengthening faith so that believers will not succumb to temptation to lose heart or slip into spiritual carelessness.

This purpose finds further expression in Paul's command to the readers to **build one another up**. This is the first occurrence of a key-concept in Paul's view of the church. Building up is a metaphor for producing spiritual growth and stability, and is associated with the picture of the church as a building. (1 C. 8:1; 10:23; 14:3–5, 12, 17, 26; Eph. 4:12, 16, 29; cf. Rom. 15:20; 1 C. 3:9; 2 C. 10:8; 12:19; 13:10; Eph. 2:21; 1 Pet. 2:5, 7). Here Paul thinks of individual believers being built up, and so the church is built up and becomes more and more what it ought to be. What the present passage makes clear (and this is confirmed by the rest of Paul's teaching) is that he envisages an activity in which the members of the church each **build one another up** or they are built up by an apostle, such as Paul himself. A believer does not build himself up, but is built up by the encouragement of other believers. This may be an accident of word-usage, but it demonstrates how much the well-being of the church depends on the growth of mutual love. The growth of the church depends on the contribution of each of the members. Paul was thankful that the church was already **doing** this, and his instruction was merely that they should so all the more. Best points out that the rest of the letter, with its instructions about life in the church community, can be regarded as an elaboration of the command in this verse.

The church today has largely lost the sense of the nearness and unpredictability of the parousia, although belief in the resurrection of the dead has gained a firm place in the Christian creed. Our problem today is not a failure to understand how the dead can share in the blessings associated with the parousia or a fear that we may be taken unawares by the parousia, but rather we have no place in our thinking for the parousia alongside our conception of death as the gateway to eternal life for the Christian.

What, then, has the present passage to say to the Christian church today? First, despite what has just been said, the reality of the resurrection of the dead can still be a matter of doubt to Christians and non-believers. It is one thing to recite a creed; it is another thing to affirm a belief in the presence of a coffin and incipient physical decay. There will always be a place for the reassertion of the resurrection of the dead on the basis of a word of the Lord.

Second, resurrection of the dead can easily become a belief akin to the immortality of the soul, a mere *form* of future expectation with no clear Christian content. What makes the Christian hope *Christian* is not that it is belief in the resurrection of the dead but that it is resurrection to new life with Jesus. Paul's teaching in the present passage brings out the way in which the Christian hope centres on being with Jesus, and it is noteworthy that what grieved the Thessalonian Christians was precisely the fear that their loved ones would miss the joys of the parousia of *Jesus*. We need to be sure that our resurrection hopes are not concerned merely with our own reunion with those whom we love but rather are centred on our common hope of union with Jesus.

Third, Paul's teaching about living in the light and being continually watchful must be properly appreciated. Best, p. 361, suggests that 'when eschatological sects have over-stressed watchfulness history has shown that other more essential virtues tend to be neglected'. This is no doubt true as a comment on sects which have spent their time *waiting* for the parousia and neglected other Christian duties in the false belief that Christian holiness is primarily a matter of individual piety. But our exposition has shown that what Paul means by watchfulness is not so much looking out for signs of the imminence of the parousia as rather living in a way appropriate to the new era which the coming of Christ has inaugurated. Watchfulness means being awake to the nature of the present age and doing one's Christian duty in it. Paul elucidates it in terms of the Christian virtues of faith, love and hope, and his whole point is that Christians do not need to look for signs of the imminence of the parousia since they will not be unprepared for it when it comes if they are living in the light. The Christian does not look anxiously for signs of the parousia; he gets on with the work that he has been given to do.

Fourth, there remains the basic question of whether we can share Paul's belief in the reality of a literal parousia of Jesus. Let it be admitted that the language is that of apocalyptic and therefore the details are not to be taken literally. Burkeen, pp. 448–92, has argued that what Paul says here in apocalyptic imagery he also says elsewhere with the minimum of imagery, and develops some ideas of K. Rahner in a helpful distinction between the apocalyptic imagery and the essential structure of Paul's thoughts and expectations. (K. Rahner, 'The Hermeneutics of Eschatological Assertions', in *Theological Investigations*, Baltimore/London, 1966, IV, pp. 323–346). Following this line we can affirm the reality of the parousia as an event which defies description other than in symbolism. Here the important point is that we do not demythologise the parousia into some timeless truth and see it merely as a way of speaking of Jesus as the ever-present eschatological event (R. Bultmann), but rather we affirm its nature as event in which the final triumph of Christ becomes a reality.

Even when viewed in this way, some may still want to reject this structure of thinking as part of a scheme which moves from a creation-event to a consummation-event and which cannot be reconciled with a scientific understanding of the universe. But the Christian understanding of the world is based on the conviction that in Jesus God came into the world and shattered the structures of natural causation by his incarnation and resurrection, events which both p rtake of the nature of history, in that they can be located in space and time and take their place in the nexus of physical and historical events, and also cannot be understood as purely historical since in them the transcendent God acts within the immanent historical process. This is sheer miracle, and as such it points to the way to understand the biblical language about creation and consummation as events which are historical and yet more than historical. It is thus possible, and indeed necessary, within the Christian framework of thinking centred on the incarnation and resurrection of Jesus, to affirm belief both in divine creation and also in divine consummation. The language of the parousia affirms that God acts through Jesus at the consummation (as in creation and redemption) and that consummation means the submission of the fallen world to its Lord, the final establishment of that Lordship which was proclaimed through the resurrection. Such a view of things may run counter to a scientific materialism which has no room for God, creation and consummation; but the Christian who believes in incarnation and resurrection has long since abandoned this closed view of the universe.

Fifth, it is worth observing that Paul's teaching underlines the importance of moral and spiritual preparedness for the parousia. There is a final Wrath from which people need to be saved, and there is the implication that those who are unprepared will miss out on final salvation. Paul's exhortations provide the doctrinal underpinning for practising the Christian virtues and show that these are of ultimate value and significance. Right and wrong matter in the end. Many people fight shy of this, adopting a relativistic view of morality and an ultimate universalism which claims that all mankind will finally be saved, no matter how they may have lived. Paul teaches the opposite in this passage, and it is fair to claim that this is the general thrust of his teaching, against which other passages that have sometimes been wrongly interpreted in favour of universalism should be understood. In any case, one is bound to say that, whatever one may hope or believe about the ultimate fate of mankind, nothing can be permitted to weaken the validity of the command to righteousness and goodness here and now.

So far, then, from this passage being timebound and no longer tenable in a Christian understanding of life, it has in fact a vital contribution to make to it.

INSTRUCTIONS FOR LIFE IN THE CHURCH

5:12-24

A new section clearly begins at 5:12. Paul has completed his specific instructions and exhortations about Christian ethics and the parousia, and now turns to a third area of general instruction and encouragement. The end of the section is placed by many commentators at v. 22. The final greetings in the letter commence at v. 25, and the problem is whether the prayer in vv. 23f. should be regarded as part of the general instructions, or as a section on its own, or as part of the concluding greetings. Since Paul can slide easily from one topic to another, a decision is not easy and perhaps we should simply recognise that there are no clear transitions or breaks at the end of the letter. However, in thought vv. 23f. would appear to go closely with what precedes, as Paul's prayer that God will enable the Thessalonians to fulfil his instructions, and therefore we adopt the view that the section concludes with v. 24. It is just possible that vv. 23f. contain a general prayer related to the whole of the contents of the letter and thus forming a concluding section; but this seems less likely.

The connection of thought within the section and its total purpose within the letter are matters of uncertainty. Best, p. 223, goes so far as to say that the section contains 'a series of largely unrelated exhortations'. He notes the parallels which exist between the instruction here and in Rom. 12, and argues that in both places Paul is dependent on a traditional pattern of instruction with a Jewish-Christian origin. The implication would appear to be that at least some of the teaching is not organically related to the Thessalonian situation but represents general Christian teaching that could be applied with little change to almost any first-century church.

Von Dobschütz, p. 215, argues that the section falls into five sections followed by the closing prayer: recognition of the leaders (vv. 12f.); spiritual counsel for the weaker members (v. 14); observance of the basic Christian principle (v. 15); the right basis for Christian living (vv. 16-18); the testing of unusual spiritual manifestations (vv. 19-22). This analysis is generally convincing. That the passage contains similarities to Romans 12 is also obvious:

I Th. 5	Rom. 12
12-13a Respect leaders	3-8 Don't think more highly of yourself than of other Christians with spiritual gifts.
13b Peace among yourselves	18 Peace with all men
14 Care for weak and unruly	(cf. Rom. 14:1 Receive the weak)

15 Not evil for evil	17a Not evil for evil
but good to one another and all men	but good to all men
16 Rejoice always	12a Rejoice in hope
17 Pray unceasingly	12c Continue in prayer
18 Give thanks	(cf. Eph. 5:20)
19 Don't quench the spirit	11b Fervent in Spirit
20 Don't despise prophecy	(6 Prophecy)
21a Test all things	
21b Hold fast to good	9b Cleave to good
22 Avoid evil	9b Hate evil

From this comparison (cf. Best, p. 241) the extent of the common material can be seen. The themes appear broadly in reverse order and the wording is quite free. A common basis in tradition exists, but Paul handles it quite freely, and it is arguable that he shaped the teaching to suit the needs of each individual community. This is particularly obvious in vv. 12–13a, 14, 19, 20, 21a, where the parallels with Romans are weakest. The situation is the very natural one of a pastor who knows that a number of specific topics are usually important in exhortation and has a rough general pattern of teaching in his mind, but who presents it in such a way that he adapts it to the particular situation which he has in mind. We may, therefore, claim that Paul's teaching here is related to the Thessalonian situation and can be used to throw light on it. A pattern of thought can also be traced in which Paul begins with specific problems of leadership in the church, moves on to general instruction about life in the church, and then returns to the question of charismatic gifts. It would indeed be improbable that Paul should write in general terms to a church of which he had particular knowledge and at the end of a letter which has throughout been directly and closely applied to their specific situation.

In view of Paul's general commendation of the Thessalonians elsewhere in the letter it would be wrong to find serious deficiencies in the life of the church reflected in this section. Nevertheless, in any church there will always be room for progress and improvement, and there will always be individual members who need special pastoral care.

12. We have already seen how **But** and **brethren** are markers used by Paul to introduce a new theme in the letter. **we beseech** has also appeared previously in 4:1 as a means of introducing an exhortation. Paul's request is for respect for those who work in the church. **to respect** is literally 'to know'; the verb is apparently used in the same way as *epiginōskō* in 1 C. 16:18 of knowing the worth of a

person and hence of showing them appropriate respect. (In 1 C. 16:18 the verb itself has this extended sense of showing respect. Here, however, the force may simply be 'to appreciate the worth of'; the consequent showing of respect is expressed in the verb 'to esteem' in v. 13.)

Those whose worth is to be recognised are described in a series of three coordinated verbs: **those who labour among you and are over you in the Lord and admonish you.** The Greek construction shows that these are three aspects of the work of the same group of people and not a list of three categories of people. They are the people who exercise leadership in the community, but Paul does not use any specific title here to refer to their office.

When Ac. 14:23 states that Paul appointed elders in the churches of Galatia, the meaning may be that he appointed leaders of the sort who later came to be known (by Luke and his readers) as elders. There is no mention of elders in Paul's writings (other than the Pastoral Epistles), but bishops are mentioned in Phil. 1:1, i.e. in a letter written only a few years later to a neighbouring church. Although most scholars think that by the time 1 Th. was written there was not yet an established form of organisation in the Pauline churches with leaders occupying the specific position of elders or bishops, it is possible that Paul refers to such people in this letter in terms of their function. The silence of 1 C., however, which does discuss a variety of spiritual gifts and functions rather tilts the balance in favour of the view that there was not yet an established nomenclature for spiritual leaders in the local churches. The most that can be said is that the persons who exercised leadership were appointed to do so, or their position was at least confirmed, by Paul himself. Von Dobschütz's claim (pp. 218f.) that there were no church 'offices' at this stage, but only voluntary and informal leadership, goes against the evidence (see E. E. Ellis, *Prophecy and Hermeneutic*, Tübingen/Grand Rapids, 1978, p. 7 n. 24).

First, the task of leadership is described in terms of **labour.** The corresponding noun has already been used in 1:3 of the hard toil which is the expression of love. Paul frequently uses this term for Christian ministry (1 C. 15:10; Gal. 4:11; Phil. 2:16; Col. 1:29; 1 Tim. 4:10) especially by travelling workers like himself, but he also uses it of work within the church by its members (1 C. 16:16; cf. Rom. 16:6, 12). He regarded such people as sharers in his own work (1 C. 16:16). The term is quite general and does not allow us to define the nature of the work. We must think of any aspect of leadership in the church and care for its members which demanded effort on the part of those who exercised it.

The meaning of the second phrase, **are over you,** is disputed.

The verb recurs in Rom. 12 :8 where it is preceded and followed by terms related to sharing one's material resources and showing mercy respectively. It is also found in I Tim. 3:4, 5, 12; 5:17 where it seems to refer to exercising authority, and in Tit. 3:8, 14 of applying oneself to good deeds. One view is that here in I Th. the word refers to the exercise of authority and direction, and this is supported by the usage in LXX and contemporary Greek. The other view is that it refers to the showing of concern and care, a meaning which is probable in Rom. 12:8 and possible in I Tim. It seems likely that the two meanings can be combined. Paul is here thinking of those whose task it is to care for and supervise the church and who consequently have a certain measure of jurisdiction over its members and its activities. This interpretation is strengthened by the addition of the phrase **in the Lord** which is more appropriate in an appeal to respect those who exercise authority than those who show care; broadly speaking, 'in the Lord' is a phrase used by Paul where the demands of Jesus as Lord are in view.

Further, the third phase, **those who . . . admonish you**, points in the same direction. This phrase is used of giving warning to those who are going astray or are in danger of doing so (v. 14; 2 Th. 3:15; Col. 1:28; 3:16; Ac. 20:31). The implication is that those who admonish have authority to do so. The three phrases taken together, then, describe the activities of those to whom the care of the church is committed, those who work for its good, who are responsible for its welfare and therefore direct its activity, and who have authority to speak a word of warning to members who are in need of it. Such authority is exercised 'in the Lord', within the context of a situation where Jesus is acknowledged as Lord and where this acknowledgment controls the behaviour of the members.

13. Paul's admonition continues with the exhortation that the Thessalonians are **to esteem** their leaders **very highly in love**. The verb (*hēgeomai*) can simply mean 'to consider, regard' (e.g. 2 C. 9:5); in which case it must be connected closely with the phrase **in love**; the whole phrase will then mean in effect 'to love'. It is an argument against this view that the verb and the qualifying phrase are separated from each other in the Greek. Further, the verb does not need to be qualified by a prepositional phrase in this way. It can be used on its own to mean 'to esteem' in the sense of having a high regard or showing honour. Those who are recognised as leaders must be given appropriate respect. Paul emphasises that such respect must be shown in full measure, **very highly**; it must not be grudging or partial. It finds its basis not in the persons of the leaders but rather in the **work** which they are doing.

In the New Testament church honour is not given to people

because of any qualities which they may possess due to birth or social status or natural gifts but only on the basis of the spiritual task to which they are called. The Christian leader is to be a servant and not to seek glory for himself, although he may have to require obedience to the authority which the Lord has given to him. Respect for the message and respect for the messenger cannot be easily separated. The warnings and admonishments given by the leaders are to be accepted and obeyed because they ultimately come from the Lord. Paul adds that such respect is to be shown **in love**. It does not spring from fear, from an unwilling submission to the power of their office but from love and gratitude for their service in the gospel (von Dobschütz, p. 218).

Finally, Paul adds **Be at peace among yourselves**. The reference is clearly to the avoidance of quarrelsomeness which leads to division and strife. The advice is paralleled in Mk 9:50; Rom. 12:18; 2 C. 13:11 and Heb. 12:14, and must have been a common piece of exhortation in the early church. The need for peacableness is taught in Rom. 14:17, 19; 1 C. 14:33; Eph. 4:3; 2 Tim. 2:22; Jas 3:18, with which we may link verses where Paul counsels believers to be of one mind (Rom. 12:16; 15:5; 2 C. 13:11; Phil. 2 :2; 4:2), and peacableness is regarded as a fruit of the Spirit (Gal. 5:22; cf. Rom. 14:17). The frequency with which this virtue is commended shows that it was a necessary injunction in the early churches; the danger of quarrelsomeness was so great then, as now, that it needed no special motive for a writer to include it in his exhortations. For this reason many commentators suggest that the injunction here need not reflect any specific situation in the Thessalonian church beyond the common need of Christians to be warned of the danger of division. If we adopt this view, the injunction may stand on its own and bears no specific relation to the preceding instruction. (Some MSS read 'Be at peace with them', sc. the church leaders. But the MS evidence favours the *RSV* text 'among yourselves', and the Greek construction, *en* with dative, also fits this reading better.)

However, it is noteworthy that Paul here speaks of peace within the church rather than with people in general, and that he gives similar advice in situations where there were divisions in the church (Rome; Corinth; Philippi). The fact that he makes a fresh start in v. 14 suggests that v. 13*b* goes closely with what precedes. It would, therefore, seem very probable that there was a real tendency, known to Paul, for some members of the church to disregard the direction given by the church leaders and to oppose them. Paul therefore issues a general directive, meant particularly for any such people who were out of step with the leadership, to respect the leaders and to avoid quarrelsomeness. Frame, p. 195, goes further and specifically identifies this group with those who were refusing to work (cf. 4:11f., which must be directed against some specific people who were living in idleness, and 2 Th. 3:6–13, which is even more concrete in its depiction of the situation). This suggestion is reasonable and should be accepted. But Frame's further speculation that the leaders had dealt tactlessly with the idlers and caused some bitter feeling goes beyond the evidence. Scepticism about the latter part of Frame's hypothesis should not lead to rejection of the former part.

14. In the immediately preceding verses Paul has spoken of the need of the community to respect its leaders. He now moves on to advise the community on how it ought to treat those with special spiritual problems and needs. The contrast expressed by **And** (literally, 'but', Greek *de*) and **brethren** is thus not between two different groups but between two different types of attitude that the same people must show to two different groups within the community. It is true that some commentators have thought that in v. 14 Paul specifically addresses the leaders who are referred to in vv. 12f. and tells them how they are to act towards the other members of the church for whom they are responsible (so Masson, p. 73). But the Greek word order shows that Paul is contrasting two exhortations (*parakaloumen de hymas*), not two groups of people (*hymas de parakaloumen*). The succeeding exhortations, which follow on without a break, are meant for the whole church. For Paul, the whole church was involved in mutual care and not just a group of leaders: 'Paul knows nothing of an inert mass, the congregation, on which the ministry operates' (Best, p. 223). Even when church leadership had assumed a more settled and precise form, Paul still insisted that the task of leaders was to prepare the church as a whole for the task of ministry (Eph. 4:11f.).

Three particular groups of people are singled out for special care. The first are the **idle**. The Greek word *ataktos*, found only here in the *NT* (but cognates are used in 2 Th. 3:6ff., 11), originally referred to people who failed to keep to their proper position, whether in the army or in civil life. Hence it meant 'disorderly', 'irresponsible', and this sense is adopted here by Rigaux, pp. 582f. (cf. C. Spicq, 'Les Thessaloniciens "inquiets" étaient-ils de paresseux?' *ST* 10, 1956, pp. 1–13; *id.*, *Notes de lexicographie néo-testamentaire*, Freiburg/Göttingen, 1978, I, pp. 157–9; G. Delling, *TDNT* VIII, pp. 47f.). Older commentators preferred the meaning 'idlers' or 'loafers' (Milligan, pp. 152–4; Frame, p. 197; cf. Best, pp. 229f.). The sense of loafing around when one ought to be working is attested in contemporary papyrus documents; it is required in 2 Th. 3:6–13, and it gives a good link with 4 : 11. In other words, the general context in the letters indicates that the specific type of disorderliness in mind here lay in a refusal to work and conform to the normal way of life of employees. Such people are to be admonished; the word is that used in v. 12 and this is one of the pieces of evidence which suggests that v. 14 is directed to the church leaders. However, while the duty of admonition will have rested especially on the leaders who could speak with particular authority, the lines between leaders and the rest of the congregation were very fluid, and any member of the church might feel that it was his spiritual duty to admonish a fellow-member.

The second group needing counsel are **the fainthearted**. The Greek word is found only here in the *NT* and means despondent or worried or sad. Its precise force remains uncertain, and it is broad enough to cover those who were lacking in strength to face up to persecution and those who were saddened or worried by the death of their relatives or friends. If the first group in Paul's mind is specifically the people addressed in 4:10–12, here he may particularly have in mind those whose problems are discussed in 4 :13–5:11. The obvious form of help for such people is encouragement, expressed by the same word as Paul used in 2:11 of his own pastoral care for the community.

Third, there are **the weak**. This word could refer to the physically ill; but nothing in the context supports such a reference. In 1 C. 8:9–11; 9:22; Rom. 14:1f. the word is used for Christians who were weak in faith and lacked the courage or spiritual insight to eat meat which might have been offered in sacrifice to an idol or which had not been slaughtered in the approved Jewish manner and so was unclean. While admitting that we have no evidence for such scruples about food and the observance of holy days at Thessalonica, Best, pp. 230f., suggests that these problems were likely to arise in any church and adopts this reference for the word here. A third possibility is that the word refers to moral weakness and has special reference to those tempted to sexual impurity (4:3–8; Frame, p. 198). Since Paul does use the word elsewhere to refer to the human weakness which is susceptible to temptation and sinfulness (Rom. 5:6) and finds it hard to do God's will (Rom. 4:19; 8:3, 26) or is overcome by difficult circumstances (1 C. 2:3; 2 C. 11:30; 12:5, 9f.), it seems probable that this general sense is in mind here. Paul will then be thinking of any who find that they are weak when assailed by hardship or temptation, and this may include those susceptible to sexual temptations, although it is doubtful whether they are primarily or principally in mind.

Paul counsels **help** for such people. Elsewhere in the *NT* this word is used of holding fast to something (sound teaching, Tit. 1:9), or of being closely attached to a person (Mt. 6:24 par. Lk. 16:13). Here the verb must mean to support and strengthen, and it refers in the most general way to providing support by standing alongside the weak and helping them to shoulder their burdens.

Finally, there is a fourth injunction, **be patient with them all**. This should probably be taken as part of the series of injunctions rather than as the commencement of a new section of exhortation. Whoever may be the object of warning or help, the persons giving it must show the kind of patience which puts up with people and their awkwardnesses and even opposition to the helper. The verb is one used of the showing of restraint towards people who deserve punishment. It refers to a quality of God himself (Rom. 2:4; 9:22; cf. Lk. 18:7; 1 Pet. 3:20; 2 Pet. 3:9), and is often commended as a Christian virtue (1 C. 13:4; 2 C. 6:6; Gal. 5:22; Eph. 4:2; Col. 1:11; 3:12; 2 Tim. 3:10). There are many people who resist all efforts to help them, or who show a lack of gratitude, or who keep falling back into the situations and attitudes from which they have been rescued. It needs patience to continue to help such people when repeated help seems of little use or is unwelcome.

15. In the previous verse Paul has been concerned with the responsibility of the members of the church to care for one another, and the final 'them all' refers to the Christian community (contrast Rom. 12:18, where the reference is probably to people at large). We now have a broadening out of the thought in the form of a general injunction which extends in scope beyond the community to all men. Frame, p. 200, understands the opening imperative **See that none of you. . . .** as a literal command to the readers as a whole (**See** is a plural imperative) to take care that none of their number breaks Paul's commandment: the whole community, he says, has a responsibility for the conduct of its individual members. But it seems likely that he is pressing the language too literally. Paul simply means 'Each of you must see to it that he does not. . .' What is opposed is the repayment of **evil for evil**, the attitude which responds to a wrong or an insult by retaliating in the same way. The command is thus a rejection of the principle that in human relationships one may take vengeance on wrongdoers by treating them in the same way.

Already in the *OT* vengeance had been limited to the exact equivalent, 'an eye for an eye and a tooth for a tooth' (Exod. 21:23–25; Lev. 24:17–21; Dt. 19:21), and this was intended as the limit. Later *OT* teaching was moving in the direction of forbidding retaliation (Prov. 20:22; cf. 25:21f.; cf. Sir. 28:1–7).

But Paul goes well beyond this with his positive command **always seek to do good**. In the context this can only mean that even when somebody does wrong to a Christian the latter must respond by doing good in return. Von Dobschütz, p. 221, claims that this goes beyond anything in Greek and Jewish ethics. It was the heart of Christian morality, and we find the sentiment repeated in Rom. 12:17, 19–21 and I Pet. 3:9 (cf. I C. 4:12f.; 6:7). Behind it lies the teaching of Jesus about refraining from taking vengeance and about loving one's enemies (Mt. 5:38–42; 43–48; Lk. 6:27–36; J. Piper, '*Love your Enemies*', Cambridge, 1979). It is related to the so-called 'Golden Rule', which in its negative form prohibits doing to others what you would not wish them to do to you, and in its positive form (the one used by Jesus) requires that we do to others what we would wish them to do to us, regardless of whether or not they actually do their part (Mt. 7:12; Lk. 6:31).

But it is not obvious that the Golden Rule is the source of Paul's principle here. Many people would be prepared to allow that if they hurt somebody else it is quite fair and just for the offended person to treat them in the same way, but it is not so common to find a person agreeing that if he suffers wrong he should repay the wrong-doer by doing good to him. It is unlikely, therefore, that Best, p. 233, is correct in arguing that Paul's teaching merely reflects the rejection of the *lex talionis* by Judaism. The force of Paul's statement is considerable with its **always** and **to all** which stretches to all occasions and to all people, not merely those within the church. The verb **seek** in no way weakens it, for its force is not that we should do something only if it is possible (and we can easily find excuses for saying that it is impossible), but rather that we must make it our definite goal to do good and strive to achieve it.

Since Paul is dealing with life in the church and immediately returns to other aspects of this topic in the ensuing verses, it seems likely that we should take the whole of this verse as being concerned primarily with this situation, but the use of the principle elsewhere suggests that usually it was applied to behaviour towards mankind generally and especially towards persecutors. Paul retains this broad reference, but without in any way limiting the thought he applies it especially to relationships within the church. The thought may well be that if we accept this principle with regard to people outside the church, we ought all the more to practise it in our relationships with other Christians. 'Charity begins at home' not in the sense that we put our duties at home before those to the outside world, but in the sense that it is shameful if we treat members of our family worse than we treat strangers.

16. The next section of the exhortation consists of three brief and pointed commands which are linked together by their common form and by the extended comment that follows the third one (v. 18*b*) and rounds off the series. They are quite general in content and describe three of the typical characteristics of the believer. Thus it is difficult to find any special motivation for them in the situation at Thessalonica. Rather, just as Paul writes at the beginning of the letter about the Christian virtues of faith, hope and love shown by the church, and thus refers to qualities that one would hope to find in any Christian church, so here he gives fairly standard Christian encouragement and exhortation simply because it is needed in any church. In the present letter the encouragement would certainly be appropriate in view of the problems faced by the church in its outward difficulties, aggravated as Paul felt them to be by his own absence, and also by the internal tensions which are reflected at various points.

Although the whole section is concerned primarily with instructions to the church as a church, the three commands here are directed to the individuals who compose the church and do not refer only to their communal gatherings. They describe basic Christian attitudes which will express themselves in the Christian life as a whole, and not simply in communal gatherings.

The first of these attitudes or activities is summed up as **Rejoice always**. This is a frequently expressed injunction (Rom. 12:12,15; 2 C. 6:10; Phil. 2:18; 3:1; 4:4; 1 Pet. 4:13), which is often associated with hardship and persecution: the Christian rejoices despite hardship and sometimes almost because of it, since he knows that the hardship will have positive and beneficial results (1 Pet. 4:13). The source of joy can lie in the hope of what God will do in the future (Mt. 5:12) but von Dobschütz, p. 223, is right to emphasise that it arises out of having found one's salvation in Jesus. It is right and proper that believers should be glad as a result of their Christian experience. One has heard criticism of Isaac Watts' hymn

Come, ye that love the Lord,
   And let your joys be known . . .
Let those refuse to sing
   That never knew our God;
But children of the heavenly King
   Must shout their joys abroad

on the grounds of its apparently exclusive attitude or suggestion of superiority. But the emotion is a legitimate one, just as it is appropriate for a couple to be joyful at their marriage. If our Christian experience does not lead to joy, we do well to ask whether it is genuine.

Paul's emphasis here, however, is not simply on joyfulness but on the possibility of rejoicing **always**. Christian joy is the normal attitude of the believer. This does not mean a superficial attitude to

life which refuses to take serious things seriously or which is fool-
ishly light-hearted: Paul can tell his readers to 'weep with those who
weep' and thus to show genuine sympathy (Rom. 12:15). Rather,
the believer's relationship with Christ and his experience of salvation
should give him a stable and deep-rooted joy which enables him to
cope with disappointments and see them in their true perspective.
Out of his joy of heart he is the better able to comfort other people.
In the present context the thought is doubtless that, no matter what
circumstances may get him down, the believer should be able to rise
above them. Such joy will be shown in the Christian community in
praise to God and fellowship with other believers. It is based in part
on the experience of answered prayer (cf. v. 17) and finds expression
in thankfulness (cf. v. 18).

17. The second basic activity of the believer is expressed in the
command **pray constantly**. Again this is a common injunction in
Paul's writings (v. 25; 2 Th. 3:1; Rom. 12:12; Eph. 6:18; Col. 4:2)
which corresponds with his own example and practice (1:2). Paul
speaks quite naturally of his own practice of praying constantly
(1:2f.; 2:13; Rom. 1:9) without suggesting that this was in any way
unusual. Rather, he was not confined to any set hours of prayer,
but could and did pray at any time. Christians may find that if they
do not observe set occasions of prayer, they may forget to pray at
any time. What Paul says does not imply that there are no set times
for prayer, but rather that the Christian should live in such communion with God that prayer, whether spoken or unspoken, is
always easy and natural. Since he goes on to speak about thanksgiving as a separate activity, he is probably thinking here more of
petition for oneself and intercession for others. Such prayer will be
a means of strength to believers facing difficulties of any kind, and
the Thessalonians would have no difficulty in applying this rather
general injunction to their own specific situation.

18. Paul's third command is **give thanks in all circumstances**.
Here again we have a common command (Eph. 5:20; Col. 3:17; cf.
Rom. 14:6; 1 C. 14:16; 2 C. 1:11; 4:15; 9:11f.; Eph. 5:4; Phil. 4:6;
Col. 2:7; 3:15; 4:2; 1 Tim. 2:1; 4:3f.) corresponding to Paul's own
example (1:2; 2:13; Rom. 1:8; 1 C. 1:4; *et al.*). Commentators differ
whether the underlying Greek phrase should be translated **in all
circumstances** or 'at all times' (Greek *en panti*). The parallelism
with vv. 16f. suggests the latter, but Pauline usage elsewhere supports *RSV*. But it is surely a pointless controversy, since either
translation is virtually equivalent to the other. Believers are to find
reason to praise and thank God in whatever situation they may find
themselves and thus at all times. This may seem reminiscent of the
attitude of Pollyanna in her 'Glad-game'—the art of feeling glad in

any situation, if not because it is positively enjoyable, at least because one can always think of something worse that might have happened instead ('I can be glad even if I have a broken leg because I might have had two broken legs'). However, Paul's attitude is different. On the one hand, the believer can always see (or should seek to believe) that even adversities can have a beneficial purpose (I Pet. 4:12f.; Rom. 8:28). On the other hand, he has access to a source of inward joy in his fellowship with Christ that cannot be disturbed by the most adverse of circumstances. Best, p. 236, rightly sums up: 'No matter what the circumstances (persecution, sickness, etc.) the Christian ought to be able to give thanks to God, not of course for the difficult circumstances but for his salvation through Christ, and when he is able to do this then he also is strengthened to endure what is difficult.'

Paul concludes his set of exhortations by stating that **this is the will of God in Christ Jesus** for the readers. The comment may mean that fulfilling these commands is what God requires of those who live a life in Christ (*GNB*) or that this is what God in Christ intends and makes possible for his people (*RSV*; *NEB*; see Ellingworth and Nida, pp. 121f.); probably the latter interpretation should be adopted (cf. Rigaux, 589). The statement is in effect repeated from 4:3 with the addition of the reference to Christ. It probably goes with all three commands rather than just the last of them, and it makes it clear that it is God's purpose and intention that Christians should live a life of joyfulness and thankfulness, expressed in prayer. The point is worth emphasising for sometimes believers suspect that God's will for them is simply a sanctification (4:3) which is self-denying and rather negative. Is not man's 'chief end' (in the words of the Shorter Catechism) 'to glorify God', a purpose which leaves no room for enjoyment of things for their own sake? The same catechism, however, adds that man's chief end is also 'to enjoy him for ever', and reminds us that in glorifying God we enter into a relationship which he intends to be a source of real joy to us. God intends that his people should be happy, even although his will for them may include hard and trying circumstances.

19. After these very general, universally applicable commands which have to do with the basic attitudes of believers, both individually and in the church, Paul gives a further set of commands which have to do specifically with the life of the church and are concerned with the place of the Spirit and his gifts. There are five statements in the imperative. The first two (vv. 19, 20) stand in parallelism with each other; the third (v. 21*a*) is in effect a repetition of the second, but expressed positively; the fourth and fifth (vv. 21*b*, 22) fill out the content of the third.

In analysing the structure in this way we are assuming that the reference throughout the section is to the same subject, the gifts of the Spirit, and rejecting the view that the last two commands are more general and ethical in content. The teaching here has no precise parallel in Rom. 12: the reference to being 'fervent in Spirit' in Rom. 12:11 is concerned with a different aspect of the ministry of the Spirit (his power to fill the believer with life and vigour). It does, however, overlap with what Paul says about the gifts of the Spirit in 1 C. 12, 14. Best, p. 237, argues that the content is probably traditional and that therefore it is not related to any specific problem in Thessalonica; had it been so, he argues, Paul would have developed the topic more fully. This conclusion would seem to require some modification. At the very least we may take it that Paul is dealing with a real problem in first-century churches, but the fact that he does not discuss it elsewhere, except in 1 C., suggests that he had a special reason for taking it up here. Where we may agree with Best is in his claim that the problem cannot have been too serious a one at Thessalonica.

Do not quench the Spirit is a command which takes up the metaphor of the Spirit as fire or the association of the Spirit with fire (Mt. 3:11 par. Lk. 3:16; Ac. 2:3; Rom. 12:12; 2 Tim. 1:6). While Rom. 12:12 and 2 Tim. 1:6 speak positively of being aglow with the Spirit or fanning the fire of the Spirit into flame, the negative form of the present command is noteworthy. The implication is that there was a tendency in the church to quench the fire of the Spirit. If so, this further implies that it was probably a reaction against what may have seemed to be an over-enthusiastic stress on the Spirit. From 1 C. 12, 14 we learn that communal church meetings included the manifestation of various charismata of the Spirit by different individuals, including the ability to prophesy and to speak in tongues. Both of these activities have been the object of much study, and we now have possibly a clearer idea of them than was formerly the case (see J. D. G. Dunn, *Baptism in the Holy Spirit*, London, 1970; id., *Jesus and the Spirit*, London, 1975; D. Hill, *New Testament Prophecy*, London, 1979).

It thus seems probable that what Paul is speaking about here is the exercise of the various charismata or spiritual gifts in the church, of which prophecy is the one particular example that he picks out, probably because it was the most important. Since the gifts were given for the benefit of the church, it would follow that where the church was hostile or indifferent towards them, their practice would indeed be quenched; those who could exercise the gift would be reticent to do so. But at this point the church needed the instruction given by the Spirit in this way. If we ask why the gift was being quenched, we can do little more than offer surmise, since we have no concrete information. It is just possible that the specific commands in vv. 16–18 were needed because the church was not sufficiently open to the inspiration of the Spirit (cf. Ac. 13:52; Rom. 14:17; Eph. 6:18; 1 C. 14:16 for the connection of joy, prayer and thanksgiving with the Spirit). The members of the church may have been too reserved and sober in outlook, and Paul wanted them to experience more of the joy of the Lord. They needed the power of the Spirit to build them up.

20. In particular, Paul laid emphasis on the importance of **prophesying**. This is not surprising in view of the way in which he ranks it in 1 C. 14:1 as the highest of the spiritual gifts which might be manifested in the local church. There Paul states that the prophet 'speaks to men for their upbuilding and encouragement and consolation'. It is interesting that the stress here is not on the presentation of revelation from God (although Paul does use this word for the prophet's message in 1 C. 14:26, 30), but rather on the spiritual effects of the message in helping the congregation. Although prophecy might well include the revelation of hidden mysteries, Paul seems to have been more concerned with the encouragement that comes from the Word of God. It was this kind of message which was in danger of being despised and regarded as of no account. Paul's negative command is in effect a positive exhortation to value and appreciate what the prophets say, and the implication is that some members of the congregation were sceptical of the value of such messages.

21. The reason for this may well have been that the prophetic messages were of varied value. In 1 C. 12 and 14 Paul had to deal more fully with spiritual gifts, and it is apparent there that he attached importance to the gift of spiritual discernment which enabled members of the congregation to distinguish true inspiration from false. As a limiting case Paul refers to the possibility that somebody speaking under inspiration might say 'Jesus is accursed'. Whether this actually happened or is merely an extreme imaginary example of what might happen, it is plain that strange things might be said under the guise of spiritual inspiration. Spiritual experiences of the kind known in the early church could easily be counterfeited. If a group of people speak in tongues, for example, the psychological pressure may easily induce other people to follow their example and acquire the ability without the need for any spiritual or supernatural explanation. Paul had, therefore, to insist on the need for doctrinal tests of what was said by prophets. The same guidance was given by John when he warned his readers against believing any person speaking under the inspiration of the Spirit and argued that the

uttering of heresy about the persons of Jesus was a sure sign of the lack of inspiration (1 Jn 4:1-3). It can very well be that at Thessalonica the variety and dubious quality of the utterances of some prophets were dragging the phenomenon into disrepute.

Paul therefore urges that his readers must **test everything**. In the context this must refer to exercising discrimination regarding the content of prophetic utterances. They must certainly assess what they hear and not let themselves be imposed upon. If they hear what is good, then they can hold fast to it, in the sense that they take the message to heart, believe it and act upon it. Thus they will profit by prophecy and be built up by it. How this discrimination is to be exercised Paul does not say. In 1 C. 12:10, however, he includes among the gifts of the Spirit 'the ability to distinguish between spirits'; he regards discrimination as itself an activity directed by the Spirit (cf. 1 C. 2:13-16). But he does not explain how it works; he merely requires that the members of the congregation must 'weigh' what the prophets say (1 C. 14:29). Presumably the standard was the accepted tradition of Christian teaching already passed on to the church.

22. But where prophetic teaching did not pass the test it was to be rejected. In language verbally reminiscent of Job 1:1, 8, Paul tells his readers to **abstain from every form of evil**. While **form** can mean outward appearance, it is more likely that it means 'kind' or 'type'. The command, taken on its own, could be interpreted as a general ethical injunction to refrain from every kind of evil practice. In its present context, however, a sudden transition to a general ethical principle is improbable, and the command must be taken to refer to rejection of every evil type of phenomenon allegedly inspired by the Spirit. (It must be admitted, however, that the verb *apechomai* might be expected to mean 'to abstain from doing something evil', as in 4:3, rather than 'to keep away from' or 'to have nothing to do with'; however, the verb can be used literally of being distant from [Mk. 7:6]. Frame, p. 208, translates 'hold yourselves aloof from'.) But the generality of the language may suggest that a broader principle has been applied to a more specific area, namely prophecy.

The relevance of Paul's teaching has been rediscovered in many areas of the Christian church in the second half of the twentieth-century with the development of the so-called 'charismatic' movement. In a number of churches and Christian groups of all denominations there has been a development of the type of phenomena described by Paul in 1 C. 12; 14. Unusual phenomena, including speaking in tongues, prophecy, and healing of the sick, have occurred and these have been attributed to the work of the Spirit. The very possibility of such things happening has been disallowed by

some writers who argue that they belonged to the early days of the
church and were not intended to be permanent in the church. So
far as prophecy is concerned, one can observe that it is linked with
apostleship by Paul and regarded as having foundational significance
in the church (Eph. 2:20; 3:5). Just as the apostles belonged to the
first-generation church and were not intended to have any successors, so it can be argued that prophecy was intended to help the
church only at its foundation, and that the provision of the written
Scriptures of the New Testament has made both apostles and
prophets unnecessary.

While this is a strong argument, two points somewhat mitigate
its force. First, regardless of whether or not charismatic phenomena
are considered theologically legitimate, the fact is that phenomena
which are *prima facie* charismatic do actually occur in the church
today, and need to be evaluated. Second, even those who deny most
strongly that the apostles and prophets were meant to have any
successors would still want to claim that in some sense the church
today must be apostolic and prophetic (cf. C. K. Barrett, *The Signs
of an Apostle*, London, 1970). Likewise, those who feel that unusual
charismatic phenomena do not take place (or should not take place)
still look for the power and guidance of the Spirit in less spectacular
ways.

Hence it follows that the church today still needs to discern the
true working of the Spirit among possibly counterfeit activities. The
charismatic revival has merely underlined the importance of Paul's
advice here. On the one hand, it has stressed the importance of
openness to the working of the Spirit, and the renewed vigour which
has come into the church shows that it is unhelpful for the church
to quench the Spirit. On the other hand, the need to be discerning
with regard to activities attributed to the Spirit is all the greater.
One may, for example, draw attention to the view that there is a
'baptism' with the Spirit, a second and deeper experience of the
Spirit than takes place at conversion, and that believers should seek
after this deeper experience, the essential characteristic of which is
the charisma of speaking in tongues. Such teaching must be tested
by Scripture, which, in this writer's opinion, knows nothing of a
'baptism' with the Spirit subsequent to the initial gift of the Spirit
at conversion or new birth, and which certainly does not regard
speaking in tongues as the essential characteristic of those baptised
with the Spirit.

23. Paul closes the main body of the letter with the expression of
a prayer for his readers and an assurance that God will fulfil it. As
indicated above, the prayer should probably be regarded as closing
the present section of the letter rather than as a separate section

linked to the letter as a whole. The theme is quite general and takes up Paul's earlier teaching about the sanctification of the readers. The prayer is expressed in the form of a wish, as in 3:11–13, which offers a close parallel in content. It is concerned with the activity of **the God of peace himself**. The emphatic **himself** is not set in contrast with what the Thessalonians themselves are to do (5:12–22) but simply stresses the personal relationship of God to the readers—it is God himself who will provide for their spiritual needs. Paul often speaks of **the God of peace** (here and elsewhere at the end of a section of teaching or exhortation, Rom. 15:33; 16:20; 2 C. 13:11; Phil. 4:9; cf. 2 Th. 3:16 and Eph. 6:23; see also 1 C. 14:33; Heb. 13:20). While he can think of **peace** as the opposite of strife and disorder (1 C. 14:33), here the thought is of peace as an all-encompassing term for salvation (1:1; Rom. 2:10; 8:6; 14:17; Eph. 6:15). Paul uses the phrase when he is thinking of God as the source of spiritual blessings for his people. The verb **sanctify** is used only here in the Epistle; elsewhere Paul uses it to refer to the character of believers as those who have already been sanctified (Rom. 15:16; 1 C. 1:2; 6:11; cf. Eph. 5:26). Here he is praying for the continuation and completion of the process. Just as Paul can refer to believers as saints or holy ones, despite their lack of actual holiness in conduct, so those who have been sanctified or set apart as God's people must increasingly show the appropriate characteristics in goodness and dedication to God's service, and Paul prays that God will work in the lives of his readers to this end. They will thus be 'entire' (*RSV* **wholly** translates what is an adjective in Greek) in the sense of totally conforming to God's purpose for them.

The second part of the verse makes clear that Paul prays for this process to be accomplished at the parousia. This raises two problems. First, Paul uses an aorist form of the verb as opposed to a continuous form: does this mean that he regards such 'entire sanctification' as a once-for-all action achieved by the agency of God? Second, does Paul regard such sanctification as something which the believer must show in order to be ready for the parousia or as something which will be brought about as a result of the parousia? We can answer the first question by comparing the wish in 3:12 which must refer to an increase in love as a gradual process but which is also expressed in the aorist form; here, too, therefore, Paul can have a process in mind, and this is confirmed by the teaching about an on-going work of God in the life of believers in Phil. 1:6, 9f. (cf. 1 C. 1:8). As for the second question, Paul's language certainly implies that he prays for believers to be completely holy in preparation for the parousia (cf. Phil. 1:10f.; 1 C. 1:7f.). The same thought is present in 3:13 and it should be taken seriously.

Since Paul believed that the parousia could occur within the lifetime of his readers, he also believed that they could be fully prepared for it at any time. Even if we take the thought to be of holiness in every aspect of the personality and of complete consecration to God rather than of the outworking of such consecration in the details of daily living, the prospect still seems daunting. The point may be that Paul's prayer represents an ideal that may not be fully realised. In the last analysis the believer's standing with God at the parousia rests on the work of Christ rather than on any achievement of his own (even though it is the work of God within him), and for Paul believers already are sanctified through Christ when they are converted. The call to full sanctification must be taken with all seriousness, but it cannot and must not be transformed into a doctrine of final salvation by works.

In the second part of the verse Paul repeats the same thought in different words, with a wish that the readers' **spirit and soul and body be kept sound and blameless**. The intention of the prayer is clear enough. The wording is somewhat difficult in that Paul begins with the adjective **sound** (i.e. whole, complete) but then proceeds to use an adverbial expression 'blamelessly' (*RSV* **blameless**). The force is thus 'May your whole personality be preserved blamelessly, i.e. so as to be blameless' (for the adverb, see 2:10). However, the adjective 'whole' is a predicate, and so we should translate 'May your personality be preserved blamelessly so as to be whole.'

The word **sound** is one used of what is physically untouched (like unhewn stones for constructing an altar, Dt. 27:6) or of unblemished victims for sacrifice (Jos. Ant. 8:118; not LXX). The thought may be, therefore, of the freedom of the readers from any blemish which would sully their holiness (cf. Jas. 1:4), and this is possible through their being free from anything that would be blameworthy.

The reference to **spirit and soul and body** has roused much discussion, since this is the only place in the *NT* where there appears to be a tripartite description of human nature. (1). The easiest way of taking the verse is as a description of human nature as consisting of three parts. Elsewhere, however, Paul seems to think of man as body and soul or as body and spirit with no very clear differentiation between soul and spirit. It may be possible to think of spirit as the highest aspect of human personality, and soul as the centre of will and emotion (G. Harder, *NIDNTT* III, p. 684). (2). In various ways attempts have been made to gain a bipartite view of man from the verse. P. A. van Stempvoort ('Eine stilistische Lösung einer alten Schwierigkeit in 1 Thess. v. 23', *NTS* 7, 1960–1, pp. 262–5) divides the sentence in the middle, and translates 'May the God of peace sanctify you wholly and in every part. May both body and

soul be preserved without fault at the coming of our Lord Jesus.'
This view takes 'spirit' as equivalent to a personal pronoun. But it
produces a very unnatural rendering of the Greek. Alternatively,
one might regard soul and body as being in apposition to spirit:
'May your spirit, namely, your soul and body, be preserved . . .'
This is the view of Masson, pp. 77f., who takes 'spirit' to mean the
human personality as a whole (cf. Gal. 6:18; 1 Th. 5:28).
(3). Jewett, pp. 175–83, proposes that Paul was dealing with enthusiasts who adopted a Gnostic type of understanding of man in
which the divinely-given spirit was contrasted with the human body
and soul; Paul takes up their language and uses it to emphasise that
sanctification extends to the whole of the personality. The weakness
of this view is that it presupposes a Gnostic type of anthropology
among the readers, for which we have no real evidence. (See R. H.
Gundry, *Sōma in Biblical Theology*, Cambridge, 1976, p. 135 n. 2).
Others suppose that Paul has taken over a traditional formula (Epist.
Apost. 24), or that he is simply piling on language for rhetorical
effect. Best, pp. 243f., is typical of commentators who insist that
the language is not to be pressed. (4). Von Dobschütz, p. 229,
notes that a trichotomous analysis of man is not found before Paul.
He holds that Paul is describing the nature of the Christian, as
distinct from man in general. The spirit is the divine Spirit which
enters into the personality alongside the human soul and body. The
difficulty with this view is that it is strange to think of the divine
Spirit being *preserved* in the believer. However, the difficulty may
not be insuperable if Paul thinks of the indwelling Spirit as becoming virtually a part of the individual. A stronger objection is
that Paul distinguishes the Spirit from the spirit of the believer in
Rom. 8:16.

In our view the most probable view remains the first, taking it in
the sense that Paul here distinguishes three aspects of the Christian's
personality, his life in relationship with God through the 'spiritual'
part of his nature, his human personality or 'soul', and the human
body through which he acts and expresses himself. The distinctions
are loose, and do not suggest three 'parts' of man which can be
sharply separated, but rather three aspects of his being. Paul lists
them together here to emphasise that it is indeed the whole person
who is the object of salvation. This may have implications for his
understanding of the resurrection life. It is not just a resurrection
of the physical body but necessarily involves the whole of one's
personal existence.

24. If the readers were in any way tempted to doubt whether they
might be prepared for the parousia, Paul proceeds to reassure them.
Their salvation depends upon the One who called them to be his

people (2:12). His call was to enter into his kingdom and glory. Since it is part of the character of God that he is **faithful** and keeps his promises (2 Th. 3:3; 1 C. 1:9; 10:13; 2 C. 1:18), it follows that he **will do it** (cf. Rom. 16:25; Phil. 1:6). Those who trust in him can be sure that they will experience his power to preserve them right through to the end. The believer can thus be sure not only of his present acceptance by God (Rom. 5:1), but also of his 'final perseverance'; although Paul would insist that those who persevere are those who put their trust in God and do not turn away from him.

CLOSING REQUESTS AND GREETINGS

5:25–28

After the expression of prayer for his readers it only remains for Paul to bring his letter to a close in the accepted manner of the time by giving his personal greetings and requests to his readers. The tone is strongly Christian.

25. Paul concludes several of his letters with a request that his readers will pray for him (2 Th. 3:1f.; Rom. 15:30; Eph. 6:18f.; Col. 4:3f.; cf. 2 C. 1:11; Phil. 1:19; Phm. 22; also Heb. 13:18). Paul's requests for prayer were certainly made on the level of brotherhood in the church. But there is also the thought that through prayer the churches share in the work of mission; those who cannot go on mission themselves can share in the work by praying for missionaries. It is clear that Paul felt himself very dependent upon the prayers of his friends. We should possibly read 'pray *also* for us' with a strong group of MSS; if so, Best, p. 245, is right in seeing a correlation between Paul's prayer for his readers (v. 23) and their prayer for him. The mechanics of intercessory prayer are mysterious. There is no explanation why we should all pray for one another and not just for ourselves, except perhaps that through mutual intercession the members of the church truly form a body of inter-dependent members instead of being a less effective collection of individual units.

26. The second request is that all the brothers be greeted **with a holy kiss**. The **kiss** was an accepted form of affectionate greeting in various areas of ancient life (G. Stählin, *TDNT* IX, pp. 118–24, 125–8, 138–46). As such, it was lacking in sexual significance. The description of it as **holy** shows that it was the mark of a Christian relationship rather than a purely secular one. It was thus a mark of oneness in Christ, and therefore Paul directs that all the members of the church are to be greeted in this fashion. Since Paul makes the request, the kiss would be seen as a greeting with which he was associated, despite his absence. He does not say who is to convey the greeting, but we may presume that at a church gathering each person would greet several others in such a way that nobody was left out or ostracised. In view of the fact that there was some tendency to division in the church, this stress on the fact that **all** belong to the one fellowship is probably intentional, especially since we find the same emphasis in the next verse. The 'holy kiss' has been revived in some Christian groups in a spirit of obedience to the letter of the *NT*. Such literal obedience may not be the best way of fulfilling the spirit of the teaching of the *NT* if kissing is not culturally acceptable outside sexual and family relationships. What is important is that the members of the church should have some way of expressing visibly and concretely the love which they have for one another as fellow-members of the body of Christ. The manner of expression may vary in different cultures; but it is doubtful whether doing nothing at all, as modern western Christians tend to do, really fulfils the spirit of the injunction.

27. The third closing request is introduced by a solemn adjuration couched in the first person singular. This is most probably explained by Paul himself taking up his pen after an amanuensis had written the body of the letter (cf. 2 Th. 3:17; 1 C. 16:21; Gal. 6:11–18; Col. 4:18). The request that the **letter be read to all the brethren** is not particularly surprising. The reference is of course to reading aloud, and it can be assumed that the letter would be read at a meeting of the members of the church, partly because this was the quickest way to make the contents known to everybody in the absence of modern facilities for multi-copying, and partly perhaps because not all members of the church may have been literate. At the same time, it is possible that Paul regarded the letter as making up for his physical absence from the church and therefore wished it to be read as part of the proceedings in the church meeting as a substitute for the sermon that he would have given had he been present. This motive may well explain the particularly strong language of adjuration with which Paul introduces the request. Paul was conscious of his authority and responsibility as an apostle, and he wished to ensure that his function of speaking authoritatively to the congregation would be carried out even when he was not there (cf. 2 Th. 3:17). The stress on **all the brethren** indicates that he is thinking of a full church meeting—it is interesting that he simply assumes that all the members of the church do gather together regularly, whereas many modern Christians are somewhat less than regular in their attendance—and there may be the thought that the letter must be particularly read to those for whom it contained a note of warning and admonition (5:12f.). A further point may simply be that Paul's affection for all the members of the church was such that he wanted them all to hear what he had to say.

28. The letter closes in the normal Pauline manner with the benediction. The form of words is found elsewhere in Paul's letters with slight variations (2 Th. 3:18; Rom. 16:20*b*; Gal. 6:18; Phil. 4:23; Col. 4:18). The wording is close to that of the opening greeting. The normal secular greeting 'farewell' (Ac. 15:29) is replaced by a prayer for **the grace of the Lord Jesus Christ** to be with the readers. Although the language could easily become formal, here it takes the readers to the heart of Paul's gospel, to the person of Jesus as the Lord and as the source of divine favour.

THE SECOND LETTER OF PAUL

to the

Thessalonians

1:1–2 The general character of the introductory greetings in Paul's letters was discussed in our comments on 1 Th. 1:1. We saw that 1 Thessalonians has the simplest and least developed form of greeting, but includes the three basic elements of the names of the writers of the letter, the name of the recipients, and the expression of Christian good wishes. These three elements are found in the present greeting with scarcely any change, since the same writers are writing to the same recipients not long after the first letter. What was said about these elements in the comments on 1 Th. 1:1 need not be repeated here. Paul, however, seldom repeats his greetings exactly, and there are two small differences to be noted. First, there is the qualification of God the Father as **God our Father**. This use of **our** to indicate that God is the Father of believers rather than merely of Jesus his Son is common Pauline usage; but in other epistolary greetings it is usually found in the expression of good wishes ('from God our Father'). Second, the source of **grace** and **peace** is named, as in all other Pauline epistles except 1 Th. Whereas **grace** is particularly associated with Christ (2 C. 13:14) and **peace** with God (Rom. 15:33; Phil. 4:7), here **God the Father and the Lord Jesus Christ** are named together as the one source of both grace and peace. The repetition of the reference to God and Christ so soon after v. 1 has seemed awkward and heavy to some commentators; one may question whether it is much more awkward than the repetition in 2 C. 1:2f.; Gal. 1:1–4; Eph. 1:2f.; Col. 1:2f.

Trilling, p. 35, who wishes to deny that Paul wrote the letter, finds it odd that the writer reproduces the introductory greeting of 1 Th. with all its unusual features and with scarcely any variation. He suggests that the changes are in the direction of conventionality, produce an awkward effect, and could have been based on a knowledge of Paul's other letters. Although in his eyes the letter stresses the apostolic authority of Paul, he finds nothing odd in the lack of Paul's official title of apostle at this point. He holds that Silvanus and Timothy play no real part in the letter, and therefore the inclusion of their names here is a pointless carry-over from 1 Th. Such details are meant to create a (false) impression of authenticity. Finally, Trilling thinks that the reference to the church being 'in God our Father and the Lord Jesus Christ' does not correspond with the picture of the church later in the Epistle, and is therefore a lifeless phrase taken over from 1 Th. To all this it can be replied that it is not surprising if a Pauline letter written soon after 1 Th. to the same people carries a very similar greeting with slight alterations that lead towards Paul's later pattern of opening greetings. Trilling's attempt to explain away the omission of 'apostle' is artificial, but in any case we may well doubt whether the Epistle was intended to stress Paul's apostolic authority to later generations. The mention of Paul's companions can be paralleled by, for example, the mention of Sosthenes in 1 C. 1:1, although he plays no part in the rest of the letter. Finally, Trilling's attempts to claim that the church is less a spiritual reality than a community of the faithful who stand *under* the authority of their Lord and are tied to the instructions of the apostle is over-subtle, and is no basis for saying that the introductory description of the church is merely conventional. The case for the inauthenticity of these verses is totally unconvincing.

OPENING THANKSGIVING

1:3–12

Just as 1 Th. begins with a thanksgiving which slides over with no real break into a description of how the readers became Christians, so too in this letter the opening expression of thanks comes to a climax in the thought of the readers' steadfastness in enduring persecution and then slides over into a comment on the situation which is meant to encourage them to continue to hold to their Christian beliefs. This statement, with its threat of divine judgment upon persecutors and its promise of future reward for the persecuted, then leads into an expression of intercessory prayer for the continuing growth of the readers in Christian virtues and their experience of divine glory. Such a shift from thanksgiving to one of the main concerns of the letter is not unfamiliar elsewhere in Paul's correspondence. In the present case it produces an extremely long and loose sentence (vv. 3–10); but sentences of comparable length occur elsewhere in Paul (see A. Q. Morton and J. McLeman, *Paul, the Man and the Myth*, London, 1966, Table 51). The content of the section shows affinities with 1 Th. in that Paul takes up the thoughts expressed in the introductory thanksgiving there and develops them. The main teaching section in vv. 5–10 is unparalleled, but this is because the writer is taking up a theme which arose out of the peculiar circumstances of the readers.

3. Instead of the usual 'we give thanks' found in his other letters, Paul begins with the words **We are bound to give thanks**, a phrase repeated in 2:13 but not used elsewhere by Paul. Commentators have detected both an un-Pauline expression and a cooler tone in the words, as if the author were almost saying 'there isn't much to be thankful about, but still we are under obligation to give thanks if at all possible.' The characterisation is inappropriate, since Paul goes on to express the reason for his thanks in an enthusiastic manner. The thought is not of giving thanks for duty's sake, but of the obligation imposed by joyfulness and relief, and this motive explains the slightly unusual wording. *RSV* takes the adverb **always** with **to give thanks**, and this appears to be correct; in any case there is little difference between 'we always ought to give thanks' and 'we ought to give thanks always'.

Paul addresses his readers right at the beginning of the letter as brothers (*RSV* **brethren**), although elsewhere he reserves this form of address for later in his letters. It is an expression of the personal relationship which he feels between himself and the persecuted community, and it is hard to see why Trilling, p. 44, regards it as stiff and impersonal. The final phrase in the clause is **as is fitting**, which roots the obligation to give thanks in the situation of the readers whose conduct merits praise to God. There may be something of a liturgical character about the language, since similar phraseology is found in later Christian writings as well as in Jewish material (Pesahim 10:5; R. Aus, 'The Liturgical Background of the Necessity and Propriety of Giving Thanks according to 2 Thess 1, 3', *JBL* 92, 1973, pp. 422–38). But somewhat similar phraseology is found in Phil. 1:7, and it may well be that Paul is simply influenced by forms of words with which he was familiar from Judaism, rather than that the epistle reflects a developed and late Christian formal language. It has also been suggested that Paul's language may reflect the fact that he is replying to a letter from the Thessalonians in which they protested that they were unworthy of the praise heaped upon them in Paul's earlier letter (Frame, p. 220). It is simpler to suppose that such natural sentiments had been conveyed by word of mouth to Paul.

In the second part of the sentence Paul proceeds to explain why he ought to give thanks to God, and gives two reasons. First, the readers' **faith is growing abundantly**. In 1 Th. Paul gave thanks for the Thessalonians' 'work of faith'; now he does so for the increase in their faith, the sign of a healthy Christian life. It may be significant that in 1 Th. 3:10 Paul wrote about a lack in their faith and prayed for it to be supplied. Whether or not he is consciously alluding to that prayer, he could now feel that God had answered his prayer and done so fully. The verb used, a compound of *hyper-*, expresses vigorous growth, and is of a form that Paul likes to use. The word occurs only here, and it has been suggested that

an inventor is hardly likely to have created it. Second, the readers'
love for one another is increasing. Again Paul takes up a motif
from the thanksgiving in 1 Th., the Thessalonians' 'labour of love',
which had been the theme of specific prayer on his part in the
earlier letter (1 Th. 3:12).

Such love was being shown by **every one** in the church, and this
again is a mark of spiritual maturity. It is noteworthy that Paul uses
verbs in the present tense, which indicate that the process of growth
was a continuous one and was still continuing. Although Paul wrote
of the need for love both to one another and to all mankind in 1
Th. 3:12, there is nothing significant about the omission of that
phrase here, where the thought is primarily of the attitudes towards
God and one another within the church. Paul does not go on here
to speak of hope, as he did in 1 Th. 1:3, but the thought of the
steadfastness which arises from hope becomes the object of special
mention in the next verse and marks the main theme of the section.
Trilling, p. 45, finds the comments too vague for a real situation
and assumes that the whole setting implied here is imaginary; there
would seem to be no real grounds for this subjective impression.

4. *RSV* breaks up the long sentence which is just getting under
way into a series of shorter ones, by substituting a co-ordinating
Therefore for the subordinating 'with the result that' of the Greek.
The connection is slightly loose in that while Paul appears to be
going on to say that he boasts in the churches because of the faith
and love of the readers, in fact he states that he boasts about
something else, namely, their steadfastness under persecution. The
point is probably that the readers were maintaining these Christian
virtues of faith and love despite persecution. The phrase **we ourselves** carries some emphasis, 'we for our part', and suggests that
an implicit contrast is present. A contrast with the people in other
churches who already knew for themselves and spoke about the
Thessalonian church (1 Th. 1:9) is hardly likely. It is possible that
Paul is drawing attention to the fact that he was going against his
usual custom of not boasting about his churches (but this view is
contradicted by the sentiments expressed in 2 C. 8:1–5; 9:2–4); or
he may be contrasting his own attitude with that of the Thessalonians themselves who, as we have already noted, may have protested
against Paul's high praise of them in his earlier letter because they
felt unworthy of it. The compound verb translated **boast** is found
here only in the *NT*, Paul normally using the simple form; but this
is no argument against authenticity since he also uses another compound of the verb in one passage (Rom. 11:18).

the churches of God is a general phrase also used in 1 C. 11:16.
Elsewhere Paul specifies the particular geographical area meant (1

Th. 2:14); but here he is referring broadly to wherever his missionary work takes him. The particular qualities which he now singles
out as the object of thankful mention (for this concept of boasting,
see 1 Th. 2:19) are the **steadfastness** and **faith** of the readers. The
former word was used in association with hope to describe the third
of the Christian virtues which characterised the church from its
foundation. It is singled out here in view of the increasingly difficult
situation with which the church was coping and it is closely linked
with faith. In the context the latter word may carry the nuance of
faithfulness (cf. 1 Th. 3:5); but the primary sense is doubtless that
of faith in God, a quality closely akin to hope which gives believers
the capacity to be steadfast. It is their trust in God that enables
them to undergo opposition without succumbing to it. Clearly such
faith contains an element of hope, so that it is false to assert with
Trilling, p. 47, that the dimension of hope has completely disappeared from the epistle. Equally it is mistaken to suppose that here
faith has become merely one of several virtues rather than the central
characteristic of the Christian. As Best, p. 253, notes, the combination of the concepts of steadfastness and faith is common later
than Paul (1 Pet. 1:5–9; Heb. 6:12; 11:1; Rev. 13:10). **persecutions**
and **afflictions** are virtually synonymous terms (for the former, see
1 Th. 1:6; 3:3, 7; Paul uses the latter in Rom. 8:35; 2 C. 12:10) and
are used together for rhetorical effect (Mk 4:17; Rom. 8:35). Any
kind of outward pressure exerted upon Christians simply because
they are Christians is meant. The final clause **which you are enduring** indicates both that the afflictions were still continuing and
that the readers were successfully standing up to them. It is not
necessary to suppose with Trilling, pp. 48f., that the reference is to
a general situation of persecution which was typical of the post-
Pauline period.

5. From expressing thanks for the spiritual growth and the steadfastness of the readers under persecution Paul moves on to a piece
of teaching which is concerned with the question of the justice of
what was happening to them. His point, which is developed over
the next few verses, is that it belongs to the character of God to act
justly by rewarding those who suffer with future ease at the parousia
of Jesus and by inflicting judgment on those who cause them to
suffer. Paul sees the **evidence** of God's **righteous judgment** in what
he has just been describing. In the Greek text there is no verb and
the noun **evidence** is loosely attached to what precedes; it may be
regarded as being in apposition to the preceding clause or as dependent upon an unexpressed 'which is' (cf. Rom. 12:1). The word
itself can mean 'proof' or 'means of proving'. It is not altogether
clear what Paul regards as constituting the evidence. Von Dob-

schütz, pp. 241f., holds that the actual sufferings of the readers are the evidence. If it belongs to God's righteous judgment to reward sufferers and punish persecutors, then the *lex talionis* will be satisfied if the Christians suffer now. Other commentators hold that Paul is referring to the endurance and faith shown by the readers in the midst of their persecution. A persecution which demands and brings out such steadfastness cannot remain unrequited by God.

But how does all this constitute a *proof* or *evidence* of a future, as yet unknown judgment by God? Although commentators generally take **judgment** as future, it does not make good sense of the passage; moreover, elsewhere Paul uses a different Greek word (*krima*, not *krisis* as here) for the future judgment. Rather the thought is of God's present process of judgment on his people which has the aim of judging them to be worthy of the kingdom. This understanding of the word gives good sense. The trials and the way in which the readers are enduring them (perhaps, as Best, p. 255, suggests, the fact that Paul could boast about this to other churches) constitute evidence of a righteous process of judgment which God is carrying out in order that he may see that they are worthy of the kingdom, granted that he will repay those who suffer with future reward. For this thought of a present judgment, we may cite I Pet. 4 :17–19. Another related passage is Phil. I :27–39, where the firm and fearless attitude of the church to persecution is a clear omen to the persecutors of their future destruction and of the church's salvation. The *RSV* translation **that you may be made worthy** correctly reproduces the passive form in the Greek; but the passive is probably a circumlocution for the action of God who alone can regard people as worthy of his kingdom. The verb means to *regard* as worthy rather than to *make* worthy, but the verdict follows on the successful endurance of tribulation. Paul's point is that steadfastness in persecution leads to entry to the kingdom of God. It goes without saying that the thought is not of salvation by works but rather of the evidencing of true faith in God by steadfastness when one is tempted to abandon faith.

The goal of faith is entry to **the kingdom of God,** here conceived, as in I Th. 2:12, as the future sphere of divine blessing to which God calls his faithful people. It is this hope **for which** the readers **are** presently enduring **suffering,** not in the sense that they endure in order to gain entry, but rather in that their sufferings are connected with, or are in the interest of, the kingdom. Von Dobschütz, p. 243, remarks that not all suffering gives a right to enter the kingdom, but only that which is endured for the sake of the kingdom.

6. The assurance that the readers will enter the kingdom depends on a firm assumption that Paul makes regarding the nature of divine justice. Although the clause is conditional in form, the introductory conjunction (*eiper*) always indicates an assumed fact in Paul; hence the *RSV* translation **since** is justified. The righteous process of judgment by God leads up to and is consistent with what is regarded as **just** at God's bar. For Paul it is manifestly just in the eyes of both God and men that suffering should be rewarded and those who inflict it should be punished. What he assumes and does not find it necessary to prove or demonstrate is that God has the power to act in accordance with this just principle and will in fact do so. He takes it for granted that God will actually do what he considers to be just. The only point at issue, then, is whether the human belief in the justice of the *lex talionis* is in accordance with the mind of God, and he declares that this is so.

Paul begins with the negative statement that God **will repay with affliction those who afflict you**. The *lex talionis*, 'an eye for an eye and a tooth for a tooth', is very conspicuous in the play on words between **affliction** and those who **afflict** you. The language may reflect Is. 66:4, where God threatens to repay sinners with their sins, i.e. to make them suffer what they have caused others to suffer. Many modern Christians and humanists would protest that this kind of thought is unacceptable, since it makes God out to be a strict martinet rather than a loving Father who will freely pardon all manner of sin. However, it must be observed, first of all, that the principle enunciated here has the effect of removing the right to inflict of punishment and vengeance from the individual, who may easily act unjustly or be motivated by vindictiveness against his persecutors. When Paul takes up the theme in Romans he emphasises that believers must not avenge themselves but rather return good for evil. They can do so in the confidence that where vengeance is necessary God himself will take care of it (Rom. 12:17–21).

It may then be objected that, if God forbids his people to take vengeance, he ought to act in the same way himself and show love to his enemies. Here, however, a second observation can be made. From v. 8 it is clear that the punishment described here is for those who reject the gospel, and the content of the gospel is that 'God shows his love for us in that while we were yet sinners Christ died for us' and that 'while we were enemies we were reconciled to God by the death of his Son' (Rom. 5 :8, 10). The God whom Paul is describing is a God who does offer love and reconciliation to his enemies, but if they refuse this offer and continue in opposition to his goodness and love, then it would seem inevitable that, having refused mercy, they must face justice. Nothing in the *NT* suggests that God's love is indifferent to justice, and that he bestows a free pardon on his enemies at the cost of failing to defend the persecuted against the persecutors. Indeed, it is difficult to see how the ultimate justice of God to those who suffer can be defended in a situation where the persecutor knows that in the end he will be freely forgiven.

7. The negative aspect of judgment is quickly followed by the positive aspect. Those **who are afflicted** by persecutors will be granted **rest** in place of their sufferings. The word **rest** signifies the relaxation of tension and is used by Paul in reference to relief from suffering (2 C. 2:13; 7:5; 8:13). The thought, it should be observed, is not of inactivity or of reward for sufferings, still less of taking vengeance, but simply of the absence of suffering, which in itself is a perfectly adequate fulfilment of the longings of those who suffer. It is, however, one of the blessings associated with the kingdom of God (v. 5) and as such is accompanied by other, more positive blessings. Paul states that his readers will experience this respite along **with us**, i.e. himself and his missionary colleagues. The phrase betrays his own experience of tribulation which is reflected later in the letter (3:2) and was prominent in his earlier letter (e.g. 1 Th. 2:15; 3:7). Von Dobschütz, p. 245, saw in this phrase a subtle indication of authenticity which an imitator was unlikely to have created; Trilling, pp. 52f., by contrast sees it as typical of a later tendency to emphasise the connection between the apostle and the church. The thought is certainly typical of early church writers in the *NT* epistles, but surely the most natural explanation of it is simply the historical one that Paul was conscious of a fellowship in suffering between himself and this church at the particular time of writing; the phrase cannot be used as an indicator of inauthenticity.

In the second part of the verse the thought broadens out in the direction of a presentation of the strictly Christian nature of the hope. While vv. 6–7a refer solely to the action of God, it is now made clear that all along Paul has been thinking of his action through Christ. The ending of persecution is to be linked with the parousia. The language used to express this thought (through to v. 10) has impressed many readers by its rhythmical character, and it has been suspected that some kind of hymn may lie behind it. The frequent use of *OT* language would point to a Jewish Christian composition. But Paul himself was a Jewish Christian and was quite capable of produing rhythmic prose. There is nothing in the passage which demands the theory that he is here incorporating earlier material by a different author. We may, therefore, assume that these verses are a composition by the author of the epistle, unless we find evidence which points in a contrary direction.

The time of God's act of recompense is fixed as **when the Lord**

Jesus is revealed from heaven. Paul here uses the less usual word 'revelation' (Gk. *apokalypsis*) to refer to the parousia. It is found with the same sense in 1 C. 1:7; cf. Rom. 2:5 (for the use of the corresponding verb, see 2 Th. 2:3, 6, 8; Rom. 8:18; 1 C. 3:13), and this usage is found also in 1 Pet. 1:7, 13; 4:13 (for the verb, see Lk. 17:30; Rom. 8:18; 1 C. 3:13; 1 Pet. 1:5; 5:1). Trilling's observation, p. 54, that the writer's failure to use this word-group for the present revelation of God in Christ reflects the weakening of the emphasis on present salvation and its future revelation which is characteristic of later writings, is unjustified; the same disuse characterises 2 C. and 1 Th. The word conveys the thought of the unveiling of that which is at present hidden, i.e. of the visible manifestation of the Lord Jesus who is at present hidden from sight in heaven. The description of the One through whom God will exercise judgment as the **Lord** is a common one; the title **Lord** is frequently associated with the parousia and brings out the status of the judge.

Three prepositional phrases colour the picture. First, he comes **from heaven**, a phrase which does not merely indicate his origin but also stresses his authority. He comes from the dwelling place of God with the authority of God to execute judgment and recompense. The thought is already present in 1 Th. 4:16 and shows that a coming to the world is in mind; it is language such as this which justifies the description of the parousia as the 'second *coming*' of Jesus. Second, the Lord comes **with his mighty angels** (literally, 'with angels of the might of him'). The essential thought here is the same as that found in 1 Th. 3:13, if we are correct in regarding 'all his holy ones' (*RSV* 'all his saints') there as a reference to the angels who attend God in his heavenly dwelling, accompany him at his coming (Zech. 14:5; 1 En. 1:9), and who also accompany God's agent, the Son of man, so as to contribute to the glory and majesty of his coming in judgment. The qualifying phrase 'of his might' is variously understood to refer to 'the angels through whom he exercises his might', or 'the angels who belong to his might', or 'the angels of his (heavenly) host', or 'his powerful angels' (a genitive of quality), or 'the angels of power' as the name of a particular class in an angelic hierarchy. The second of these possibilities seems to be best supported. It is interesting that elsewhere 'might' is an accompaniment of the parousia (Mk. 13:26). The precise force of the words is not important; what matters is the impression of divine power and authority with which the Lord Jesus is invested.

Third, the Lord comes **in flaming fire** (literally, 'in fire of flame'; the phrase is punctuated as part of v. 8 in *GNB* and the Greek text). This is a curious phrase, and one might have expected the variant wording 'in flame of fire' which is found in a significant group of

MSS (including B D G vg sy co Ir^{lat} Tert). The same phrase with the
same textual variant is found in Ac. 7:30 in a description of the
revelation to Moses at the burning bush. In LXX we have the same
variations in Exod. 3:2, and the phrase 'flame of fire' is found
frequently elsewhere (Isa. 29:6; 30:30, *v.l.*; 66:15; Dan. 7:9; Ps.
104:4 [cited Heb. 1:7]). If we accept the difficult wording 'in fire of
flame', the other reading can be seen as an attempt to ease a harsh
phrase under the influence of a common LXX phrase. However, R.
Aus, 'The Relevance of Isaiah 66:7 to Revelation 12 and 2 Thessalonians 1', *ZNW* 67, 1976, pp. 252–68, has argued that, since there
is considerable influence from Isa. 66 in this section of 2 Th., we
should adopt 'in flame of fire' as an allusion to Isa. 66:15 and regard
'in fire of flame' as an assimilation to the account of the theophany
in Exod. 3:2. It is true that Isa. 66 has influenced the passage as a
whole, but it is possible that a later scribe brought the text into
closer conformity with Isa. 66; also it should be noted that we
cannot be sure that the copy of Exod. 3:2 used by the scribes who
are said to have assimilated the text to that verse had the required
wording (in fact A, which has 'in fire of flame' here has 'in flame of
fire' in Exod. 3:2). In any case, the phrase does not point simply to
a theophany, but underlines the fact of judgment, and it should
probably be linked with the immediately following phrase 'inflicting
vengeance' (*pace* Best, p. 259).

8. Having described God as the One who judges persecutors in
v. 6, Paul now repeats and expands the thought in terms of the
activity of the Lord Jesus (v. 7) as the one who inflicts **vengeance**.
The phraseology is drawn from the *OT* (Dt. 32:35; Isa. 66:15; Ezek.
25:14), where it is used to describe the activity of Yahweh himself;
his work of judgment is here entrusted to the Lord Jesus (cf. Jn.
5:22). Best, p. 259, emphasises that the term **vengeance** is justified
as the translation of Gk. *ekdikēsis* rather than simply 'punishment';
this follows from the usage in LXX and from the general *NT*
understanding of God's judgment as retributory (cf. Rom. 12:19;
Heb. 10:30). One might say that in order that justice may be seen
to be done the punishment must fit the crime. In the present case
it is particularly the persecutors whom Paul has in mind, but they
are described in terms of the class to which they belong as **those
who do not know God** and **those who do not obey the gospel**.
The Greek construction shows that two groups of people are being
listed, but there is considerable uncertainty regarding the identify
of the persons mentioned. The phrase **those who do not know God**
is used in the *OT* (Ps. 79:6 par. Jer. 10:25) to describe the Gentiles
in contrast to the Jews (see especially, 1 Th. 4:5). (1). It is thus
possible that Paul is referring first to the Gentiles and then, second,

to the Jews as those who do not obey the gospel (cf. Isa. 66:4; Ac. 6:7; Rom. 10:16). Against this distinction it has been observed that the second clause could refer to Gentiles as well as to Jews. (2). Lightfoot, p. 103, therefore suggested that the first group is Gentiles and the second is both Gentiles and Jews; but this is surely a very artificial type of grouping. (3). It is more plausible to argue that the two groups are in fact identical in composition despite the apparent differentiation in the Greek text. In this case, the reference could be to Gentiles throughout. (4). Alternatively, since it is quite possible that Jews can be included in the category of those who do not know God (Jer. 9:6; Jn. 8:55), it is arguable that Paul is referring generally in both groups to both Jews and Gentiles (Best, p. 260).

In our opinion, however, suggestion (1) is best. Two groups should be distinguished. Paul refers, first, to the Gentiles, describing them in traditional Jewish terms as people who are ignorant of God, and he sees in this ignorance the cause of their attacks on Christians. Then, second, he includes the Jews who have some knowledge of God, but who have refused to believe and obey the good news of our Lord Jesus, i.e. the good news that Jesus is the one exalted by God as Lord. It has been objected that the inflicting of vengeance on those ignorant of God is unjust. Paul's answer would have been that the ignorance of which he is writing is the wilful ignorance of those who 'although they knew God . . . did not honour him as God or give thanks to him', people who 'exchanged the truth about God for a lie and worshipped and served the creature rather than the Creator', and all this although 'what can be known about God is plain to them, because God has shown it to them' (Rom. 1:18–25).

9. Having emphasised the fact of divine vengeance against the persecutors (vv. 6, 8), Paul goes on to comment briefly on the nature of the fate which awaits them. Such people as those whom he has described (this is the force of the Gk. *hoitines*) will pay a penalty which consists in eternal destruction. The phrase 'pay a penalty' (*RSV* **suffer the punishment**) comes from Classical Greek and indicates the suffering of the deserts that one merits as the result of a legal judgment. **destruction** is a word that can be used of physical dissolution (1 Th. 5:3; cf. 1 C. 5:5) and metaphorically of disaster (1 Tim. 6:9). It is not used elsewhere in the *NT* of punishment after death (unless this is meant in 1 Tim. 6:9). The use of **eternal**, i.e. never-ending, and the context of the parousia indicates that what is commonly called 'eternal punishment' is meant. The same phrase is found in 4 Mac. 10:15, and similar phrases are used in Mt. 18:8; 25:41, 46; Heb. 6:2; Jude 7. The opposite condition is eternal life (Mt. 25:46).

There has been some argument as to whether the phrase signifies

'destruction that lasts for ever', i.e. annihilation, or 'everlasting
punishment', i.e. continuing pain. Exegesis of the passage must not
be determined by what is more congenial to modern feeling. In
favour of everlasting punishment it can be argued: (1). Jesus believed in it, and Paul will have shared his outlook (Mt. 5:29f.;
12:32; 18:8f.; 25:41, 46; Lk. 16:23–25); (2). Jewish teaching of the
time accepted the fact of eternal punishment (1QS 2:15; 5:13; Ps.
Sol. 2:35; 15:11; 4 Mac. 10:15); (3). In the present context the
reference to separation from the Lord is of little significance if those
punished are not conscious of their separation (Best, p. 262). These
points are of varying strength, and several of the texts cited are as
uncertain in interpretation as the present one.

It is clear elsewhere that Paul believed that all men would be
raised up to stand before the divine judgment seat (Rom. 14:10; 2
C. 5:10), and that sinners would face the wrath of God with consequent tribulation and distress (Rom. 2:5–9). As various commentators have observed, in no place does Paul discuss the fate of the
lost in any detail. There is no suggestion of any gloating over their
punishment, and, although Trilling, p. 58, permits himself the
observation that the author of the letter comes dangerously near to
an unethical position, he has nevertheless to admit that neither Paul
nor any other *NT* writer actually crosses this boundary. The simple
fact is that Paul does not say sufficient here or anywhere else to
enable us to comment in detail on his beliefs. The one thing that
can be said with certainty, however, is that he did not believe in
annihilation in the sense that the wicked lose consciousness at death
and never recover it. He undoubtedly believed that all men without
exception would appear before the judgment seat (*pace* H.-A. Wilke,
pp. 151–5, cited at 1 Th. 4:13 note). But whether the sentence
passed upon them would mean eternal consciousness of pain or not
is not clear.

The question may indeed be a meaningless one since we are
concerned with eternity rather than time. What mattered for Paul
was the fact that their destruction was synonymous with exclusion
from the presence of the Lord. This is an image familiar from the
teaching of Jesus (Mt. 7:23; 8:12; Lk. 13:27f.; Mt. 25:30, 41) and
found elsewhere in the *NT* (Rev. 22:15). Here Paul expresses it in
language reminiscent of the dire refrain in Isa. 2:10, 19, 21, where
men flee 'from before the terror of the Lord and from the glory of
his majesty' (some commentators have taken **from** in other ways
than as a preposition expressing separation, but this is the best way
of taking it; see Best, p. 263). The *OT* language is used to convey
something of the awe and majesty of the Lord as judge, and it is
significant that language originally used of Yahweh is here applied

to Jesus. To be separated from God and his blessings—and to be for ever in this situation—is for Paul the worst of prospects. This is the reality for which the other pictures used are merely symbols.

10. The final section of the long sentence is in form an expanded temporal phrase which repeats the substance of v. *7b* and emphasises that the exclusion of the persecutors takes place **when** the Lord **comes.** *RSV* has brought forward the temporal phrase **on that day** from its position at the very end of the sentence after the parenthetic clause **because our testimony to you was believed.** The inclusion of this phrase shows how the *NT* writers take up the *OT* concept of the day of the Lord (1 Th. 5:2) and identify it as the day of the parousia. The stereotyped phrase **that day** refers to this final day, following an *OT* usage in which it often refers to the day of the fulfilment of prophecy (Isa. 2:11; Mk. 13:32; 14:25; Lk. 10:12; 17:31; 21:34; 2 Tim. 1:18; 4:8). For the parousia as the coming of the Lord, we have a background in Dan. 7:13 (Mk. 8:38; 13:26, 35f.; 14:62; Mt. 10:23; 16:28; 24:44; Lk; 18:8; Jn 14:3; 1 C. 4:5; 11:26; Rev. 1:4, 7; *et al.*). However, although the clause is grammatically temporal, its content suggests that its real function is to provide the positive contrast to the description of the fate of the wicked.

The expressed purpose of the Lord's coming is **to be glorified in his saints, and to be marvelled at in all who have believed.** The wording reflects a number of *OT* passages which speak of God being glorified among his saints (Ps. 89:7 [88:8 LXX]) and being wondered at among his holy ones (Ps. 68:35 [67:36 LXX]). The structure of the clause (**when . . .**) is probably due to Isa. 2:10, which influenced the previous part of the sentence. It is doubtful how far Paul was consciously quoting the Psalms, and it is perhaps more likely that familiar phrases sprang readily and almost unconsciously to his pen. This will help to explain the fact that, although in Ps. 89 the original reference is to God's heavenly attendants, here the **saints** are plainly Christian believers (cf. 1 Th. 3:13). The force of the preposition **in** with **his saints** is not clear, and various suggestions have been offered: (1). The Lord who is *in the midst of* his saints is glorified by them—and so implicitly they share in his glory (von Dobschütz, p. 251); (2). The Lord is glorified *by* his saints (or in the eyes of his saints); (3). The Lord is glorified *on the ground of* his saints, i.e. in that they have developed Christ's character (Frame, p. 237); (4). The glory of the Lord is *seen in* his saints in that 'they are the mirror in which his glory shines' (Lightfoot, p. 104). The first of these suggestions gives the best sense; especially since it will also fit the second phrase **to be marvelled at in all who believed.** It is not stated to whom the glory is revealed, but doubt-

less the believers themselves and the heavenly attendants of God are
in mind.

It is interesting that the emphasis lies on the glorification of the
Lord rather than of his people. Paul will write later of the glorification of the saints (1:12; 2:14; cf. Rom. 8:30), but here his emphasis is on the glory of the Lord and the thought of his people
sharing in it is implicit rather than explicit. This is certainly significant in the present context. It means that Paul has avoided any
suggestion of a selfish, self-centred self-congratulation on the part
of the saved over against the lost; their attention is to be centred on
the One who has saved them. He is the One who is glorified and is
the object of wondering praise. The passage makes it clear that the
saints are those who **have believed** (the aorist is used of their initial
act of faith, or perhaps it looks back from the time of the parousia
to their earlier commitment to Jesus). No distinction between the
two groups (e.g. between Jewish and Gentile believers) is intended.
Finally, there is the parenthetical statement **because our testimony
to you was believed** (the weakly-attested variant 'was confirmed',
favoured by Hort and Moffatt, is not worth serious consideration).
The statement is awkwardly placed and its inclusion must have had
a special motive. Most probably it is Paul's way of encouraging his
readers by assuring them that they belong to the company of believing saints who will share in the parousia. The Lord will **be marvelled at in** all those who believed—and therefore in you—because
our witness which was directed to you was believed. The only
difficulty here is the rather unusual use of **to you** (Gk. *eph' hymas*)
with **our testimony**; but this is not serious. For the Christian message preached by the apostles as a testimony, we may compare I C.
1:6.

II. The lengthy opening sentence is now complete. Paul has given
thanks for the spiritual progress of his readers despite their difficult
situation and has assured them of a reversal in their condition at the
coming of the Lord. But the fact of their past progress and the
assurance of the righteous judgment of the Lord are not sufficient
to guarantee that the readers will stand firm in their faith and share
in the future blessings. Christian perseverance is a matter of continuing prayer and continuing faith. So Paul at last expresses how he
prays that his readers will eventually reach the kingdom of God
through continuing to show the evidences of a living faith.

To this end is a somewhat loose connection with what has just
preceded. It takes up the content of vv. 5–10 and above all the
thought of the readers being included among those worthy (v. 5) to
be with the Lord (v. 10). It is with a view to this hope being fulfilled
that Paul and his colleagues engage in continual prayer for their

converts. (There is an 'also' in the Greek which, if it has any force at all, suggests that Paul prays as well as giving thanks; cf. O'Brien, p. 178.) The rest of the sentence can express both the content and the purpose of the prayer, since one states in prayer what one hopes will happen as a result of the prayer. The thought goes back to the fact that God had originally issued **his call** to them to be his people and so to enter ultimately into 'his kingdom and glory' (1 Th. 2:12). God's call is thus much the same as his choice or election of his people (1 Th. 1:4). Paul's prayer is that the readers will be **worthy of** this **call** in the sense that their lives will show the characteristics expected in those who have responded to it. *RSV* translates the verb as **make worthy,** but a number of commentators insist that elsewhere the verb means to deem worthy (just as 'justify' is commonly taken as 'regard as righteous' rather than 'make righteous'). The same problem arose in v. 5 where a compound of the same verb is used. In both verses it is probable that the literal meaning of the word is to deem worthy, but it is equally true that God cannot deem worthy any whom he himself has not made worthy by his action rather than by their good works; hence the force of the verb is tantamount to 'make worthy' (Whiteley, p. 95).

This is made clear by the rest of the clause. Those whom God deems worthy are those in whom he can **fulfil every good resolve and work of faith.** The verb suggests the bringing to completion of a process already started. The Thessalonians already display good resolves and works of faith. The former phrase is literally 'every purpose of goodness' (for 'goodness', see Rom. 15:14; Gal. 5:22; Eph. 5:9). Although the noun is often used of God's will and purpose (Lk. 2:14; 10:21; Eph. 1:5, 9; Phil. 2:13), and some commentators wish to adopt that meaning here, it should undoubtedly be taken of human resolves (Rom. 10:1; Phil. 1:15). **work of faith** is a phrase already familiar from 1 Th. 1:3 and refers to the efforts which spring from faith. The two phrases form a hendiadys in that it is difficult to detect any difference between resolves of goodness and works of faith; if faith indicates the source of the desires, goodness indicates their character. Concretely Paul is no doubt thinking of loving actions as the evidence of real faith and of a heart which is thus controlled by the desire to do what is good.

The phrase **by his power** indicates the means by which God achieves his purpose, but it is also possible to translate the underlying Greek phrase as 'powerfully', in the sense that God will fully and completely accomplish his purpose in the lives of the readers. Their perseverance thus depends on the work of God in them. But, as we have seen earlier, this does not mean that there is no need for human response to the promptings of the Spirit. There is the added paradox that God's working in the readers appears to be dependent in part on the effectiveness of Paul's prayers. These tensions are inevitable in any attempt to correlate the working of God in the human heart with human purposes and actions.

12. Finally, Paul comes to the ultimate purpose of God which he prays may be fulfilled through the completion of his work in the readers. It is **that the name of our Lord Jesus may be glorified in you**. The language is ultimately based on Isa. 66:5 (cf. 24:15; Mal. 1:11), where, however, it is the name of Yahweh which is glorified. It also reflects what Paul has already said in v. 10 in his description of the parousia. In effect, therefore, v. 12 expresses the hope that the Thessalonian Christians will be found worthy to participate in that event, a thought which admittedly was already adumbrated in v. 10. The difference is perhaps that v. 10 deals with their initial act of faith which gave them a place in the Lord's people, while the present verse deals with the perseverance in faith and good works which they must show until the coming of the Lord. The reference to **the name** of the Lord stands in contrast to the mention of the Lord himself in the parallel expression in v. 10, and arises simply from the use of language echoing LXX. We should not, therefore, attach too much significance to the use of the word, for example, by asking which particular name or title of Jesus was in Paul's mind. The thought is simply that the Lord Jesus is glorified. The context suggests that the thought is of the glorification of Jesus at the parousia, as in v. 10, and not of a present glorification of Jesus (*pace* von Dobschütz, p. 257).

The phrase **in you** raises the same problem of interpretation as 'in his saints' in v. 10. In the present case the phrase is followed by the comment that the readers too will be glorified in him (i.e. Jesus), and it would seem probable that both phrases should have the same force. This suggests that glory is brought to Jesus through or as a result of his people who live in a way that brings honour to him, and that they share in glorification through him and what he has done for them. This is more probable than taking the phrase to refer to the readers giving glory to Jesus (equivalent to 'by you'). O'Brien, p. 182, has argued for a local sense (cf. v. 10), but it is quite possible to take the phrase in a different sense here from that in v. 10 since here the context is slightly different. There it was Jesus who was to be glorified; here it is his name. There the thought was purely of Jesus, whereas here there is the element of reciprocity. This last point is new. What was merely implicit in v. 10 now comes fully into view, and it is to be noticed that the glorification of the readers is associated more with their showing the Christian virtues of goodness and active faith than with their being rewarded or recompensed for their suffering persecution.

The prayer closes with the comment that all this takes place **according to the grace of our God and the Lord Jesus Christ**. It is divine grace which is the source of salvation and future glorification. The phrase is reminiscent of Rom. 4:4, 16; 12:6; 1 C. 3:10. What is unusual is the wording. Although Paul frequently links God and Jesus as the sources of spiritual blessings such as grace and peace (1:2), he does not elsewhere append both nouns in the genitive to the word 'grace', and when he does use the two names together he does not employ the odd wording found here, literally, 'of our God and Lord Jesus Christ'. This could be taken to mean that Paul is describing Jesus as both God and Lord (cf. Tit. 2:13; 2 Pet. 1:11; N. Turner, *Grammatical Insights into the New Testament*, Edinburgh, 1965, pp. 13–7). *RSV* assumes that 'Lord' can be used as a title without the article, so that God and the Lord Jesus are named side by side. Von Dobschütz, p. 258, found the expression so harsh that he argued that the second part was a scribal addition—despite the lack of any supporting textual evidence. Frame, p. 242, and others hold that two standard formulae have been run together without the author being conscious of the grammatical irregularity which he was creating. This would be especially possible as a result of dictation (Best, pp. 272f.). The effect of the whole phrase is to direct the minds of the readers again to the source of salvation and to lessen the temptation to dwell in any kind of self-centred way on the thought of personal reward. All this is surely genuinely Pauline, and the post-Pauline impression which some commentators have found here and in the chapter as a whole seems to be illusory.

THE COMING OF THE DAY OF THE LORD

2:1–12

A new section begins at 2:1. Even more clearly there is a break at the end of the chapter. But it is doubtful whether the whole chapter should be regarded as one section. It seems best, however, to regard vv. 1–12 as forming a section of teaching, since v. 13 starts afresh in the form of a thanksgiving. The theme of the section is clear enough. It is meant to allay uncertainty or excitement caused by assertions that the day of the Lord is already present. The basic answer given by Paul is that certain other events must happen first, namely, the appearance of the so-called lawless one. He is at present restrained from appearing, but will eventually appear in order to deceive sinful mankind. Then he will be destroyed at the coming of the Lord Jesus. The argument is difficult to follow, partly because of the way in which Paul tackles the theme in a non-chronological manner; vv. 5–7 go back to the period before his appearance described in vv. 3–4, and vv. 9–12 go back to the period of his appearance before his destruction described in v. 8. The effect of the teaching is, first, to assure the readers that, although certain events must precede the Day of the Lord, the 'run down' has already begun (v. 7); and, second, to comment on the way in which the ungodly will be deceived by the lawless one and thus share in his judgment and destruction. This last thought links up with Paul's warning to the readers not to be deceived into mistaking the epiphany of the lawless one for the parousia of the Lord Jesus.

The content of the teaching is largely peculiar to this section, and has little parallel elsewhere in Paul, although it is implied that some instruction on these matters had been given by Paul orally. Indeed, it is precisely because Paul feels that he can assume so much on the part of his readers that the modern reader has so much difficulty in understanding the passage. The uniqueness of the teaching is of course no argument against its originating with Paul. The problem rather is whether it is in harmony with his other teaching and whether its development is conceivable at the time of his correspondence with Thessalonica.

1. The beginning of a new section is indicated in the Greek text by the opening words **Now we beg you, brethren**, whose order has been altered in *RSV*. The use of the address **brethren** to mark a new section is a familiar stylistic feature. The verb **beg** is used to introduce a request or exhortation in 1 Th. 4:1; 5:12 (cf. Phil. 4:3). The content of the request follows in v. 2, but first Paul refers to the subject which is on his mind and thus achieves a link with the preceding chapter. It is important to observe that the present section is in fact closely connected with what has just preceded, and deals with the possibility of misunderstanding by the persecuted community concerning the imminence of **the coming of our Lord Jesus Christ**. Paul here uses the word *parousia* which despite its absence from ch. 1 was evidently his usual expression for the appearing of Jesus (1 Th. 2 :19), and he gives Jesus his full title by way of underlining the solemnity of the theme in this opening phrase. He explains the significance of the coming by closely linking with it the thought of **our assembling to meet him**. This motif goes back to the Jewish hope of the gathering together of the scattered exiles in their own land (Isa. 52:12; Zech. 2:6; 2 Mac. 1:27; 2:7) and was taken over by Jesus and the early church to refer to the final gathering together of his people with the Messiah (Mk 13:27; Mt. 23:37; Lk. 13:34). Paul has already written about this in 1 Th. 4:17;

the stress is more on the motif of being with the Lord than on the thought of the gathering together of a community. It was this hope which encouraged the Thessalonians, and therefore it would have been very natural for them in a situation of persecution to long for its speedy fulfilment and to be very open to persuasion that it was imminent.

2. In such a situation it was clearly appropriate for Paul to urge them not to be excited by any intimation **that the day of the Lord has come**. Paul had already written about the day of the Lord (1 Th. 1 :10; cf. 5:2) as the occasion on which Christian hope is centred. He now feared that the Thessalonians had heard that it had come. The verb used is the perfect tense of the verb *enistēmi* which has the sense 'to be present, to have come' (Rom. 8:38; 1 C. 3:22; Gal. 1:4; Heb. 9:9). There is fairly general agreement that the verb cannot mean anything else (*pace* A. M. G. Stephenson, 'On the meaning of ἐνέστηκεν ἡ ἡμέρα τοῦ κυρίου in 2 Thessalonians 2.2', *TU* 102, 1968, pp. 442–51). It is not so certain what the readers may have understood by the phrase as a whole, but the most probable view is that they thought that the last day in its traditional apocalyptic sense had already dawned. Plainly the expression did not mean literally twenty-four hours, but a lengthier, limited period which would culminate in the coming of the Lord. Other views which assume that the readers would have 'demythologised' or 'spiritualised' the concept completely fail to do justice to the context. It should be noted that the readers' problem was thus not the delay of the parousia, but their belief that it was overwhelmingly imminent (Burkeen, p. 318).

Those who felt that the last day had dawned would certainly be in danger of being **quickly shaken in mind**. The verb suggests being tossed about in a stormy wind, and is used metaphorically of being so perturbed as to lose one's normal composure and good sense. **quickly** refers to the swift effect that the news could have on an excitable people. The phrase refers to the initial shock which they would feel. This would be followed by a continual feeling of being **excited**, or better 'disturbed' and 'upset', by the news (cf. Mk 13:7, which suggests that the word was used in eschatological teaching).

But what was the source of this idea which Paul feared was being entertained by his readers? He refers to the possibility of being **excited, either by spirit or by word, or by letter purporting to be from us**. Of these three possibilities the first will refer to a message given under prophetic inspiration (cf. 1 Th. 5:19; 1 Jn 4:1–3) and the second to some other kind of teaching, presumably no less inspired but not given in the form of prophecy (cf. 1 Th. 4:15). The third reference is of course to a letter from Paul. *RSV* assumes that **purporting to be from us** qualifies only the last of these three possibilities and that the phrase calls in question the genuineness of any letter which offered such teaching. Both of these assumptions are dubious. It is more likely that the phrase goes with all three nouns, and that it refers not to whether the sources of teaching were truly Pauline but to whether the message attributed to Paul was a faithful representation of his teaching. Since Paul had given teaching about the coming of the Lord at Thessalonica (v. 5), and since he had also spoken about the imminence of judgment in his earlier letter (1 Th. 2:16; 5:2), it is probable that he is referring generally to any of his utterances from which the Thessalonians might have drawn more than he intended to say. This is not quite the same thing as saying that Paul did not know what had misled the readers and therefore named all the conceivable possibilities. Either of these suppositions, however, makes the best sense of the verse.

It is wholly unlikely that at the date of 2 Thessalonians, assuming it is authentic, there should have been any pseudonymous letter purporting to be written by Paul and containing teaching contrary to his own; we know of nothing that would suggest that he had opponents who might do this. The only evidence to the contrary would be 3:17, and it is doubtful whether this verse implies the existence of forged letters. Those who regard the letter as inauthentic take the reference to be to any utterances attributed to Paul (whether by himself or by others claiming his name or authority) which might contain contrary teaching. A. Lindemann, 'Zum Abfassungszweck des Zweiten Thessalonicher briefes', *ZNW* 68, 1977, pp. 35–47, claims that the reference is to 1 Thessalonians, and that by his comments here and in 2:15 the pseudonymous author meant to claim that *his* letter was the only authentic letter of Paul to Thessalonica and thus to put 1 Thessalonians out of circulation as a genuinely Pauline letter, replacing it by his own. This theory attributes to the author a degree of literary depravity which is scarcely conceivable. One may surely take it as a working rule that a Christian author is honest unless there is no other solution to a problem than his deceitfulness. In the present case this theory would appear to be totally unnecessary. Trilling, p. 24 n. 21, argues that it is hard to see why the author should have wanted to discredit the whole of 1 Thessalonians simply to get rid of its eschatology and why his own views should have been thought to be contrary to those in the earlier letter.

3. Whatever Paul may have said to the church at Thessalonica, certainly some person or persons were declaring (whether on his or on their own authority) that the day of the Lord had come. Paul therefore begins his detailed teaching by a strict injunction that the readers are to **let no one deceive** them **in any way**. The language is reminiscent of the warning given by Jesus in Mk 13:5; 'Take heed that no one leads you astray', which occurs in a similar context of misleading teaching that the Messiah has come. There is a real danger of the church being misled by such teaching – as is evidenced by Paul's fears that his readers were already being upset by it. But the similarity of the wording to Mk 13:5 may suggest that there was a standard pattern of response to a situation which could recur at different times and in different places. The effect of the false teaching is not clear. On the one hand, it looks as though the readers may have been deluded into supposing that the parousia was nearer than it really was and thus becoming the victims of illusory hopes. On the other hand, their expectations may have led them to mistake an impostor for the Messiah, just as in Mk 13, and this possibility is strengthened by the reference to deception in vv. 9–12; the readers are to beware of being misled along with the rest of mankind. Paul, therefore, has to make very clear the nature of the events that precede the real parousia.

His next sentence forms an anacolouthon in the Greek. Literally it runs **for unless the rebellion comes first. . .** *RSV* has correctly given the sense by interpolating the words **that day will not come**. Giblin, pp. 122–31, offers a different solution, supplying such a clause as 'the Lord will not have come in judgment to end definitively the deception that is the work of Satan', and he claims that Paul is not discussing the temporal aspects of the parousia but rather its qualitative aspects; his concern is not signs of its coming but rather the conditions for the manifestation of God's judgment. This interpretation is unlikely since it requires the readers to supply the missing phrase from what Paul has not yet written rather than from the immediately preceding context, and in any case it is hard to see how it does away with the temporal 'before and after' element in Paul's argument.

Two related elements must occur first. The first is described as **the rebellion**, literally the apostasy. Paul says nothing to elucidate the word, unless we are to assume that it is more narrowly defined by the second element, the revealing of **the man of lawlessness**. Although various commentators think that two consecutive events are in mind, it seems more probable that one complex event is in mind. (The *RSV* rendering makes it clear that **first** refers to the relation of both events to the day of the Lord.) **rebellion** is a word used in secular Greek for political or military revolt; it was used in the LXX for rebellion against God (Jos. 22:22; 2 Chr. 22:19; 33:10; Jer. 2:19). In particular it referred to the declension of some of the Jews from the Law at the time of the Maccabean revolt (1 Mac.

2:15). In apocalyptic writings the idea of a rebellion against God in the last days became an important motif (Jub. 23:14–21; 2 Esd. 5:1–12; 1 En. 91:7; 93:9). In the *NT* there is a general belief that in the last days the opposition of men to God and immorality and wickedness will greatly increase (Mt. 24:12; 2 Tim. 3:1–9). This is associated with an increase in warfare between nations (Mk 13:7f.) and with the activity of false prophets and teachers (Mk 13 :22; 1 Tim. 4:1–3; 2 Tim. 4:3f.) who attempt to lead the church astray; along with all this there is intensified persecution of the church (Mk 13:9–13). Since Paul can here refer to the **rebellion** as something well known to his readers and requiring no explanation, it is probable that he is taking up this general motif, found in the teaching of Jesus and current more widely in the early church, and reminding his readers that this is an integral part of their expectation for the future. The thought is of a general increase in godliness within the world at large rather than a large-scale apostasy within the church, although the probability of the attitude in the world at large affecting some within the church should not be overlooked. Giblin's view, pp. 81–8, that the event involves the separating out of believers from unbelievers, reads something into the text. Nor is there anything to suggest that a specifically Jewish phenomenon is in mind.

The second element is the revelation of **the man of lawlessness**. *RSV* has preserved the Hebraic form of expression, Anglicised in *GNB* as 'the Wicked One' (cf. 'son of lawlessness', Ps. 89:23; R. D. Aus, 'God's Plan and God's Power: Isaiah 66 and the Restraining Factors of 2 Thess 2, 6–7', *JBL* 96, 1977, pp. 537–53 [p. 538, n. 11], following W. Bornemann). Many MSS have 'the man of sin', but it is probable that this reading is due to the replacement of a rare word by a more common one. The phrase is a unique one, although the idea of a major evil figure opposed to God in the last days is well attested. Elsewhere in the *NT* we read of the expectation of 'antichrist' (1 Jn 2:18, 22; 4:3; 2 Jn 7) or of a false prophet and a beast (Rev. 13). It is probable that these various motifs are related. In the present context the person in mind is evidently a human being and is therefore not to be identified with Satan or some other superhuman figure (cf. v. 9).

Although **lawlessness** may make us think primarily of disobedience to the Jewish law, it is probable that we should take the term, as in 1 Jn 3:4, with particular reference to rebellion against the will of God as it is manifested in the last days. The motif of 'law' has been submerged below the general concept of opposition to God (I. de la Potterie and S. Lyonnet, *The Christian Lives by the Spirit*, Staten Island, 1971, pp. 37–55). All that the phrase tells us, then, is that the individual in question is the arch-opponent of God. In the light of vv. 6–7 the fact that he is to be **revealed** may well imply that he is already in existence somewhere, waiting to be manifested; but it is possible that the verb was chosen simply by analogy with the revealing of the Lord. His characterisation by another Hebraism, **the son of perdition**, means that he is doomed to destruction (cf. 1 Sam. 20:31; Jn 17:12). Paul introduces the phrase at the very outset of his exposition to assure his readers that God's opponent will not succeed.

4. The opposition of the rebel to God is emphasised by the rest of the description. He **opposes and exalts himself against every . . . god**. This echoes Isa. 66:6 (according to R. D. Aus, art. cit., p. 539) and above all Dan. 11:36, where we read of a king who 'shall do according to his will; he shall exalt himself and magnify himself above every god, and shall speak astonishing things against the God of gods.' The common element is the phrase **against . . . every god**. Paul's rewording of the *OT* text stresses the enmity of the rebel against every existing god and his self-exaltation to place himself on the highest level. In Daniel the text applies to a king of the north who is generally identified as Antiochus Epiphanes who plundered the temple in Jerusalem and set up an altar to Zeus. Paul takes over the language, but it is not clear whether he regarded the prophecy in Daniel as pointing primarily to a still-future person or as having a primary fulfilment in the career of Antiochus and a further, final fulfilment in a person yet to come. In any case Jesus and the early church looked forward to a future fulfilment of at least some of the prophecies in Daniel. In taking over the passage Paul adds the words **so-called** and **or object of worship**; the former may stress the unreality of the gods in the ancient world (cf. 1 C. 8 :5) or indicate that *every* object regarded as divine by men is in mind (Masson, p. 96), while the latter brings into the picture all the paraphernalia of idolatry.

The extent of the rebel's opposition to God is seen in its result and climax: **he takes his seat in the temple of God, proclaiming himself to be God**. Although *RSV* translates the clause as an achieved result, it is possible that what is described is merely an attempt to do so. To sit **in the temple** is tantamount to claiming that one is a god, worthy of worship. Behind the imagery may lie the accusation of Ezekiel against the ruler of Tyre (Ezek. 28 : 2) and the stories of Antiochus who himself entered the temple in Jerusalem, of the Roman general Pompey who made his way into the holy of holies, and perhaps also of Caligula, the Roman emperor who attempted to set up an image of himself in the temple in AD 41 (Jos. Ant. 18:261–309).

(1). In the light of these stories it may seem plausible to argue that Paul expected a repetition of this action by the rebel. Certainly such an action could have been regarded as a possible one, and it would probably have seemed utterly blasphemous to Jews and Christians alike. However, there are obvious difficulties with this interpretation. If we accept the Pauline authorship of the passage, we are faced by the fact that the prophecy was not fulfilled, unless we are to identify the destruction of Jerusalem and the desecration of the temple by Titus as the fulfilment. If we date the passage after AD 70, we are confronted by the problem of the writer referring to the desecration of a temple which no longer existed. It is no answer to this difficulty to say that Irenaeus could repeat the prophecy in his own day (Trilling, p. 86, n. 324) and that the writer was using apocalyptic symbols and could treat them as freely as he liked. Irenaeus was repeating what had for him the authority of Scripture, and he may have shared the later view of Hippolytus and others that the temple would be rebuilt. Moreover, it is one thing for apocalyptic writers to use existing imagery freely and another thing for them to produce pictures that would be historically incredible to their readers. Other possibilities than a literal reference to the pre-AD 70 temple must be investigated.

(2). The view just mentioned, namely, that the Jewish temple would be rebuilt at the end of the age, is still defended by adherents of the dispensationalist school of interpretation (Thomas, p. 322). It is part of a total understanding of biblical prophecy which rests on an over-literal interpretation of apocalyptic imagery.

(3). It is possible that Paul is using the imagery of a heavenly temple, presumably regarded as having come down from heaven to earth (see Ps. 11:4; 1 En. 14; 2 Bar. 4; T. Levi 5; b Hag. 12b; for the concept, see R. J. McKelvey, *The New Temple*, Oxford, 1969). However, the idea of a heavenly temple plays no part elsewhere in Paul's thought, and in any case it is difficult to see how Christians could have envisaged the setting up of a new temple in the future.

(4). Paul could have been referring to the church as the temple of God (1 C. 3:16f.; 2 C. 6:16; Eph. 2:21; Giblin, pp. 76–80). This suggestion is tied up with Giblin's view that the rebellious man is a false prophet; sitting in the temple refers to his teaching or judging activity. It seems unlikely, since the context of Paul's remarks suggests a manifestation in the non-Christian world rather than in the church.

(5). Finally, the suggestion may be offered that Paul was using a well-known motif metaphorically and typologically. Taking up a motif derived from Ezekiel and Daniel and given concrete illustration in previous desecrations of the Jewish temple, both actual and attempted, he has used this language to portray the character of the culminating manifestation of evil as an anti-theistic power which usurps the place of God in the world. No specific temple is in mind, but the motif of sitting in the temple and claiming to be God is used to express the opposition of evil to God. Just as Paul goes on to describe the downfall of the rebel in apocalyptic language, so he calls on apocalyptic language to depict his appearance and activity. This of course raises the question whether the rebel himself is merely a symbolic representation, a point to which we must return later. A further problem is whether Paul's readers would have taken his language symbolically rather than literally. This same problem arises with all the apocalyptic pictures in the *NT*, especially in Revelation, and the answer is that probably different readers understood the text with different degrees of literalness and symbolism, just as is the case today. What matters, however, is the spiritual truth conveyed by the imagery, namely, the reality and menace of the power of evil which attempts to deny the reality and power of God.

5. Having shown that the day of the Lord cannot come before the revelation of the rebel, Paul now goes on to show why the rebel has not yet appeared. The reason is one which should have been known by the readers—just as, indeed, they should already have known that the rebel would appear before the coming of the Lord. Paul therefore underlines what he is saying by reminding his readers that he has told them previously about all this, and that they ought to have remembered it. Verse 5 goes closely with v. 6, but at the same time it sums up what has just been said. There is gentle criticism of the readers who ought to **remember** what Paul had told them right back at the time of his visit to the church; note how he reverts to the I form (cf. 1 Th. 2:18; 3:5) and uses the imperfect form of the verb to signify repeated instruction. The thought is paralleled in 1 Th. 5:1f., where again we learn that Paul had instructed the Thessalonians orally about the coming of the Lord (cf. also 1 Th. 3:4; 4:2).

It has been objected that it is odd that, while Paul refers back to what he said at Thessalonica, he makes no reference back to what he wrote on the same topic in 1 Thessalonians (Trilling, p. 88, n. 333). But the problem is unreal, since the theme in 1 Thessalonians was a different one, namely, the nature of the events surrounding the return of the Lord. Admittedly one might claim that there is a difference between the teaching of 1 Th. 5 and of the present passage: here the day of the Lord is preceded by the appearance of the rebel, whereas there it is unheralded by signs. But the 'sign' in the present passage is one that should be recognised by *believers* whereas the point of 1 Th. 5 is that the day takes *unbelievers* unawares, and according to 2 Th. 2 unbelievers do not recognise what is happening but are even deceived and deluded by it. A different explanation of the passage is given by defenders of pseudonymity. For Trilling, p. 88, the verse is meant to assure readers, who knew well that Paul had said nothing like the contents of the present passage in his acknowledged letters, that the teaching really went back to Paul himself who had declared it in his (now inaccessible) oral teaching. This seems to be a very artificial understanding of a verse which makes good sense on the assumption of authenticity.

6. Some linguists make a distinction between 'old information' and 'new information'. The former is 'shared information . . . a kind of starting point based on concepts already "in the air", to which the new information' can be related' (W. L. Chafe, *Meaning and the Structure of Language*, Chicago, 1970, p. 211). This useful distinction can be applied to a text like the present one where Paul assumes a community of existing knowledge ('old information') between himself and his readers, expressed in **And you know** . . ., and then proceeds to draw fresh insights and make new points ('new information'). If the task of exegesis was simply to elucidate the new information supplied by the text, it would be comparatively simple. Unfortunately this text is the classical example of a situation where the modern reader does not share the old information possessed by the original recipients of the letter. Just what was it that they already knew? It could be something that they had been taught earlier by Paul (whether orally or in a previous letter), or something that they knew by personal experience. The Greek verb used here (*oida*) has been thought to have the latter nuance (Giblin, pp. 159–66), although what the readers knew personally may well have been something that they recognised only in the light of Paul's earlier teaching.

The adverb **now** should probably be taken with the verb **you know** (*contra RSV*). Logically and temporally it gives a contrast with the preceding verse: 'You remember what I told you then, and now you know for yourselves' (Trilling, pp. 88f.). Frame, pp. 262f., and Best, p. 290, prefer to follow *RSV* and see a contrast with the future events described in the following verses (cf. 'And then' in v. 8; but the contrast here is rather with the 'already' in v. 7). The readers are acquainted with 'that which restrains in order that he may be revealed in his (own) time'. The Greek is terse and cryptic here and in v. 7, but our translation gives the probable sense.

Paul uses a neuter phrase, **what is restraining** (*to katechon*, article with participle), but in v. 7 he uses the masculine form instead. This suggests that he is thinking of some entity which can be regarded both as a principle and as a person. The meaning of the

verb translated 'restrain' is disputed (for a summary of the possibilities see H. Hanse, *TDNT* II, pp. 829f.). Normally the verb
means 'to hold fast', and it can be used of physical restraint (Lk.
4:42; Phm. 13) or of holding things fast in one's memory and
obeying them (Lk. 8:15; 1 C. 11:2; 15:2; 1 Th. 5:21; Heb. 3:6, 14;
10:23). It can also mean to occupy a place (Lk. 14:9) or to hold a
person or thing in bondage (Rom. 1:18; 7:6). In the passive the
verb can be used of being 'held' by a supernatural power in a state
of religious inspiration or ecstasy.

Attempts have been made to suggest a Semitic background to
Paul's use of the Greek word here. O. Betz, 'Der Katechon', *NTS*
9, 1962–3, pp. 276–91, thought that it was equivalent to Hebrew
tamak, used in 1Q27 (but see Giblin, pp. 168–76, who notes that
the word is never translated by *katechō* in LXX), and R. D. Aus,
art. cit., has suggested Hebrew '*āsar*, used in Isa. 66:9 of shutting
up the womb; the strength of this proposal rests on whether Aus's
claim that Isa. 66 provides other elements of background for this
passage is found convincing. Three main possibilities of translation
have been proposed: (1). The majority of commentators translate
'to hold back, restrain', hence 'to delay'. (2). Frame, pp. 258, 264,
and Best, p. 299 take the verb intransitively as 'to hold sway'.
(3). Giblin, pp. 167–242, takes it actively as 'to seize', in the sense
of spiritual possession by a demonic, pseudo-prophetic force that
was captivating the readers. This view was adequately refuted by
Best, pp. 298f., who notes that the active use of the verb with this
meaning is unusual, and that in 1 Th. 5:21 Paul uses the verb in a
good sense rather than in a bad sense (as here).

Perhaps a stronger objection lies in the words **so that he may be
revealed in his time**. This phrase expresses purpose, and, despite
the objections of Giblin, pp. 204–10, it seems impossible to deprive
it of a purposive content and link it with 'you know' so that 'the
link . . . is little more than an expression of temporal consequence
between the present experience of a force analogous to the
ἄνθρωπος τῆς ἀνομίας and the future manifestation of this latter
figure at the determined moment' (Giblin, p. 210). Rather what
Paul is saying is that the readers know what is restraining the
rebellious man in order that he may be revealed at the appointed
time *and not before it* (cf. *NEB*, 'that he shall be revealed only at
the proper time'. See, however, M. Barnouin, 'Les problèmes de
traduction concernant II Thess. ii. 6–7', *NTS* 23, 1976–7, pp. 482–
98, who translates 'vous connaisez ce qui le tient gardé, avec comme
but qu'il soit révélé, lui, au temps qui sera le sien'.). Our exposition assumes that the **he** (*RSV*) who is to be revealed is the rebel,
as in v. 3; attempts to interpret 'he' as Jesus or the restraining

power are misguided. **his time** (*RSV*; UBS adopts the variant reading 'his own time', but the sense is unaffected) is the time appointed
for his appearance by *God* whose purpose is in process of fulfilment
(Ac. 1:7). The question of what is delaying his appearance will be
best examined after we have looked at v. 7.

7. Paul's next move is to explain the significance of what his
readers already know. The loose conjunction **For** shows that he is
explaining how it is that the rebel will not be revealed until the right
time: although it is true that **the mystery of lawlessness is already
at work,** it is under restraint for the time being. The effect of the
contrast between the two parts of the verse is to make the first
clause have a concessive force. The first point, then, is that the
appearance of the rebel is preceded by the present working of
lawlessness; note how lawlessness has its personal and impersonal
aspects, just like the restraining force. The **mystery of lawlessness**
can hardly mean 'the secret about lawlessness' despite the analogy
of other places where 'mystery' refers to a divine secret now revealed
to God's people about some aspect of his saving purpose (Mk. 4:11;
Rom. 11:25; 1 C. 4:1; Col. 1:26f.; *et al.*). It must refer rather to the
secret, hidden activity of lawlessness, 'not something incomprehensible, but something hidden' (K. Haacker, 'Erwägungen zu Mc iv
11', *NovT* 14, 1972, pp. 219–25). The correct parallel to the expression is to be found in Jos. Bel. 1:470 which describes the life of
Antipater as 'secret evil' (literally 'a mystery of evil') rather than in
the phrase 'the mysteries of sin' in the Qumran texts (1QH 5:36;
cf. 1 QM 14:9; 1Q27 1:2, 7). As in v. 3 we take **lawlessness** in the
more general sense of rebellion against God. The verb **is at work** is
best taken as a Greek middle (intransitive) form rather than as a
passive ('is caused to work, *sc.* by God').

The second part of the verse runs literally 'only he who now
restrains until he is out of the way'. It can be understood in two
main ways: (1). M. Barnouin, art. cit., pp. 486–90, translates:
'Quelqu'un le tenant seulement gardé actuellement jusqu'à ce que,
sortant de là, il vienne.' On this view the subject of the subordinate
clause is the same as the object of the participle: someone keeps the
rebel back until the latter appears. On this view the restrainer is
not removed from the scene (cf. R. D. Aus, art. cit., p. 551).
However, this interpretation leaves the sentence without a main
verb and gives a dubious rendering of the phrase 'is out of the way'.
(2). It is better, therefore, to understand the form of the sentence
in the light of the close parallel in Gal. 2:10, where we have a similar
case of the ellipse of the main clause (to be supplied from the
preceding context) and the placing of the subject of the subordinate
clause before the conjunction. This gives the translation: '(it is at

work) only until he who now restrains is out of the way'. The restraining force is now personal (masculine participle) and **now** means 'at the present moment', with perhaps a hint of temporal limitation (cf. 1 Th. 3:6). R. D. Aus, art cit., p. 542, holds that the expression is a Hebraism based on Dan. 11:31; 12:11 (where *sûr* is used of the removal of the continual burnt offering). The phrase is paralleled in 1 C. 5:2; Col. 2:14, where it signifies removal from the scene of action or banishment. H. W. Fulford, ' "Ἕως ἐκ μέσου γένηται," 2 Thes. 2:7,' *ExpT* 23, 1911–12, pp. 40f., adduced parallels from Plutarch which show that the phrase can mean 'retires from the scene.' Once the restraining power has been removed, rebellion will no longer take place in a hidden fashion; there will be an open manifestation of evil.

We must now try to determine what Paul means by the 'restraining power' and the 'rebel.' It is necessary to distinguish between the origin and character of his language and what he may have meant by it.

There is some precedent in Jewish apocalyptic for the idea of keeping back an evil power. Two great monsters, Behemoth and Leviathan, are kept, until the time when the Messiah will begin to be revealed, for food for those who survive until then (2 Bar. 29:4; cf. 2 Esd. 6:49–52, where the eschatological motif is not apparent). In Rev. 7:1–3 restraint is placed on the winds until the servants of God have been sealed. There may be traces of the same motif in Job 7:12. We also have the thought of the binding of Satan during the millennium in Rev. 20:1–3, an idea which has some pre-history in Isa. 24:21f.; Tob. 8:3; 1 En. 10:4–12; 18:14–16; 19:1f.; 21:1–6; Jub. 23:29; 48:15; T. Levi 18:12, where we read of the binding and imprisonment for temporary periods of demons, fallen angels, Mastema and Satan. Against this background Dibelius, pp. 47–51, argued that the Pauline teaching ultimately rests on a myth in which a heavenly being restrains the forces of evil. Best, pp. 296f., has offered some criticisms of this theory, in particular that it fails to identify satisfactorily the restraining force and the nature of its activity. However, the main thrust of his case appears to be that the theory does not go far enough. It illuminates the imagery but it does not explain how Paul was using it. In short, in terms of the distinction made above, we have here a theory of the origin and character of Paul's language. It still remains to determine how Paul was using it and what he wished to convey by it.

(1). One early interpretation of the passage finds the restraining force in the Roman Empire as personified in the Emperor himself. This view has much to commend it, since it gives a convincing explanation of the mixture of genders and it draws on Paul's own experience of the Empire as a force making for law and order. Paul's attitude to Rome is generally favourable; the administration was basically just, even if there were plenty of unjust governors and officials. It is no objection to this view to say that Rome does not play this role in Jewish apocalyptic; Paul could well have innovated here. A greater difficulty is whether Paul could have envisaged the Emperor (or the Empire) being removed to make way for the rebel. If the passage were post-Pauline, some consideration might be given to the Nero-redivivus myth, according to which Nero was believed not to have died but to have hidden in the east among the Parthians and to be ready to lead them in an invasion against Rome. Traces of this myth may be present in Rev. 13:13f. On this view the restrainer would be the reigning Emperor and the rebel would be the returning Nero. (For details of the myth, see G. R. Beasley-Murray, *The Book of Revelation*, London, 1974, pp. 210f.) But this myth is too late to have influenced Paul himself, and even fear of the Parthians was not an important factor in the fifties. It has also been objected that the rebel appears to be more of a religious seducer than a political tyrant, but it is certainly not unknown for political tyrants to claim divine honours for themselves.

(2). Since the Roman Empire did not come to an end in the kind of way just envisaged, some commentators have tried to salvage Paul's reputation as a reliable prophet by arguing that the restraining force is not the Empire as such but the principle of law and order which was typified by it and which still continues in the form of other political systems. On this view the force is given a literary personification in v. 7 (Lightfoot, p. 114; Morris, pp. 226f.).

(3). B. B. Warfield, 'The Prophecies of St Paul. 1 and 2 Thes-salonians', *Exp* 3:4, 1886, pp. 30–44, identified the Jewish state as the restraining power. Once Judaism had effectively ceased to exist and Christianity could no longer shelter under its protection, the latter would be exposed to the full force of persecution by Rome. In particular, James of Jerusalem was the personification of this restraining force. This hypothesis appears to have found no followers.

(4). Frame, pp. 261f., considered that the force holding sway is none other than Satan, whose influence is already at work in the world as 'the mystery of lawlessness'. When the time appointed by God comes, Satan will be put out of the way, so that the rebel can take the stage. Frame saw a possible allusion to this limited role of Satan in the Freer logion, a textual variant to Mk. 16:14 in the Washington or Freer Codex (W): 'The term of years for Satan's power has been fulfilled, but other terrible things draw near;' he suggested that his being put out of the way might correspond to his being cast from heaven to earth in Rev. 12. This view requires that the verb *katechō* be translated as 'to hold sway.' A somewhat similar view is held by Best, pp. 299–302, who thinks that the power which holds sway, 'the hostile occupying power,' is an evil agent (but not Satan himself) who will step aside when the rebel appears.

(5). A diametrically opposite view is that the restraining force is God himself; he delays the final revelation of evil in all its fullness. This view was especially developed by A. Strobel, *Untersuchungen zum eschatologischen Verzögerungsproblem auf Grund der spätjudisch-urchristlichen Geschichte von Habakkuk 2, 2ff.*, Leiden, 1961 (see also J. Ernst, *Die eschatologischen Gegenspieler in den Schriften des Neuen Testaments*, Regensburg, 1967; D. J. Stephens, *Eschatological Themes in 2 Thessalonians 2:1–12*, unpublished thesis, St Andrews, 1976; Burkeen, pp. 348–50; Thomas, pp. 324f., holds that the Holy Spirit is in mind). It has been developed by Trilling, pp. 90–102, who argues that the restraining force is simply the delay of the parousia which the readers were experiencing and which is ultimately due to God himself. Trilling argues that there is no essential difference between the neuter and masculine forms of expression, although he recognises that it is God who stands behind the delaying action. It is surprising that Trilling makes no attempt to answer the criticisms which Best, pp. 300f., had already made of this interpretation. Best argues that this is a highly odd way to refer to the action of God, that the theory requires that 'is out of the way' be taken to mean 'withdraw' (but see above for this possibility), and that to take *katechō* in the sense of 'to delay' is abnormal.

(6). A related view is that the restraining factor is the proclamation of the gospel (neuter) by Christian missionaries and in particular by Paul himself (masculine); when Paul is 'out of the way' then the End will come (O. Cullmann, 'Le caractère eschatologique du devoir missionaire et de la conscience apostolique de S. Paul', *RHPR* 16, 1936, pp. 210–45; in German translation in *id.*, *Vorträge und Aufsätze 1925–67*, Tübingen, 1967, pp. 305–36; J. Munck, *Paul and the Salvation of Mankind*, London, 1959, pp. 36–42). The theory suggests that Paul christianised the principle that all Israel must repent before the End can come (SB III, pp. 640f.). Best, pp. 297f., argues against this view that Paul is not especially conscious of his apostolic position as the missionary to the Gentiles in these epistles; but this is not a strong point in view of the evidence of 1 Th. 1–2. A much stronger objection is that, according to 1 Th. 4:13–18, Paul reckoned with the possibility of his own survival until the parousia (Whiteley, p. 102), and this must be pronounced fatal to the theory in this form. It is also very dubious whether Paul, though insistent on his position as the apostle to the Gentiles, saw himself as the essential factor in God's saving plan for mankind.

(7) Finally, as we have seen, Giblin takes *katechō* in the sense 'to seize' and argues that false prophets were misleading the Thessalonians; they were led by one particular individual whom Paul believed must be ousted before there could take place the manifestation of the rebel and his destruction by the Lord. This view is unlikely philologically, and it fails to explain why the removal of false prophets in one local church should occupy such a crucial position in the development of God's plan.

We have now examined the main views of this passage, and it is safe to say that none of them is free from difficulty. (*a*). The view that the restraining or occupying power is good rather than evil in character seems essential to making sense of the passage. A contest between two opposing evil forces is most improbable, and the idea of one evil force disappearing to make room for another also seems unlikely. If so, we may rule out views (4) and (7). (*b*). If Paul regarded Rome as the restraining power, we are left with the problem of finding a candidate for the rebellious man. On this view it can hardly have been a Roman Emperor, although the parallels of Pompey and Caligula would surely have pointed strongly in that direction. This consideration speaks against views (1) and (2). (*c*). We are brought back to the view that God himself is involved in the restraint. Just as the rebel is an apocalyptic figure, about whose identity and nature Paul does not speculate, so too the restraining force is of supernatural dimensions and must be understood as having a divine origin. The view that sees the preaching of the gospel to all nations (Mk 13:10) as the factor which causes God to restrain the final outbreak of evil is attractive, provided that it is not linked to the activity of any single individual, such as Paul himself. It may be that Paul had in mind some angelic figure who was keeping evil under restraint during the period of preaching until its final, open manifestation; if so, it is not too difficult to think of this figure 'withdrawing' at God's command at the appointed time.

We thus adopt a modified version of view (6), according to which it is ultimately God who will allow the rebel to be manifested only when the present opportunity for preaching and hearing the gospel is brought to an end by the removal of the angelic figure who is now in charge. Then the power of evil, which has been at work secretly in the world, but none the less effectively, will be openly manifested so as to produce the final showdown.

The advantages of this view are: (i). It recognises the essentially apocalyptic nature of Paul's language. (ii). It links Paul's teaching to other strands of apocalyptic in the *NT*, and in particular it makes use of the one clearly expressed condition that must be fulfilled before the End, namely, the preaching of the gospel (cf. 2 Pet. 3:9; Rev. 14:6f.). (iii). It avoids the problems caused by regarding Paul as the personification of the restraining force, and it also avoids speaking of God himself being put 'out of the way'. (iv). It provides an understanding of the passage which will fit in with its Pauline origin. Since Paul shows knowledge of the synoptic apocalyptic teaching, there is nothing here that need be pronounced un-Pauline. In particular, it must be emphasised that there is nothing here that is incompatible with 1 Thessalonians. If, however, the passage is not from Paul, we are faced by the insuperable difficulty that the author expressed himself in a manner that would have been almost incomprehensible for his readers, especially since v. 5 cannot now refer to previous instruction given to the readers (see R. D. Aus, art cit., p. 549 n. 68). (v). Without forcing the language of the passage, we have found that the most probable exegesis of it gives an interpretation which can still be valid today, no doubt after a longer period than Paul could have envisaged.

8. Once the restraining or occupying force is out of the way, the final stage in the apocalyptic drama takes place. **And then** contrasts with 'now' in v. 7 (rather than with 'now' in v. 6); but the phrase is a common one in prophecies of series of apocalyptic events (Mk 13:21, 26, 27). **the lawless one** is the normal Greek phrase for the person described as 'the man of the lawlessness' in Hebraic fashion in v. 3. In contrast to the secret working of evil in the present time, he **will be revealed** openly (cf. vv. 3, 6). Paul has thus arrived back at the same point of time as in v. 3 after the parenthesis in vv. 6–7. The condition has been fulfilled for the appearance of the Lord Jesus. We are not told how long the rebel will act openly and unhindered; instead all the attention is concentrated on his downfall. This takes place at the time of, and as a result of, the **appearing** and **coming** of the Lord. This phrase is in the dative, expressing instrumentality, and here for the first time Paul places alongside the word *parousia* another term, *epiphaneia*, to describe the appearing of the Lord (cf. 1 Tim. 6:14; 2 Tim. 4:1, 8; Tit. 2:13; in 2 Tim. 1:10 it is used to describe the incarnation of Jesus). The word has the same basic meaning as *parousia*, so much so that some commentators think that Paul is simply piling up words for effect. But the word was used in the *OT* for an epiphany or revelation of God, especially but not exclusively in a hostile sense (2 Sam. 7:23; 2 Mac. 2:21; 3:24); and it was also used in Hellenistic Greek for visits by emperors and other dignitaries. Something of these senses may well be present here as Paul emphasises the powerful and sovereign character of the appearance of the Lord.

Paul draws on *OT* language to describe how **the Lord Jesus** ('Jesus' is omitted by some MSS and bracketed by UBS, but should probably be retained in the text) **will slay him with the breath of his mouth and destroy him**. Behind this statement with its two clauses in synonymous parallelism we may trace the influence of Isa. 11:4 LXX: 'And he shall smite . . . with the word of his mouth, and with the breath of his lips he shall slay the wicked'. Paul has identified the 'wicked' (a collective expression in Isa.) with the rebellious man, and he has altered the wording of the citation from 'the breath of his lips' to 'the breath of his mouth' by running together the two phrases in Isa., possibly under the influence of Ps. 33:6. The verb **slay** is probably original in Paul's wording; some MSS have 'consume', but this may be due to a copying error. The thought is of the powerful **breath** of the Lord (cf. Exod. 15:8; Job 4:9); but probably not of a fiery breath (as in 2 Esd. 13:10f.; Rev. 11:5), unless we are to take 'in flaming fire' (v. 7) as indicating this. Calvin held that the reference was simply to his word (so Whiteley, p. 102). Its effect is to kill the rebellious man and **destroy** him, i.e. render him powerless. The action is depicted with a notable lack of detail; Paul merely uses appropriate *OT* phraseology to emphasise the sovereign power of annihilation demonstrated by the Lord. Nothing further needed to be said.

9. Somewhat surprisingly at first sight Paul continues the sentence started in v. 8 with a rather awkwardly placed 'whose', which must refer back to the rebellious one (hence *RSV* begins a new sentence and paraphrases with **The coming of the lawless one**), although the nearest antecedent is 'the Lord Jesus'. Such loose sentence construction is not unknown elsewhere in Paul (see, for example, Rom. 9:22–26). Temporally, Paul reverts to the description of the open manifestation of the rebellious man, which he describes as a **coming** (Gk. *parousia*) in order to underline how it is a Satanic counterpart to the coming of the Lord and hence a source of deception. *RSV* translates the Greek verb 'is' by **will be**, which is contextually justified. Commentators differ as to what is the predicate of the clause, but Best's view, p. 304, that **by the activity of Satan** forms part of the predicate and is not a phrase attached to the subject (as in *RSV*), is most likely. Paul is thus saying that the rebellious one's manifestation takes place as a result of (literally, according to) the inspiration of Satan; he uses the word *energeia* (cf. v. 11) which normally is used of the power of God. Just as God empowers the Messiah, so **Satan** empowers the 'antichrist' (cf. Rev. 13:2).

Thanks to this satanic inspiration the rebellious man is equipped **with all power** to do mighty works. There is an interesting contrast in Rom. 15:18f. where Paul describes 'what Christ has wrought through' him 'by the power of signs and wonders, by the power of the Holy Spirit'. Through this satanic power the rebellious man too is able to work **signs and wonders** (cf. Mk 13:22, where the false messiahs and prophets perform signs and wonders to deceive men), only they are **pretended**. This last word is literally 'of falsehood', a genitive of origin, which may indicate the source, the nature or the intention of the rebellious man's activity. Probably the epithet should go with all three nouns (i.e. including 'power' contrary to *RSV*) and it expresses the source of the miraculous activity—there is no suggestion that the miracles are in any way unreal. The activity described is paralleled in the description of the beast and the false prophet in Rev. 13 and makes it clear that we are dealing with different forms of the same tradition, which is also found in Mk 13:22. The plasticity of the imagery (one evil figure here, two in Rev. 13, several in Mk 13) warns against taking the apocalyptic symoolism over-literally. On the other hand, it is unnecessary to argue with Trilling, pp. 103f., that two originally separate images, one of a potentate and the other of a false prophet, have been run together by the author.

10. The description of the activity of the rebellious man continues with a further phrase parallel to the previous one and describing its effect. His activity takes place **with all wicked deception**. Again the thought is paralleled in Mk 13:22 and Rev. 13:13f. where the aim of the evil powers is to lead people astray. **wicked** is literally 'of wickedness' and may refer to the character (von Dobschütz, p. 288) or the origin (Frame, p. 270) of the deceitful activity; probably both ideas should be included, since what is evil in origin becomes evil in nature. The noun is virtually synonymous with 'lawlessness' or 'rebellion' (Rigaux, p. 675), and is used particularly of the opposition to God which reaches its climax in the last days. (Ps. Sol. 17:23–29; Diog. 9:1); in the *NT*, however, it is used more generally of all evil conduct. The activity of the rebellious one has this deceptive effect on **those who are to perish** (literally, 'the perishing'; we take the phrase as a 'dative of disadvantage' with 'deception' and not with the verb 'is' in v. 9). This is a Pauline phrase (1 C. 1:18; 2 C. 2:15; 4:3), used in contrast with 'those who are being saved'. The thought is not of two pre-determined classes of people whose character and destiny is fixed by God, but is simply descriptive of the actual character of certain people as being on their way to destruction (and thus in a sense already experiencing something of that process) and of others as being on their way to salvation (and already experiencing the saving power of God).

Two important things follow from Paul's description. The first is

that the deceptive power of the rebellious one is for those who are
on the way to destruction and not (it is implied) for those who are
being saved. The saved, as von Dobschütz, p. 288, finally puts it,
certainly experience the coming of the rebellious one as severe
persecution. But the miraculous signs are not a source of danger to
them—their deceptive effect is confined to those who are perishing.
The second thing is that the perishing are deceived and hence
brought to destruction **because they refused to love the truth and
so be saved**. Whatever one may say about divine predestination,
the lost carry the responsibility for their own perdition. It takes
place **because** (an unusual conjunction found only here in Paul, but
used by Luke in the context of judgment upon wrong-doing, Lk.
1:20; 19:44; Ac. 12:23) they did not welcome the love of the truth.
This is a somewhat unusual phrase, perhaps coined as a contrast to
'deception of wickedness' (von Dobschütz, p. 289). **the truth** is
manifestly for Paul the gospel message, since he is thinking primarily of those who have rejected the Christian message and persecute those who have accepted it (*pace* Best, p. 308, no particular
reference to the Jews is intended). Trilling, p. 110, explores the
possibility of a wider understanding of 'truth', so that the passage
may throw some light on the fate of those who have not heard the
gospel but respond positively or negatively to such truth (or whatever they consider to be truth) as has been revealed to them. This
is an attractive idea, since, even if for Paul the gospel represented
the fullest revelation of truth, he did not deny that the truth is
revealed fragmentarily in other ways (Rom. 1:18–20).

The proper attitude to truth is to **love** it; the use of 'love' with
an objective genitive is common enough (cf. 'the love of God', Lk.
11:42; 'love of the Father', 1 Jn 2:15). It is the use of the verb 'they
did not receive' with the object 'love' (paraphrased by *RSV*: **they
refused to love**) which is unusual. Von Dobschütz, p. 289, offers
the explanation: they had had no love for the truth at all, and
consequently, when it was offered to them in the gospel, they did
not receive it. Frame, p. 271, suggests that what was offered to
them was not just the gospel, which might be received merely on
an intellectual level, but the more difficult love for it; in other
words, what was offered to them as a result of the Spirit's call
through the Word (1 Th. 1:5; 2:13) was the possibility of love for
the Word. This explanation fits in nicely with Pauline thought where
the possibility of receiving the gospel is offered to men along with
the gospel (Eph. 2:8; 2 Tim. 2:25; cf. Ac. 5:31; 11:18 for hints in
this direction). The result of accepting the truth would of course
have been that they would **be saved** (cf 1 Th. 2:16).

11. Paul picks up the last clause in v. 10 and proceeds to explain from it how those who are destined to perish are deceived by the rebellious man into believing his false claims. It is because they refused the truth that **therefore God sends upon them a strong delusion**, literally 'a power of delusion', in order that they may **believe what is false**. The present tense **sends** is probably futuristic in sense, 'is going to send' (cf. 'is' in v. 9); but it would probably not be wrong to see here an expression of a principle which is always at work. Those who refuse to believe and accept the truth find that judgment comes upon them in the form of an inability to accept the truth. The accent in the verse lies on the fact that this is a deliberate action of **God**. Various commentators have rightly warned against any attempt to weaken the force of Paul's statement, no matter how unwelcome it may be to modern readers; we must not twist Paul's words to make him say what we should like him to say. The belief that God can use evil spirits and send them upon men in order to accomplish his purpose is found in the *OT* (cf. 2 Sam. 24:1 with 1 Chr. 21:1; 1 Kg. 22:23; Ezek. 14:9). And in Paul's classical exposition of sin and its consequences in Rom. 1:24ff. we may see the same emphasis on how God deliberately gives up sinners to further sin. Lightfoot, p. 117, found three stages in the present passage: rejection of the truth; a divinely willed infatuation; and, consequently, a final punishment; and he argued that the same three stages can be traced in Rom. 1, 'the second being there dwelt on with a fearful earnestness'. The attempt by Trilling, pp. 112f., to dispute the exactness of the comparison is not convincing. The links with Rom. 1:25 where we have the same idea of accepting 'the lie' (*RSV* **what is false**) seem fairly obvious.

12. The closing part of the sentence indicates the ultimate purpose of God which is the condemnation of all **who did not believe the truth but had pleasure in unrighteousness**. Thus Paul lays the final emphasis upon the human responsibility of those who are condemned. The phraseology used is slightly unusual. The phrase **did not believe** represents an aorist participle and is followed by an object in the dative case, whereas normally Paul uses the present participle of this verb and uses a preposition with the object. The unusual construction here is explained, first, by Paul's wish to show that a *prior* act of unbelief leads to condemnation; secondly, by his use of an impersonal object with the verb in the same construction as occurs in the phrase 'to obey the gospel' (Gal. 5:7); and, thirdly, by his attempt to gain close parallelism with the immediately following phrase.

Instead of accepting the truth, the persons condemned had taken **pleasure in unrighteousness** (the same word as is translated by 'wicked' in v. 10). (Elsewhere, when Paul uses this verb with an object, he inserts a preposition, 1 C. 10:5; 2 C. 12:10; but these two instances are hardly sufficient to substantiate a rule.) Frame, p. 272, rightly notes that this antithesis shows that Paul is thinking of truth 'more on the moral than on the purely intellectual side'. The biblical connection of right belief with right conduct (and false belief with evil conduct) is thus exemplified. It becomes clear that divine condemnation results not from human intellectual errors but much rather from delight in what is evil and immoral.

The effect of v. 12 is to generalise to some extent what Paul has been saying. We do not have to wait until the point when we can, as it were, identify the arrival of the final climax of evil in order to see the outworking of the divine process of judgment. It is true at all times that sin consists in delighting in what is wrong, and that those who persist in sin find that they become unable to do anything else. Paul's insight lies in the recognition that sin is contrary to the intention of God for man, and that slavery to sin is the divinely imposed penalty which leads in the end to condemnation. Yet that process is not an inevitable one, and the final accent in the passage lies on the possibility of a different pattern in the life of man. It follows that the primary significance of the passage is not that we should be trying to calculate whether or not the End is near but that we should be concerned about the moral and spiritual issues which are involved.

THANKSGIVING AND ENCOURAGEMENT

2:13–17

A new section begins here, marked off by the change in style from what has preceded. It takes the form of an expression of thanksgiving for the divine election and calling of the readers to salvation and a share in the glory of the Lord. This expression is meant to have a teaching and reassuring function over against any doubts that they might have regarding the possibility of their apostasy from the faith, and so it serves as a basis for the encouragement in v. 15 to stand fast in what they have been taught. This command is then matched by a prayer that God will encourage and strengthen them in faith and action. Thus the whole passage is meant to be an antidote to the feelings of uncertainty aroused by the suggestions that the Last Day had already come, and it reassures the readers that they will have their share in the glory associated with the parousia.

The occurrence of a second thanksgiving in the Epistle, for which we may compare 1 Th. 2:13–16, has raised problems in the minds of some commentators. But it is hard to see why the writer should be deprived of the freedom to structure his letter as he chose and not in accord with some twentieth-century rules of form criticism. Bjerkelund, p. 139, argues that we have here the conclusion of the opening thanksgiving which was interrupted by Paul's teaching on the future (so Burkeen, pp. 256–8).

13. Opinions differ whether the opening **But** is simply a particle of transition or marks a contrast with the preceding section. If it is the latter, it would appear at first to contrast **we** with what precedes, but this is unnatural since there is no obvious noun with which to make the contrast. More generally, there may be a contrast between the present verses which treat of God's election of the readers to salvation and the preceding verses which speak of his condemnation of the lost. As for the use of 'we', there is no special stress on the word; von Dobschütz, p. 297, observes that Paul frequently inserts a personal pronoun at the beginning of a new section. The opening phrase **we are bound to give thanks to God always for you, brethren,** is virtually identical with 1:3, in the same way as 1 Th. 2:13 is similar to 1 Th. 1:2. The repetition of the earlier phrase is fairly natural—such things often occur unconsciously—but it may be deliberate in that Paul is reassuring his readers by reminding them that he has already said that he cannot help giving thanks for their Christian state. But, whereas in 1:3 he gave thanks for their demonstration of Christian virtues, here the stress lies more on what God is doing in their lives, and it is on this fact that he would build their assurance.

This motif comes out immediately in the expansion of the address **brethren** by the phrase **beloved by the Lord**. Here **Lord** must be a reference to Jesus (the contrast with the immediately preceding and following occurrences of **God** guarantees this identification), and this distinguishes the phrase from the close parallel in 1 Th. 1:4 where the thought of God's love is associated with his act of election. But why has Paul shifted the emphasis from God to Jesus? A certain tendency to ascribe to Jesus what was ascribed to God in 1 Th. has been noted (3:3, 16a, b; cf. 2:16). Commentators have not been able to produce convincing reasons for the change in the present passage, whether by Paul or an imitator. The fact is that Paul has no stereotyped phraseology for divine love. The change has the effect of closely associating the Lord Jesus with God in the act of election through his love for the elect (cf. Rom. 8:35; Gal. 2:20; 2 C. 5:14). In the present context it may be deliberate in order to reassure the readers that the Lord Jesus, who is coming for his own people and who will destroy the wicked, loves them in particular and will keep them in safety for final salvation. Why Trilling, p.

119, should regard the whole expression as lacking in warmth is beyond comprehension.

Arising out of this love, we have the fact of divine choice for which Paul gives thanks to God. **chose** translates a somewhat unusual verb (*haireō*), possibly under the influence of *OT* usage (Dt. 26:18), where it concerns God's choice of Israel. The thought corresponds with that in 1 Th. 1:4 where a noun is used. We accept the text adopted by *RSV* **from the beginning** (Gk. *ap 'archēs*) rather than the variant reading 'as the first converts' (literally, 'as firstfruits'. Gk. *aparchēn*) adopted by UBS. The latter reading has limited but strong MS support and offers a Pauline word (Rom. 8:23; 11:16; 16:5; 1 C. 15:20, 23; 16:15) rather than a phrase which Paul does not use elsewhere. The decisive argument against the variant, however, is that it does not make sense in the context; one cannot see of what greater harvest the readers can be said to be the firstfruits. A simple scribal error (cf. the confusion in the MSS at Sir. 24:9; Rom. 16:5; Rev. 14:4), coupled with the influence of the better-known Pauline phrase, is probably the cause of the change. **from the beginning** must refer to the distant past (cf. Mt. 19:4; Jn 1:1) and has the effect of placing the act of election in association with the purpose of God for the world before creation (Eph. 1:4). Such statements assert that, if God made his plan so long ago, it is unlikely to be altered, and they thus form a source of assurance for the readers. God's choice of them was for them **to be saved**, literally 'for salvation', and this forms a deliberate contrast with the thought of those who are lost or perishing in v. 10. From 1 Th. 5:8 we see that the term refers especially to the fact of future deliverance, but in the present context it should be given a wide application to the whole of God's saving action in the lives of his people.

Paul proceeds to name two factors which determine the actual realisation of this salvation in the lives of the readers. On the one hand, there is **sanctification by the Spirit**. The phrase is paralleled in 1 Pet. 1:2. Literally 'sanctification of spirit', it could be taken to mean the sanctifying of the human spirit (cf. 2 C. 7:1; 1 Th. 5:23); but this is less likely than the act of sanctification by the Spirit (1 Th. 4:3–8). On the latter view we get a better parallelism with the immediately following phrase. Alongside this action of God there is the human action of **belief in the truth**, which stands in strong contrast with the attitude in v. 12. The **truth** is of course the divine revelation contained in the gospel (cf. Gal. 4:7; the language here seems to be perfectly possible for Paul, *pace* Trilling, p. 122). The logical relation of the action of the Spirit and the development of faith is not certain. The mention of the divine action first may well imply that it is this which gives rise to faith, but nothing in Paul suggests that faith and unbelief are unrelated to human responsibility.

14. To this represents the same Greek phrase as 'to this end' in 1:11 and sums up the general content of the preceding verse. In order that God might bring about the purpose of salvation through sanctification and faith which he had planned for the readers he **called** them (some MSS insert *kai*, 'also', but this could be assimilation to 1:11). Here the verb is used of the initial summons to faith (cf. 1 Th. 4:7, and contrast the continuing character of the call in 1 Th. 2:12; 5:24). The call came **through our gospel**, i.e. by means of the message preached by Paul and his associates (1 Th. 1:5). Paul is following the same pattern as in Rom. 8:29f. where God's predestination leads to his calling and ultimate glorification of his people. Trilling, p. 122, however, disputes that we have Pauline thinking here. He argues that Paul never elsewhere sees God's call as taking place through the preaching of the gospel; it is exclusively the act of God and stands 'over' the act of preaching. 'Gospel' and 'calling' are never linked, for 'calling' is an exclusively theocentric idea. As with so many of Trilling's attempts to detect non-Pauline nuances in this letter, this comment is unconvincing. Election and the preaching of the gospel follow one another closely in 1 Th. 1:4f. In 1 Th. 2:13 Paul goes so far as to claim that the words of the missionaries were received as the word of God (note that 'calling' is present in the previous verse). In Gal. 1:6 and 7 the relationship between God's call and the gospel could not be closer. Nor can one see any basis in Paul's theology for Trilling's surprising assertion that he could not have regarded God's call as taking place through the preaching of the gospel; the whole way in which Paul links the Spirit with the gospel in 1 Th. 1:5 shows that the call comes through the gospel rather than alongside it. One is tempted to say that with some attackers of authenticity, Paul can never win: if an expression is parallel to one in an acknowledged epistle, it must have been copied from it; but if it differs, then Paul could not have expressed himself in a different way from usual.

The ultimate purpose of the calling is **that you may obtain the glory of our Lord Jesus Christ**. The thought is paralleled in Rom. 8:30 and the language is similar to that in 1 Th. 5:9, 'so that we may obtain salvation through our Lord Jesus Christ'. The change from 'salvation' to **glory** is appropriate; salvation has already been mentioned in the preceding verse, and glory catches up the thought of 1:10–12, bringing out more fully the fact that believers themselves are glorified along with Jesus (Rom. 8:17). Trilling, pp. 123f., finds problems in this part of the verse if **obtain** is taken in the sense of earning (*sc.* by human effort), but argues that the phrase can have the broader meaning of 'achieve' or 'acquire'. It may be doubted whether any of this is in Paul's mind, since the phrase simply means 'to obtain possession' and allows (but does not demand) human co-operation with God in attaining that goal (see 1 Th. 5:9 note).

15. The Pauline conjunction **So then** links an exhortation closely to the preceding verse (cf. 1 Th. 5:6), and confirms that the purpose of what preceded was to lay a foundation in teaching for the command which now follows. This consideration speaks against the suggestion advanced by Trilling, pp. 124–6, that we should regard the section on the Day of the Lord as concluding at 2:14 and a totally new section of exhortations and injunctions as beginning at 2:15 and extending through to 3:16. It seems quite clear that v. 15 at least must be regarded as summing up the instructional section.

Paul's command is twofold. First, the readers must **stand firm**, a command already addressed to them in relation to affliction and persecution in 1 Th. 3:8 and now applied to the danger of their slipping away from the truth through false teaching. The command is thus appropriately related to the context and is not a mere generality (*pace* Trilling, p. 127). Second, they must **hold to the traditions**. Best, p. 317, suggests that for Paul the readers will stand firm by holding to the traditions. The thought expressed is Pauline (1 C. 11:2), but this is the only place where he uses this particular verb (except for Col. 2:19, of holding fast to the head). The thought of the teaching of the apostles, whether relating to the gospel itself (1 C. 15:1–11; Gal. 1:11f.; 1 Th. 2:13; Col. 2:6–8) or to Christian behaviour (Rom. 6:17; 1 C. 11:2, 23–25), as a tradition handed down authoritatively over the years and from place to place, is also typically Pauline. While he was conscious of preaching what he called 'my gospel' and insisted that he did not first get it from men, nevertheless he insisted that what he taught was in line with the teaching of the other apostles as it had been handed down to him and he regarded himself as passing on a tradition to his converts. Such material could be regarded as something that was taught to the converts (1 C. 4:17; Rom. 6:17; Col. 2:7; Eph. 4:21). All this is genuinely Pauline, and Trilling's comment, p. 128, that the actual expression used here, 'to hold to the traditions', is unparalleled in Paul (the closest parallel is Rev. 2:14) is beside the point.

What is unusual is the added comment that the traditions were taught **either by word of mouth or by letter**. It goes without saying that there is no reference here to the distinction between the written Scriptures and an unwritten tradition preserved in the church (as the Roman Catholic scholar Rigaux, p. 689, correctly and finally comments). Paul's reference is to what he taught orally during his visit to Thessalonica and to what he wrote in his earlier letter, and he links these two together rather than separating them as two different entities. The reason for mentioning them specifically lies in the context: in v. 2 he had drawn attention to the false statements which were being made on the basis of what he was thought to have said or written; now that he has made clear what he meant by repetition of what he had said (v. 5), he exhorts the readers to stick to what he had actually said and written and not to accept other views. This is a fully satisfying explanation of the statement, and makes other explanations unnecessary and unconvincing. First, there is no attempt on Paul's part to 'canonise' his earlier letter (or letters, if there were more than one). However, those who regard 2 Thessalonians as pseudonymous generally see the statement as a later attempt to give authority to what Paul taught and wrote. Trilling, pp. 128–30, holds that the verse refers generally to Paul's teaching (and not specifically to his teaching on the parousia), that the combination of word and letter is unparalleled in Paul, and that the thought is of the whole basis of faith as being the tradition. Paul's oral and written teaching is here starting to be canonised, and the text invited the later Catholic distinction between written and oral authorities, although this is not present at this stage of development. Trilling's arguments depend largely on his separation of the verse from its preceding context, which we have already seen cause to reject; as a result he attributes to the expressions a generality and a purpose which they do not have when read in context. Second, A. Lindemann argues that the 'letter' referred to here is 2 Th. itself (since the author wrote to discredit 1 Th. and to replace it by the present letter); he rejects Best's objection, p. 318, that the absence of the article with 'letter' is fatal to this view, but gives no reason for rejecting it. The point is part of Lindemann's whole thesis that 2 Th. is a pseudonymous composition intended to deliberately discredit 1 Th. and stands or falls with it (see on 2:2).

16. In 1 Th. 3:11–13 we have an example of a prayer following an expression of thanksgiving (and then in turn followed by a new section beginning with 'Finally, brethren'). This pattern reappears here in 2 Th., with the difference that between the thanksgiving and the prayer we have an exhortation (v. 15). The content of the prayers is fairly similar, and both are characterised by a certain degree of generality in expression. It seems clear that the passages are the work of an author proceeding along the same general lines of thought, but it is unlikely that a pseudonymous writer would have copied and altered his pattern in this fashion. The form of words differs first in the way in which Jesus is named before God the Father. There is nothing unusual about this, as Paul has the same order in 2 C. 13:13 and Gal. 1:1.

Jesus receives his full title as **our Lord Jesus Christ** (by contrast
with 1 Th. 3:11), but this form is so common in Paul as to require
no special explanation. Paul also writes **God our Father** (the MSS
vary as to whether there should be an article before *theos*) rather
than 'our God and Father' (1 Th. 3:11); but again his usage is so
varied that this unique form is not problematic. Although we have
a plural subject, there now follows a descriptive phrase, **who loved
us and gave us**, which is expressed in the singular, and the main
verb of the sentence ('comfort . . .', v. 17) is also in the singular.
It is disputed whether God alone should be regarded as the subject
(in which case the placing of God as the second part of the subject
could be due to Paul's desire to make him the real subject of the
sentence; cf. Trilling, p. 131 and n. 567), or whether both Jesus
and God are to be regarded as constituting one single subject (in
which case the placing of Jesus first may be because Paul's thought
in the preceding verses tends to be centred on Jesus; Rigaux, p.
690). As in 1 Th. 3:11, it is more likely that the latter is the case.
For Paul, God and Christ together are the source of spiritual blessings (cf. 1:2).

The basis of confidence for Paul's prayer is that God and Christ
have shown love for believers. The precise reference of **loved** is not
stated, but since the tense is past we should think of the love shown
in election or in the giving of Christ in incarnation and death. The
stress, however, is not so much on what God did to demonstrate his
love as on the fact that the love was demonstrated to **us**, to Paul
and the readers (cf. Jewett, p. 319, who thinks that the reference
is to the divine election of the Thessalonians). This emphasis on the
personal experience of God's love is confirmed by the addition **and
gave us eternal comfort and good hope through grace**. This expresses the outworking of divine love, and has the force 'and *so* he
gave . . .' **comfort** translates *paraklēsis*, which can also mean encouragement; this nuance of the word should be adopted rather
than the idea of consolation. Paul is thinking of an inner source of
encouragement that will enable the readers to face up confidently to
whatever trials may lie ahead of them. It is **eternal**, not in the sense
of being unfailing (cf. *NEB*), but rather of lasting through this age
and into the next, like eternal life. Almost synonymous is **good
hope**, another phrase unique in the Greek Bible but explicable from
the non-Christian world as a current phrase for the hope of life after
death (for evidence from the cult of Demeter and Persephone, see
P. Otzen, ' "Gute Hoffnung" bei Paulus', *ZNW* 49, 1958, pp. 283–
5). The gift is characterised in good Pauline fashion as being given
through grace (cf. especially Gal. 1:6, and also 2 C. 1:12). This
final phrase re-emphasises that God's gifts are dependent on his

goodness and not on the worthiness of the recipients and thus gives further ground for assurance that he will answer the prayer which is now at last expressed.

17. The thought of **comfort** or rather of encouragement for the readers is frequent throughout these epistles (1 Th. 2:11; 3:2, etc). Having already referred to the encouragement given by God, Paul prays that he will continue to encourage the readers in their hearts (cf. 3:5; 1 Th. 3:13). Along with this inner strengthening he also prays for God to **establish** (again cf. 1 Th. 3:2) **them in every good work and word**. Their inward hope must be expressed outwardly in all aspects of their lives despite every temptation to live at a sub-Christian level. The combination **work and word** is found in Lk. 24:19, but elsewhere Paul has the order 'word and work' (Rom. 15:18; Col. 3:17); the change in order is probably insignificant. The whole section on the future and its problems thus closes with a prayer for a Christian hope based on experience of the love of God and issuing in a fruitful life; apocalyptic speculation has disappeared from view.

PRAYER FOR PAUL'S MISSION

3:1–5

The structure of the epistle at this point is not altogether clear. Although 'Finally' (v. 1) need not indicate that the epistle is almost complete or that what follows is unimportant, the request by Paul for prayer for himself usually comes at the end of an epistle rather than just before a section of exhortation. The explanation in the present case is probably that the request is closely connected with the preceding teaching. Having spoken about the afflictions faced by the readers both now and in the future, Paul appropriately asks for prayer for the continuing work of the gospel so far as he himself is involved in it, and at the same time gives fresh assurance to his readers of the faithfulness of the Lord and of his own confidence in them. Thus, as he makes known the fact of his prayers for them, Paul also invites them to join in prayer. The thought is tightly woven, but it does form a unity, despite the feeling of some commentators that the author here was trying to patch together a section on the service of the apostle without adequate resources for doing so.

1. The beginning of a new section is marked, as often, by the address **brethren**. It is also indicated by the use of **Finally**. This word could be used to announce the end of a letter (2 C. 13:11; Eph. 6:10; Phil. 4:8), but it was also used when a letter was far

from its end (1 Th. 4:1 and note; Phil. 3:1) to introduce material of a more practical nature. **pray for us** is a request that was expressed in 1 Th. 5:25 in almost identical wording, and that was regularly made by Paul to his friends in the churches. Whereas the request was made in the most general terms in 1 Thessalonians, here it is much more specific. It is unlikely, indeed, that there is any special nuance in the actual form of the request, such as '*keep on* praying for us' (Frame, p. 290) or 'pray in addition to observing our teaching', but the request is developed in two parallel clauses, each of which indicates the content and the purpose of the prayer.

The first clause relates intercession for Paul to the progress of the gospel: it is **that the word of the Lord may speed on** (literally, 'run') **and triumph.** The **word of the Lord** (1 Th. 1:8) is of course the message of the gospel preached by the missionaries, but Paul treats it almost as a separate entity with a life of its own (compare the remarkable language used by Luke in Ac. 6:7; 12:24; 13:48). The picture of it 'running' has been traced to two sources. On the one hand, we have the *OT* imagery in Ps. 147:15, 'He sends forth his command to the earth; his word runs swiftly' (cf. Wis. 7:24, of Wisdom). On the other hand, there is the Greek picture of runners in a stadium (1 C. 9:24; cf. Rom. 9:16; Gal. 2:2; 5:7; Phil. 2:16) which was familiar to Paul. It is not necessary to choose between these two sources (Frame, p. 291, opts for the latter), since the metaphor of the race was also Jewish (Ps. 19:5); Paul is able to make use of an *OT* picture which would be meaningful to Greek readers. The idea is of the swift and victorious spread of the gospel. There may be the thought of its progress unhindered by the obstacles placed in its way by adversaries (Frame, p. 291); but this probably reads too much into the text.

The word is also said to **triumph.** Literally, it is 'glorified'. This is unlikely to be a continuation of the metaphor referring to the 'glorification' of the person who receives a crown at the end of a race. More probably it refers to the way in which people give praise and honour to the gospel by receiving it with faith and thanksgiving; the honour of course is really given to the Lord whose word it is. It is strange that recent commentators overlook the close parallel in Ac. 13:48 (see also 2 Th. 1:12) which speaks of converts glorifying the word of God. Paul adds the comment that his prayer is that this may happen to the word in the same way **as it did among you.** Since there is no verb or time-note in the phrase, however, it could refer to the initial success of the mission at Thessalonica, or to the continuation of the mission in the present time. The implication is that the mission in Thessalonica was particularly successful. The question has been raised whether Paul had specifically in mind the hope of the rapid completion of the mission in order that the essential condition for the parousia might be realised (Mk 13:10), but there is no positive evidence that this thought was in his mind.

2. The second clause which indicates the content of the prayer that Paul wishes his readers to offer is **that we may be delivered from wicked and evil men**. The close connection between the two clauses is evident. The obstacle to the triumphant progress of the gospel in Paul's own area of mission lay in the human opposition which he had to face. Essentially the same request was made by Paul in Rom. 15:31 at the time when he was contemplating a visit to Jerusalem and apprehended danger from unbelievers. Here the same verb is used (*rhyomai*; cf. especially 2 C. 1:10; 2 Tim. 3:11; 4:17f.; the verb is used eschatologically in 1 Th. 1:10). But the diction is closer to that of the *OT* (Isa. 25:4; cf. Ps. 140:1). The collocation of **wicked** and **evil** is possibly significant. The latter word, which has the original sense of 'out of place', hence 'odd' in a bad sense or 'perverse', is found only here in the *NT* of persons. In the LXX 'wicked' is regularly linked with 'lawless', and von Dobschütz, p. 306, suggests that Paul has replaced 'lawless' in this stock phrase by 'evil' because he was referring to Jews as his specific opponents at this time. This would fit in with what we know from 1 Th. 2:16 and from Ac. 18 about the concrete situation of Paul in Corinth at the time of writing the epistle. Best, pp. 325f., prefers to be agnostic about this suggestion, and argues that Paul's choice of word may be due to a desire to avoid the word used in a technical sense to characterise the rebellious man in 2:3–8. This proposal seems less likely than the one offered above; all in all, it still seems more probable that Paul includes a reference to his Jewish opponents.

The final clause, **for not all men have faith**, is meant as an explanation of their hostile conduct. **faith** here may be taken in the sense of trust (not all men exercise faith) or, less probably, as the body of belief (not all men accept the faith). The renderings offered by Frame, p. 292, 'For not for all is the faith' and 'it is not everybody who is attracted by the faith', are less probable than that of *RSV* which understands the clause as a mirror of Paul's experience. The statement may seem rather banal and unnecessary. It acquires greater significance if it is seen not so much as a conclusion to what has been just said but rather as an introduction to the next verse; that is to say, Paul wrote it to make a link with the next verse rather than as an important statement in its own right. At the same time, the clause conveys Paul's recognition that, although the prayer is for the successful preaching of the word, not all men do believe or will believe. Trilling, p. 136, finds in the whole verse a later, stylised picture of the apostle who is the restless preacher despite continual opposition. This verdict is surprising, since Trilling recognises that Paul himself frequently writes about the sufferings which are part of the apostle's lot. One may point especially to 1 C. 16:9 and Phil. 1:27f. as expressing similar sentiments to the present passage; there is no good reason to regard it as post-Pauline.

3. With the comment that not all have faith, Paul has already begun to move from his own immediate situation to that of the world in general, and this prepares the way for what appears at first to be a surprising turn in thought. Instead of claiming the assurance of divine help for himself, he turns his thought back to his readers and his concern for them in the midst of their afflictions; as Calvin rightly observed, he is more concerned about them than himself. Here, then, although Paul has begun to think about himself and his needs, he turns back under his strong pastoral compulsion to his readers and assures them **But the Lord is faithful**. There is a play on words between 'faith' and 'faithful' (although this does not require us to translate 'faith' as 'faithfulness' in v. 2). The thought is one that is frequently expressed by Paul when he wishes to assure his readers that prayers and wishes will be honoured by God (1 Th. 5:24), but here Paul speaks of the faithfulness of **the Lord** (i.e. Jesus) rather than of God. This change fits in with the emphasis on the Lord in vv. 4–5, an emphasis which is characteristic of this letter (cf. 3:16). Since the Lord keeps his promise to his people, he can be relied on to **strengthen** the readers. The verb is repeated from 2:17 (cf. 1 Th. 3:2, 13) and was evidently in the forefront of Paul's mind as he thought of the afflictions surrounding his readers. Paul does not use the verb **guard** elsewhere of divine protection for the believer, but this use is found in the *OT* (Ps. 121:7; 141:9). *RSV* takes the adjective **evil** as a neuter form, but the margin recognises that it could be masculine and refer to the devil. The arguments are fully assembled by Best, pp. 327f., who defends the latter view against Dibelius; he observes that the activity of Satan is prominent in the letters (2:9; 1 Th. 2:18; 3:5), that the context is personal, and that the title 'the evil one' was current in the early church (Eph. 6:16; Mt. 13:19, 38; 1 Jn 2:13f.; 5:18f.). This case is strengthened if the phrase is also masculine in the Lord's Prayer; whether or not Paul was personally acquainted with the prayer, its language would both reflect and influence the language of the early church. Trilling, p. 137, makes the suggestion that the word should be taken generally; the masculine and neuter senses cannot and should not be distinguished.

4. The same tone of confidence in the Lord sounds in the next verse which expresses Paul's certainty that his readers will carry out his instructions. The connection of thought is very similar to that in 2:13–15 where an expression of thanks to God for the spiritual state of the readers was followed by a consequent appeal to them for their part to stand fast and hold to what they had been taught. Here Paul's confident statement that the Lord will guard them is followed by an expression of his confidence that they will do what they are instructed. Although the verse is thus formally a statement of confidence, it can also be regarded as an implicit command to the readers. The verb **we have confidence** used in this way is typically Pauline (Rom. 15:14; 2 C. 2:3; Gal. 5:10). It is not clear whether **in the Lord** states the ground of confidence ('we trust in the Lord [*sc.* that he will enable you to . . .]') or the sphere in which it operates ('since we [*sc.* Paul and his readers] are in the Lord, we are confident that you will do . . .'). In both cases the confidence of Paul is **about** (Gk. *epi*) the readers (so *RSV* correctly; cf. 2 C. 2:3; contrast the use of *eis*, Gal. 5:10). Probably the latter understanding of the sentence is correct.

Paul's confidence about the readers is one that arises as a result of the new situation which arises from the death and resurrection of the Lord through whom they have all become part of the church. From this it follows, of course, that the confidence which Paul has is ultimately a confidence in the power and faithfulness of the Lord (see further, R. Bultmann, *TDNT* VI, pp. 4–7).

What Paul is confident of in this situation is that the readers **are** already **doing** (in Paul's absence) **and will** continue to **do** (when they receive the reminder in this letter) the things that he commands. The thought of continuing what they have already begun to do is paralleled in different words in 1 Th. 4:1 (a passage which Trilling, p. 138, regards as the pattern for the present verse), but the pattern of tenses is Pauline (2 C. 1:10; cf. 1:13f.). The verb **command** was used in 1 Th. 4:11 (cf. the noun in 1 Th. 4:2) and applies particularly to ethical and ecclesiastical instructions rather than to doctrine. The present tense would appear to refer to the instructions in this letter; but this is at first sight difficult in view of Paul's confidence that they are already doing what he commands. The solution is probably that Paul regards himself as repeating instructions that he has previously given (or at the most enlarging upon them) and can therefore be confident that what he instructs in this letter is already in part at least being obeyed by the readers.

It can be argued that Paul is preparing the way for the particular instructions (introduced by the same verb) which follow immediately in vv. 6–16. The difficulties with this interpretation are that it makes for an awkward connection of thought between vv. 1–3 and the present verse, and that v. 5 interrupts the sequence of thought; put otherwise, v. 4 appears to interrupt the connection between vv. 1-3 and 5. Trilling, pp 137f., argues against the view that the connection of thought is that v. 3 gives the Lord's side and v. 4 the human side of Christian progress; rather the thought of the apostle and his authority is determinative, and this has been emphasised by including in a rather wooden fashion an independent statement patterned on 1 Th. 4:1 which stresses the authority of the apostle. This solution is far from satisfactory, crediting the unknown author as it does with a curious combination of subtle imitation of 1 Th. and a wooden style. Another solution seems preferable, and this is that the primary reference in v. 4 is to the writer's request for the prayers of his readers in vv. 1f. The fact that Paul then uses the same verb 'to command' in v. 6 can be simply explained by the tendency of any writer to repeat a word which is already in his mind (Rigaux, p. 701). This raises the possibility that v. 3 is concerned primarily with the spiritual temptations which may keep the readers from prayer. Verse 4 is then closely connected with what precedes by the reference to the Lord. The alleged stress on apostolic authority then disappears from the passage.

5. Paul's implicit command to his readers is followed by a further prayer-wish which is coupled formally to the preceding verse by being addressed to **the Lord** (i.e. Jesus). The verb **direct** is repeated from 1 Th. 3:11, where, however, it was used more literally of the Lord opening up the way for Paul and his friends to revisit Thessalonica. Here the use is spiritual (as in Lk. 1:79, the only other occurrence of the verb in the *NT*) and is concerned with directing the hearts of the readers (the whole phrase is based on a Septuagintalism: 1 Ch. 29:18; 2 Ch. 12:14, etc). The **love of God** is a phrase that can be construed to mean our love for God (objective genitive) or God's love (*sc*. 'for us'; subjective genitive), or the kind of love shown by God (and which we ought to show; genitive of quality). Although the first construction is grammatically possible (cf. 2:10 and note; Masson, p. 112; Trilling, p. 139), it is the least likely, in view of Pauline usage elsewhere. Most commentators prefer the second possibility (Rom. 5:5; 8:35, 39; 2 C. 13:13) and argue that Paul is encouraging the readers by directing their attention to the love which God has for them. However, there is perhaps most to be said for the third possibility. Paul wants his readers to show the same kind of love as God has shown to them (cf. 2:13, 16) and in the present context to do so by their prayerful concern for Paul. The second phrase **the steadfastness of Christ** should probably be taken in the same kind of way. It has been variously understood as expectation of (the parousia of) Christ (von Dobschütz, p. 309) or, more precisely, as steadfastness in awaiting the parousia of Christ

(cf. 1 Th. 1:3; Jewett, pp. 320–2; in a more general sense of stead-fastness directed towards Christ; Trilling, p. 139). But more prob-ably it means the kind of steadfastness shown supremely by Christ (cf. Jas. 5:11; Poly. Phil. 8:2) or, less likely, the steadfastness given by Christ (cf. Rom. 15:5; Best, pp. 330f.). Rigaux, p. 700, takes the thought a step further and suggests that the readers are to take their share of the patient suffering of Christ (cf. 2 C. 1:5; Phil. 3:10), and this gives a good sense. The readers are to participate in the love shown by God and the steadfastness shown by Christ. The thought is of steadfastness in the midst of afflictions. For the link of love with prayer, see Rom. 15:30, where the idea of striving is also present (for the latter cf. Eph. 6 : 18). Thus the whole section forms a unity.

THE DANGER OF IDLENESS
3:6–16

Without any apparent link with what has preceded, there now comes a section in which the members of the church are urged to withdraw from contact from some of their number who were living idleness. Such conduct is condemned as not being in accord with the example of Paul and his missionary companions who ignored their right to be kept at the church's expense and insisted on working for their food so as not to burden the members. This example had been reinforced by a specific instruction that food was not to be given to the lazy. Despite these previous instructions (which had been re-peated in 1 Th. 4:11f.; 5:14), the trouble still continued. Paul, therefore, first exhorted the culprits directly to work hard and to do good, and, second, urged the rest of the church to withdraw fellow-ship from them to such an extent that they might amend their ways. The section concludes with a benediction.

As we noted in discussing the material on this point in 1 Th., it appears possible that, although no direct connection is made be-tween the two themes, it was the heightened sense of belief that the day of the Lord had come which was leading to this continuing attitude of indiscipline and laziness. Von Dobschütz, p. 183, rightly comments that the problem must have had some sort of religious origin, and in the absence of any indication of any other source, this one commends itself as the most likely. Moore, p. 115, however, observes that no explicit reference to the parousia occurs in Paul's discussion of the matter (see also, B. N. Kaye, 'Eschatology and Ethics in 1 and 2 Thessalonians', *NovT* 17, 1975, pp. 47–57). The problem had evidently continued from the earliest days of the church. The parallel with the situation in Corinth may suggest that another factor was also at work, namely, that the richer members of the church felt an obligation to help the poor, perhaps especially at communal meals where the Lord's Supper was celebrated as part of a fuller meal. Perhaps also there was a distribution to the poor on the same lines as in the early days of the church in Jerusalem (Ac. 2:44f.; 4:32–5:11; 6:1–6). It them becomes probable that some members of the church were taking advantage of the generosity of others and not attempting to keep themselves. This unwillingness to work could have been encouraged by the belief that the parousia was at hand, so that there was no need to provide for the future. Although this reconstruction of the situation is hypothetical, it makes good sense, and in particular it explains why the disciplinary measure proposed involves the depriving of such people from food provided by the church.

The passage is differently understood by those who adopt a later date for the letter. Trilling, pp. 141f., 151–3, draws attention to the authoritative, mandatory character of the section—it is not to be classed as exhortation—and to the way in which Paul's own conduct is now made into a pattern intended to be followed by later Christians. These characteristics of the passage are, he thinks, better explained by the hypothesis of pseudonymity. The actual fault condemned is nothing worse than laziness, and Trilling doubts whether it was necessary or practicable to adopt the disciplinary measures recommended here. The issue is that of a Christian 'work-ethic', typical of the post-Pauline period, and the outlook which is condemned has nothing to do with the parousia; rather we must see the situation in the light of such a passage as Didache 12, where the church is warned against travelling preachers who were unwilling to do anything towards their own keep. These comments show that the problem of laziness was one that continued in the church. They do not explain why it is treated at such comparative length in 2 Th. in particular. The authoritative tone is not unknown in Paul's writings (1 C. 4:21; 5:1–5, 9–13; 2 C. 13:2, 10). Nor was Paul averse to using his own conduct as an example (1 Th. 1:6; 1 C. 11:1). Further, the situation described here has closer affinities with the problem of care for the poor within the church in Jerusalem and Corinth than with the travelling preachers in Didache. The claim that the passage makes better sense when interpreted from a later perspective than that of Paul fails to convince.

6. Paul's exhortation begins with **we command**, the same verb as in v. 4 (where, we argued, the reference is not to the present exhortation) and also in 1 Th. 4:11, where the topic was the same as the present one. Although the address as **brethren** is Paul's fairly common device for introducing a new section, it is never merely formal but indicates that those who are addressed are fellow-members in the church, and it may speak against any tendency to see an over-authoritative tone on the part of the author. The formula **in the name of our Lord Jesus** is also typical of Paul's usage and indicates that Paul gives his instructions on the authority of Jesus and as his representative (cf. 1 Th. 4:1; 1 C. 1:10; 5:4). A somewhat rare construction is used to express the requirement to **keep away from** those members of the church whose conduct needs correction. The phrase means to draw back from somebody. Although this is repeated in v. 14 in different words as a means of disciplining the recalcitrant members of the church, the force of Paul's command here may be rather that the other members of the church are to avoid being led into similar action through contact with those who were setting a bad example (cf. 1 C. 15:33f.). The 'purpose is to keep the community pure rather than to purge it from unhealthy elements' (K. H. Rengstorf, *TDNT* VII, pp. 589f.). Those who are behaving in an unacceptable fashion are still called by the name of brother (cf. 1 C. 5:11) and are not excommunicated. They are **living in idleness**, literally, walking in an idle manner. The adverb (*ataktōs*; also v. 11) is from the same root as the adjective used to describe the same kind of people in 1 Th. 5:14. There we saw that the meaning was 'disorderly' or 'idle'. The latter element is undoubtedly present in the word, as the context makes clear, and the only problem is whether the word has the fuller sense of general disorderliness which was expressing itself particularly in refusal to work. In any case, the point is that the people concerned were not simply unemployed, but that they were positively refusing to do work and consequently being a nuisance to other people. This is certainly what Paul emphasises, and it appears to be the dominant thought in the passage.

Such conduct was **not in accord with the tradition that you received from us**. The notion of **tradition** has already been seen in 2:15, where the thought was of doctrinal teaching, both oral and written. Here the thought is of teaching handed down about Christian behaviour, conveyed both orally (v. 10) and in writing (1 Th. 4:11f.), and also by Paul's own example. **you received** represents the text found in a small number of Greek MSS; others have 'they (*sc.* the idlers) received' (UBS, followed by *GNB*). The latter text incorporates a slightly unusual form of the verb, and the third person might have seemed inappropriate to scribes who would have expected a second-person form; hence the form 'they received' should be preferred. Paul is emphasising that it was the very people who had received his instructions who were disobeying them.

7. For you yourselves know is a formula already used in 1 Th.
2:1 (cf. 3:3; 4:2; 5:2). Paul is giving a basis for the command in the
previous verse by showing that the conduct of the idlers in the
community is inconsistent with what the readers already know of
the Christian way of life as practised by himself during his stay in
Thessalonica. They know that they **ought to imitate** the behaviour
of the apostles. Literally the wording is 'how you ought to imitate
us', which is an elliptical way of saying 'how you ought to live so
as to imitate us'. The thought of imitating or following the pattern
of life of other Christians occurs in 1 Th. 1:6f. and 2:14 (cf. 1 C.
4:16; 11:1; Eph. 5:1; Phil. 3:17; cf. 4:9; Heb. 6:12; 13:7) and
generally conveys the idea of taking as a model the lives of those
who are modelling their own lives on that of the Lord. Where the
apostles present themselves as an example to imitate, there is the
further thought of obedience to the teaching which they were ex-
emplifying in their own lives (cf. W. Michaelis, *TDNT* IV, pp. 666–
73). Thus the tradition which the Thessalonians had received (v. 6)
was given in both the instruction and the example of the apostles.
The authoritative nature of the tradition and the example is conveyed by the verb **ought**; the phraseology is related to that in 1 Th.
4:1. This reference shows that the thought is quite Pauline, the verb
ought fulfilling the same logical function as the expressions of command and the imperatives found in other occurrences of the motif
('I urge you', 1 C. 4:16; 'Be imitators', 1 C. 11:1; Eph. 5:1; Phil.
3:17; 'do', Phil. 4:9). Hence the view of Trilling, pp. 145f., that a
note of authoritative command to imitate the apostle is present here
for the first time and reflects the later attitude of looking back to
the apostles as authoritative examples to follow, is simply not justified by the evidence. If there is any stress on the duty of following
the example of the apostles, this is amply justified by the fact that
the trouble at Thessalonica was taking so long to disappear. Paul,
then, puts himself and his companions forward as examples of
people who were not guilty of idleness. The verb used comes from
the same root as the adverb in v. 6, and is found only here in the
NT. On top of their spiritual work for the church the apostles
worked hard for their own keep.

8. Having stated that the apostles had not been idle, Paul elaborates the point by referring to the effects of idleness. Those who
do not work for their living are compelled to be dependent on the
generosity of other people, and it is his dislike of this practice which
gives particular point to Paul's attack on idleness. So he is able to
claim that he and his companions **did not eat any one's bread
without paying**. 'To eat bread' is a Hebraism which means 'to take
food' (Gen. 3:19) and can be used more generally of receiving

maintenance from somebody (2 Sam. 9:7; cf. Am. 7:12; Ps. 41:9).
We know that Paul and his companions stayed for at least part of
the time in Thessalonica with Jason (Ac. 17:7). They did not receive
board and lodging from their host without paying something towards it (cf. 2 C. 11:7). Rather than be idle and sponge on other
people, they **worked with toil and labour night and day**. The
language is very close to that of 1 Th. 2:9 where, as here, Paul goes
on to say that they did this that **we might not burden any of you**
(here the wording is identical). Paul thus reiterates his principle
that he would not seek any material return for his preaching of the
gospel. The closeness of the wording to 1 Th. 2:9 is noteworthy,
and has led various scholars to affirm that here a copyist was making
use of the earlier letter. It must, however, be admitted with Trilling,
p. 147, that Paul himself could have used the same expression twice
within a short interval. Trilling, however, argues that the transfor-
mation of Paul's theology and thought in the present passage rules
out this possibility. This conclusion is unjustified. We can see no
reason whatever why Paul, having referred to his habit of working
in relation to the nature of the gospel in 1 Thessalonians (cf. 1 C.
9:3-18; 2 C. 11:7), should not also use the same practice as an
example of diligence to his converts. (The fact that the wording
differs slightly from that in 1 Th. 2:9 is not decisive either way.
But it is significant that some of the phraseology is used by Paul in
other contexts; cf. 2 C. 11:7, 27. It is just possible that the variant
form *nukta kai hēmeran* found in some MSS should be preferred to
the better attested *nuktos kai hēmeras*, which could be assimilation
to the phraseology in 1 Th. 2:9; this would heighten the differences
in wording.)

9. Paul proceeds to explain the motive for his conduct. The
missionaries, he says, did not behave as they did because they did
not have the **right**, *sc.* not to work. This is the right to which Paul
alludes in 1 Th. 2:6 and which he states at some length in 1 C. 9:4–
6, 14 (cf. 1 Tim. 5:18). On the contrary, they had given up that
right and worked hard instead in order that they might give themselves as an **example** so that the readers could **imitate** them. The
thought is expressed elliptically and both in *RSV* and the above
paraphrase extra words have been supplied to give the sense. It
should scarcely need saying that it was not the missionaries' waiving
of their rights that constituted an example to the readers but rather
their willingness to work and not to be a burden to others. The
English **give . . . an example** does not bring out the force of the
Greek 'give *ourselves* as an example' which may suggest a certain
element of self-sacrifice in the matter (by contrast with the weaker
phrase in Phil. 3:17); but this is perhaps an over-interpretation of

a perfectly normal phrase (the force of 'we were ready to share with you . . . our own selves' in 1 Th. 2:8 is somewhat different). Paul here draws out a different purpose for his conduct from that given in 1 Th. 2:9, where he argues for the purity of his motives and his unwillingness to lay any burden on the converts. But there is nothing inconsistent about his stressing a further motive implicit in his conduct here, and certainly no ground for seeing a later hand at work.

10. From his example while he was in Thessalonica, Paul turns to the instruction which he and his companions repeatedly **gave** (the verb is in the imperfect). The *RSV* translation **For even when we were with you** lays the emphasis on the clause referring to the missionaries' presence in Thessalonica. But von Dobschütz, p. 312, is probably right in claiming that Paul is unlikely to have stressed this here (contrast 1 Th. 3:4), since he has just been referring to it in vv. 7–9, and that the stress lies on the oral instruction alongside the example: 'For when we were with you we *also* gave you this command.' The verse thus stands parallel to vv. 7–9 and fills out the nature of the traditions mentioned in v. 6. It becomes clear that teaching about the necessity of work was given right from the time of Paul's evangelistic mission in Thessalonica, and the fact that such teaching was a common part of Christian instruction for new converts is reflected in Didache 12:3. This suggests that the motives for the idleness at Thessalonica did not lie merely in heightened expectation of the End, when work would be unnecessary, but rather in a general attitude to manual labour which was current in the Hellenistic civilisation of the time.

The command **If any one will not work, let him not eat**, is similar in content to a Jewish saying based on Gen. 3:19, 'If I do not work, I have nothing to eat' (Gen. R. 2; SB III, pp. 641f.). This, however, is a statement of fact from a person who felt that he was ill-treated compared with others. Paul's statement differs in being an imperative and in being concerned with unwillingness to work. Similar statements are in other ancient sources, both Jewish and Greek, but no precise parallel has been found. A. Deissmann (*Light from the Ancient East*, London, 1927, p. 318) suggested that Paul was quoting a popular maxim coined perhaps by a master dealing with lazy slaves; but it is equally possible that the formulation is Paul's own. The saying is addressed to those who may be responsible (out of duty or charity) for caring for the hungry and directs them not to give to those who are unwilling to work. But, although this is its syntactical form, it is primarily addressed to the lazy as a warning against idleness (cf. v. 12). The effect of the principle is to establish the dignity of work over against any suggestion that people might feel that they were excused from the obligation to care for themselves, and this has been a continuing Christian principle (for the early history of the motif, see Trilling, pp. 148f.). Best, p. 339, is very hesitant about drawing conclusions from the text about the nature of work and its status today, but his attitude is unnecessarily pessimistic. The text is a relevant part of biblical teaching on the matter, although it must be taken in the context of other biblical teaching. Thus it must be balanced by teaching on the necessity of giving aid to those who are in need. It is also to be noted that it is *unwillingness* to work rather than *lack of opportunity* which stands in the text, and this is of great importance in discussions about provision for the unemployed.

11. In v. 6 Paul introduced the subject of the idle members of the church in wording which addressed itself to the church as a whole and directed against close association with the idle. Having given his teaching on the matter, he now proceeds to address it directly to any of the readers who fell into the category of the idle. This explains why he now refers again to the existence of a problem in a sentence that explains (**For**) why he has given the previous teaching. **we hear** is probably to be taken as equivalent to a perfect 'we have heard' (1 C. 11:18) rather than as a continuous 'we keep on hearing', and refers to news brought to Paul from Thessalonica whether by word of mouth or just possibly by letter. The vague form of allusion to **some of you** is typically Pauline (cf. 1 C. 5; 2 C. 2:5f.; 10:2, 12; Gal. 1:7; 2:12) and does not necessarily mean that he was unaware of the identity of the culprits. The actual wording 'some in you', i.e. 'some in the midst of you', is slightly unusual and may be meant to bring out the responsibility of the community for those who are bringing shame upon it. The description of the offenders as **living in idleness** is repeated from v. 6. But a new element is added: they are **mere busybodies, not doing any work**. The Greek contains a play on words, well brought out in *NIV* 'They are not busy; they are busybodies' (cf. Moffatt: 'busybodies instead of busy'), and aptly rendered in *NEB* 'minding everybody's business but their own'. Paronomasia of this kind was a common device in Greek (cf. Rom. 12:3; 1 C. 7:31; 2 C. 3:2; 6:10), and this particular play on words was anticipated by Demosthenes (Phil. 4:72[150]); the Latin parallel cited from Quintilian 6:354 is somewhat different. This evidence is not sufficient to show that it was a current word-play and that therefore it should not be taken at its face value (*pace* Trilling, pp. 150f.). The point is quite clear and definite: as a result of their inactivity, these people were able to spend their time in being a nuisance to other people (cf. 1

Tim. 5:13), presumably by keeping them back from their work and
by wasting time talking.

12. Having prepared the way in v. 11 for a direct address to the
idlers in the church, Paul now does so. But the form of address
which he uses is couched in the third person and is somewhat
indirect; for this use of **such persons**, compare Rom. 16:18 and 1
C. 16:16–18, which show that it is used in a generalising manner,
'anybody whom the cap fits'. The form of the injunction, too, is
intended to avoid an abrupt and categorical injunction: **we command** (vv. 4, 6) is a verb which in itself can be hortatory rather
than mandatory, and here it is linked with **and exhort** (1 Th. 4:1)
which introduces a persuasive note. Moreover, the command is
given **in the Lord Jesus Christ** (cf. 1 Th. 4:1), which conveys not
just the thought of the authority of the Lord behind the command
issued by his representatives but also the thought of the new situation of writer and readers alike which is determined by the saving
event of Jesus and leads to fellowship in the church. It is plain that
the stress on apostolic authority which Trilling claims to find in this
section and uses as a sign of post-Pauline authorship is simply not
present in this summing up of Paul's instructions to the erring
members of the church. The point may be underlined: this was the
third occasion at least on which Paul had had to raise the matter,
and yet he still does so in a brotherly fashion on the basis of their
standing in Christ; the threat of 1 C. 4:21 has not yet materialised
in Paul's relationships with Thessalonica. The readers are encouraged **to do their work in quietness**. The noun expresses the same
thought as was expressed by the verb in 1 Th. 4:11, that of not
being a nuisance to other people. The same ideal is found in 1 Tim.
2:11f., where women are not to exercise authority over men; the
thought is that of minding one's own business. This has been seen
here as the opposite of being excited by expectations of the imminent
End, but a more general reference is probable. Trilling, p. 151,
finds the picture of a quiet, well-ordered bourgeois way of life (cf.
1 Tim. 2:2, 11f.; 1 Pet. 3:4), typical of later post-apostolic teaching.
But the roots of this kind of teaching lie earlier, and there is no
reason to suppose that the emphasis is post-Pauline (Rom. 13:1–7;
1 Th. 4:11f.). The result of such diligence will be that the readers
will be able **to earn their own living**, literally, 'eat their own bread',
the opposite of living off the charity of other people (v. 8). The
teaching of the verse has been well summed up as 'Stop fussing;
stop idling; stop sponging'.

13. The fact that there is a change in the persons addressed is
indicated by the introductory 'But you' (not translated in *RSV*)
followed by the address **Brethren**, which indicates that Paul is **again**

addressing the church as a whole after directing his instruction particularly to the idlers in vv. 11f.; more precisely, he is now addressing the rest of the members of the church. They may have been tempted to **be weary**, i.e. to lose heart (Gal. 6:9; Eph. 3:13; cf. 2 C. 4:1, 16; Lk. 18:1) **in well-doing**. The phrase has a close (but not identical) parallel in Gal. 6:9, which might suggest that here it is to be taken in a fairly broad sense. Trilling, p. 154, in fact regards the verse as beginning a new subsection (vv. 13–16) and thinks that it gives a perfectly general injunction which is not connected with what precedes. This view is unlikely. It ignores the connection of vv. 14f. with the preceding section (which Trilling also denies; see below). Moreover, the context in Gal. 6:9 is that of material gifts to teachers in the church (and also more widely). It is probable that the thought of caring for the needy is still in mind here. Some commentators prefer the translation 'do the right thing' (Rom. 7:21; 1 C. 7 : 37f.; 2 C. 13:7; Jas 2:8, 19), but this does not yield the right sense in the context. The verb must mean 'to treat well' (as in Mat. 12:12; Lk. 6:27; Ac. 10:33; Gal. 6:9; Phil. 4:14).

In the context the hard-working members of the church may have been tempted to give up being charitable because they felt that advantage was being taken of them by the idle. It is not clear whether Paul is urging them to continue being charitable to the other needy members of the community or also to continue the same attitude towards the idle, but probably the latter is included, particularly in view of the spirit of the immediately following verses. This would be entirely in accord with the early Christian spirit of showing love to those who do not deserve it and do not return it. Paul thus deals with the situation of idleness in the church, not by telling the church to cut off supplies to the idlers but by admonishing the idlers to change their ways. This does not mean of course that some kind of disciplinary action is excluded in the case of persistent failure to heed Paul's commands, and this point is taken up immediately.

14. At the outset of the section in v. 6 Paul had spoken of the need to keep away from members of the church who were living in idleness. Now the instruction is repeated with more detail. There is the possibility that some members (probably the possibility that there will only be a few is indicated by the switch to the singular **any one** as contrasted with the plural 'some of you' in v. 11) will still continue to do what is wrong and so refuse **to obey what we say in this letter**. The Greek construction shows that Paul is thinking of his word or command as given in particular by means of a **letter**, and *RSV* correctly recognises that it is **this** letter which is meant. The context undoubtedly suggests that Paul in thinking of the command about the idle given in 3:6–13 and not of the instructions given in the letter as a whole (*pace* Trilling, pp. 154f.). This latter view is improbable because the other commands in the letter are few and are concerned with holding fast to traditions concerning the parousia and with praying for Paul. But there is no indication that the church as a whole was failing in these respects, and there is certainly no overt identification of any members who were deceiving the others. Moreover, the content of this verse is so close to that of v. 6 that a different reference is unlikely. The reference is to persistent idlers. The members of the church are to **note** any such person, an expression which is somewhat vague and need not indicate any kind of official striking off a roll. (We may doubt whether a church roll was kept at this date, although it would be clear enough who was baptised and who was not; those who were idling could of course include both the baptised and those who were, as we would say, 'adherents'.)

The members of the church were **to have nothing to do with them**, literally, not to mix with them. This expression is used by Paul in a similar context in 1 C. 5:9. What is meant? The application of discipline to members of the church is discussed in Mt. 18:17f.; 1 C. 5; 2 C. 2:5–11; 1 Tim. 1:20; 5:20; Tit. 3:10. From these passages we see that official church action was to be preceded by informal attempts to persuade the offender to admit his fault and seek reconciliation. Where such private persuasion was of no effect, the church as a whole could exclude such a person from fellowship.

The principle of having nothing to do with persons promoting unacceptable doctrine is found in 2 Jn 10f. and also in an important Pauline passage, Rom. 16:17–20. This last passage is particularly close to the present verse with its reference to obeying Paul's teaching, its stress on the need to avoid those who cause trouble, and the allusion to the God of peace. The closeness of the parallel may indeed suggest that Paul was concerned not only with the practice of the idlers but with their teaching. This might be used to support the view that the disciplinary action is concerned with the false teaching about the parousia which is condemned in ch. 2 (note the references to deceit in 2:3 and Rom. 16:18). However, in Rom. the thought of self-indulgence is also present, and it would seem that Paul is concerned in both cases with false teaching which was being used to justify an unchristian way of life.

A second passage which provides a significant parallel is 1 C. 5:9–11, where the members of the church are commanded to have nothing to do with brothers who were committing various sins of immorality and idolatry; the members of the church are not to associate with them—and not even to eat with them. This passage shows that lack of association includes the avoidance of common meals, and this would be particularly appropriate in the situation at Thessalonica, if common meals were the occasion for the distribution of charitable relief. But this appears to raise some problems.

First, if the common meal (including the Lord's Supper) is in mind, it is difficult to see why avoidance of eating with the offenders is apparently a lesser thing than associating with them (1 C. 5:11*b*). This problem, however, disappears if (with H. Greeven, *TDNT* VII, pp. 854f.) the sense of this verse is 'not to associate . . ., that is to say, not to eat with them', since the church meal was the occasion for the members to meet.

The second problem is that in the Thessalonian situation the offenders were evidently still within reach of brotherly admonition (v. 15), so that they can hardly have been excluded from the church meetings. According to G. Forkman, *The Limits of the Religious Community*, Lund, 1972, pp. 132–9, 179, they were excluded from the common meal, but not from the possibility of admonition. Probably also any private hospitality in the homes of other Christians was discouraged. This would of course prevent the idlers from sponging on the other members of the church. But the main purpose of the action was that they might be ashamed (1 C. 4:14), in the sense that they would realise that they had been acting in an unworthy manner and so turn from it. The purpose of the action was thus intended to be reformatory and reconciliatory.

Third, some have found difficulty in envisaging just how Paul's instructions were to be put into practice. Trilling, p. 156, asks how one can avoid contact and yet still offer brotherly admonition. The probable answer is that Paul was dealing with a situation involving personal relationships in which it is difficult, if not impossible, to frame precise binding rules. It may be adequate to say that the members of the church were to avoid making social contacts, but that when contacts arose they were to make use of them for admonition, or again that the church leaders were to give the admonition.

15. One of the problems of exercising discipline is the temptation to allow personal feeling to affect the application, especially through using the act of discipline as a means of exercising feelings of pique and enmity towards the offender. It is not easy to exercise discipline on behalf of justice and to avoid personal malice creeping in as a motive. It is, therefore, extremely important that Paul urges that a disciplined offender must not be treated **as an enemy**. This word is ambiguous, since it can mean a person who treats me in a hostile manner and/or a person whom I treat in a hostile manner. It is more likely that the second meaning is intended here. The offender must not be the object of personal hostility; feelings of anger and annoy-

ance are not to be given free rein against him. On the contrary, the readers are to **warn** him, or, as the same Greek word (*noutheteō*) is better translated in 1 Th. 5:12, they are to 'admonish' him. Not only so, but in so doing they are to regard him **as a brother**, which means both that the discipline must be exercised in love and that the offender is still to be regarded as a member of the church. This makes it plain that the process envisaged here is not one of excommunication, but rather of the refusal of intercourse (cf. J. Jeremias, *TDNT* III, p. 753, n. 84). Best, pp. 343f., argues that admonition was a matter for the church as a whole rather than for individuals in private contacts with the offender, but this does not seem to be a compelling conclusion. In any case, the informality of the whole procedure by the church is to be noted. Against Trilling, p. 156, who argues that the procedure is impracticable and therefore part of the fictitious setting of the letter, Best, p. 345, rightly claims that it is undeveloped and early.

The application of the teaching of such a passage as this to discipline in the church today is far from easy. Paul and the other *ŇT* writers appear to envisage a situation where the offence was obvious and admitted, and where the application of discipline could be expected to lead to the repentance of the offender in many cases. Although the situation in Judaism is not entirely clear, there is sufficient evidence that similar procedures were practised (I. H. Marshall, *Kept by the Power of God*, Minneapolis, 1975, pp. 41f., 47–9). The church today lives in a world where discipline is under a cloud, partly as a reaction perhaps against abuse in earlier days. If an attempt is made to exercise discipline, there may be great difficulty in establishing that a breach of the code of conduct has taken place. It is not unknown for the leaders of a church to be taken to court for alleged defamation of character by a person placed under discipline. If this obstacle is overcome and some form of discipline is imposed, the most probable result is that the offender will withdraw himself from the congregation completely and either join another or simply abandon church attendance and all that goes with it. There is along with this much uncertainty as to what grounds would justify disciplinary measures. The holding of beliefs that are incompatible with a church's doctrinal statements is no longer a matter of concern in many churches, and a person's conduct would have to be particularly scandalous before any notice was taken of it. One may suspect also that the nature of the Christian community has changed. Discipline is possible and necessary within a fairly compact, closely-related group, but this may not be so in the rather loose association typical of many modern congregations.

Such are the problems. There are no easy answers to them, but this does not mean that the issue should be easily forgotten. A passage of Scripture such as this one may have the effect of making us ask whether the church has become lax in the standards of Christian living expected of its members. Perhaps the problem today lies in the large numbers of people whose membership of the church is very nominal, in that they rarely attend services or take any fuller part in the life of the congregation; are we admitted to church membership without sufficient realisation of our obligations?

16. This section of the letter closes with a benediction. Some commentators (e.g. Best, p. 345) regard v. 16 as the beginning of the closing section of the letter, but it is better to see it as the conclusion to what precedes. Having dealt with a situation which was the cause of tension within the church, Paul prays that there may be peace in the church. The prayer falls into two parts. The first part has close similarities to 1 Th. 5:23, with its reference to the God of peace. Here, however, Paul refers to **the Lord** instead of to God. This fits in with a certain tendency in this letter to ascribe to Jesus qualities or activities elsewhere ascribed to the Father (2:13 note). **peace** is associated with Christ in Col. 3:15 and in the introductory greetings of most Pauline letters where grace and peace are the joint gifts of the Father and the Son. Here the thought is probably of the absence of disorder and strife within the church (1 C. 14:33), but should not be limited to this. 'Peace' is a broad term for salvation, and, although the prayer is linked closely to the preceding verses, it is nevertheless also to be seen as moving towards the conclusion of the letter as a whole. It is noteworthy that Paul refers to peace in other letters where tension within the community may be suspected (Rom. 15:33; 16:20; 1 C. 16:11; 2 C. 13:11; Gal. 6:16; Phil. 4:7, 9). The broadening out of the wish is seen in the qualifications **at all times** (Rom. 11:10) and **in all ways** (Phil. 1:18; for the rather full style, cf. Phil. 1:3f.; 1 Th. 1:2). The double use of 'peace' in the sentence is slightly harsh, but is not altogether surprising in the fulsome style of a prayer (cf. perhaps 2 C. 13:11).

The second part of the prayer is **The Lord be with you all**, a wish which has no precise parallel in Paul. Elsewhere Paul can pray that the God of peace will be with his readers (Rom. 15:53), and this parallel effectively makes the point that to pray for a certain gift of God to be with his people is the same as praying for God himself to be with them. The wish 'The Lord be with you' goes back into *OT* times (Jg. 6:12; Ru. 2:14) and recurs in Lk. 1:28; 2 Tim. 4:22 (for 'with your spirit' instead of 'with you', cf. Gal. 6:18; Phm. 25); for its history, see W. C. van Unnik, 'Dominus vobiscum', in A. J. B. Higgins (ed.), *New Testament Essays*, Manchester, 1959, pp. 270–305. While, then, it is true that this is the only place

in the Pauline corpus where the wish occurs, it is difficult to see
how it can then be concluded that it must also be un-Pauline, in the
sense that Paul could not have used it (as Trilling, p. 157, apparently
states). One may say, if one desires, that an imitator has elaborated
the greeting in Rom. 15:33 and developed it christologically. But it
is equally possible, if not more likely, that the wish in Romans is
developed from Paul's earlier phraseology in 1 Th. 5:23 and here.
The inclusion of the wish here may possibly be motivated by the
desire to stress yet again that all the readers are included in Paul's
prayer.

CONCLUDING GREETING

3:17–18

As in 1 Th., the closing greeting is quite brief. There is an absence
of personal remarks, and there is a certain amount of stress on the
fact that it is Paul's own greeting. Following his normal custom, he
himself would write the closing words of the letter, even if the main
part had been dictated to an amanuensis.

17. the words **this greeting** are seen by Best, pp. 346f., as a
reference back to v. 16 with its mention of the familiar Jewish word
of greeting 'peace'. However, Paul has other closing greetings which
do not mention 'peace', and the analogy of other letters (Gal. 6:11;
Col. 4:18) may suggest that Paul's personal handwriting begins at
this point, so that 'this greeting' in fact refers to vv. 17 and 18.
More frequently Paul uses the verb 'greet' to convey the good wishes
of his companions at the time of writing a letter and to urge the
recipients to share a kiss of greeting (1 Th. 5:26), but he uses the
noun here and in 1 C. 16:21; Col. 4:18 (literally, '[This is] the
greeting of me, Paul'). The words, then are themselves the greeting,
as *GNB* rightly translates: 'With my own hand I write this: *Greetings
from Paul*' (cf. Ellingworth and Nida, p. 211). It is only when this
is correctly perceived that we can avoid the mistake of regarding
the following words as the main point in the verse.

This is the mark in every letter of mine is a unique phrase. The
reference is not clear, but, however we take the syntax (the relative
pronoun translated **This** is neuter in Greek, agreeing with **mark**,
but the word **greeting** is masculine), the reference is to the greeting
in Paul's own handwriting. But in what sense is it a **mark**, and of
what is it a mark? The reference may be either to the fact that Paul
himself is writing the greeting or to the fact that it is in his own
particular handwriting. Since the 'mark' is most probably to be
interpreted as a sign or proof of authenticity (K. H. Rengstorf,

TDNT VII, p. 259, argues that here *sēmeion* has the same force as *symboulon*, an addition to a letter in the author's own hand as a sign of authenticity), it would follow that the reference is to the handwriting, which would have been known to the readers from the previous letter. One may doubt if this attempt at authentication would have carried weight in the case of a later forgery, and of course it certainly would not be effective if A. Lindemann is right in suggesting that the purpose of 2 Th. was to discredit 1 Th. It is true that Trilling, p. 158, draws attention to secondary versions of the *Letter to Abgar* in which Jesus says, 'This is written in my own hand', and to the *Testament of our Lord Jesus* which is authenticated with the signatures of three apostles. But the former of these works is no earlier than the time of Eusebius, while the latter also is hardly any earlier. Any attempt to draw analogies between what was credible in the fourth or fifth centuries and later and in the first century must be pronounced highly questionable. It is possible of course that first-century readers with no access to any other MS of Paul would assume that this was his autograph simply because the letter said so; after all, truthfulness was presumably an accepted virtue in the church. But if so, this means that the author was, as defenders of pseudonymity now freely admit, engaged in deliberate forgery calculated to deceive. We may question whether such motivation is at all likely; it would certainly be a case of using Satan to cast out Satan (2:3, 9–11).

But why is the attestation of authenticity present at all? On the assumption of genuineness, the possibilities commonly advanced are that Paul wished to enable his readers to distinguish this letter from other, inauthentic letters which may have been in circulation (cf. 2:2), or to stress the authenticity of this particular letter to any of the idlers or opponents of Paul's teaching who might try to discredit it. We have already seen that the former of these two possibilities is unlikely, and it seems more probable that Paul's purpose is to emphasise the authority and authenticity of this letter rather than to deny the authenticity of other alleged letters of his. We may compare the way in which he emphasises the authority of his teaching and the importance of his message in Gal. 6:11. There is also the analogy of 1 C. 16:21–23 where the declaration that Paul writes the greeting with his own hand is promptly followed by a solemn curse, which gains its weight from being in Paul's handwriting. In 1 Th. 5:27 the letter also closes with a solemn adjuration in Paul's own handwriting. The stress here on Paul's **own hand** conveys a similar emphasis: here is a letter, which, with its demands for right teaching, Christian living and the exercise of discipline, must not be ignored. The apostle's signature underlines the importance of the contents in each of his letters.

18. The greeting is followed by the usual closing benediction, which is identical with that in 1 Th. 5:28, save for the addition of **all** (cf. 1 C. 16:24; 2 C. 13:13). We should not overstress the force of the addition, since it is found elsewhere in Paul's letters; but it certainly shows that Paul had no conscious desire to exclude any of his readers from the blessing of the Lord.

INDEX OF AUTHORS

GENERAL INDEX